INTO THE
SWARM

INTO THE SWARM

STORIES OF RAF FIGHTER PILOTS IN THE SECOND WORLD WAR

BY
CHRISTOPHER YEOMAN
& TOR IDAR LARSEN

FONTHILL

To Oscar David Yeoman & Oscar Rasmus Whittall.

Fonthill Media Limited
Fonthill Media LLC
www.fonthillmedia.com

First published 2013

ISBN 978-1-78155-246-9

Typeset in 10pt on 13pt Sabon LT
Typesetting by Fonthill Media
Printed in the UK
Connect with us

 facebook.com/fonthillmedia  twitter.com/fonthillmedia

Contents

Junkers Ju88. (*EN Archive*)

Introduction

Sometimes it is far too easy to fall into the romanticised world of Second World War aviation. After all, it is difficult not to when so many images and accounts present Supermarine Spitfires, with their perfect elliptical wings, sporting red, white, and blue roundels, soaring high through blue skies and fluffy white clouds. This alone is often enough to make the chest swell with pride. Those dashing pilots, so innocent and young, are often seen running to their machines, ready to duel with enemy aircraft in glamorised dogfights. The sound of Merlin engines, the chattering of machine guns, the sigh of falling aircraft trailing smoke and distant explosions are, perhaps, a common perception of those legendary battles.

When the victorious fighter boys return home for the day they appear almost nonchalant with their war. There is no 'line shooting', but rather a quiet drink in the Mess to ease any unspoken nerves. However, there is no hiding from the sullen faces, the strained eyes and the obvious exhaustion evident in many wartime photographs of fighter pilots. A closer look at their day-to-day routine reveals tormenting spells of boredom and anxiety while the fighter pilots wait around in readiness for the next action.

Experience varies among the airmen. Experience, which can often be the difference between life and death when in mortal combat with the enemy. Yet no matter how capable or experienced these fighter pilots might be, there is no escaping bad luck. As the battles drag on there are many fliers that do not return home. Seats and beds are left empty, but no one can allow themselves to think about what that really means. New faces begin to replace the old ones, but with the way things are going it's almost better not to get to know the green replacements.

New pilots spend private moments working out survival tactics in their minds, despite knowing the odds are heavily stacked against them.

At dispersal the fighter boys are reading, playing cards, or sleeping until the telephone rings and shatters the silence as well as their nerves. The call to 'scramble' puts them in motion, jumpstarting brave and willing hearts.

Mad dashes, stomachs churning, the pilots soon settle down into open cockpits, ignoring their fears by concentrating on take-offs. Moments pass, then monoplane fighters can be seen racing across grass runways to get airborne. It's a desperate climb for height.

The sky seems endless. Pilots concentrate on keeping formation while straining their necks as they search the arena for any telltale signs of enemy aircraft. On some patrols they get lucky when dots can be seen in the distance revealing the enemy's position, but other times they're not as lucky and contact arrives with unwelcomed surprise.

Suddenly aircraft from all sides are twisting and turning in a frantic melee. The pilots, fuelled with a surge of adrenaline, try to make sense of the chaos that has erupted at terrific speeds around them. Bullets whizz through the air, metal twists, glass shatters and blood spills. Aircraft break apart in mid-air, cockpits burst into flames, and parachutes fail to open. Then in an instant the sky seems to clear and pilots find they are curiously all alone. Propellers spinning, they turn for home.

Eager ground crews step up on to the fighters and help weary pilots out of their cockpits, keen to hear any snippets of the action. Some pilots climb down from their mounts ready to report successes while others struggle to make sense of such a fleeting scene of aerial anarchy. Doused in sweat and exhausted, they have survived another ferocious battle.

Such was a typical day in the life of a fighter pilot. Far from being glamorous, the reality of aerial warfare was bloody and violent, but essential to securing victory over Nazi Germany. Many young men were killed, wounded, maimed and captured. It is with sincere hope that this book serves as a simple tribute to the airmen and the battles they fought during the Second World War.

Authors' Notes

Tor and I first met by an F-15E at Duxford in Cambridgeshire. It was a beautiful summer's day and we were getting ready to watch the magnificent aerial displays at Flying Legends in July 2012.

We had corresponded for some time before meeting, after discovering that we were both running numerous Second World War aviation pages on a popular social networking website.

Tor's book, *Viking Spitfire,* had just hit the stalls at Duxford that day and I was pleased to get a signed copy of a most interesting book. At this time my book, *Rise Against Eagles,* was still in production with Fonthill Media, but we were excited to be writing for the same publisher and began to exchange ideas for a future project.

Two months later we met up once again at Duxford and began to finalise a collaboration that would pay tribute to a selection of airmen we had previously researched before meeting. There had been several pilots that I wanted to include in *Rise Against Eagles* but due to time constraints they unfortunately missed the deadline.

I have opened this book with the Woods-Scawen brothers because they are local heroes to me. I live in the same town and very close to the house that they grew up in, so I really wanted to pay my respects to them in this small way by remembering their story.

Butch Barton is a pilot who I had read snippets about here and there but until meeting Wing Commander Tom Neil I didn't know too much about him. Tom's admiration for Barton as a fighter pilot and a man had an infectious effect on me, so to write about him soon become essential.

John Mungo Park was a name that I heard regularly when in company with Wing Commander John Freeborn. Mungo was a good friend of John's and I have often wanted to pay tribute to his incredible service with 74 Squadron.

I have had the honour of meeting Group Captain Allan Wright on several occasions. He is a gentleman in the truest sense of the word, exuberating modesty and intelligence. I have always found Allan an engaging character and his experiences with 92 Squadron are nothing short of inspiring.

Last but not least I have written about Pat Lardner-Burke. A couple of years ago I was given the opportunity to sit in Duxford's famous Spitfire MH434 and since that day I have endeavoured to find out more about the pilot who flew it in combat. In so doing, I came in to contact with Lardner-Burke's son Martin and Sarah Hanna, which was a privilege and a tremendous help to this work.

Likewise Tor has researched pilots from his homeland, Norway, and written about their service in the RAF during the Second World War.

Given the nature of the seemingly random selection of pilots between us, we decided to combine them in one book to remember their service and sacrifice.

Christopher Yeoman
April, 2013

Norway and Great Britain has a long tradition of cooperation and friendship. The special bond between our two countries grew strongly after the Second World War, and has not faded one bit since those past days of war. We are connected in many ways; our love for English football, our royal families, an similar sense of humour, and we're both sporting a bit of the same 'stiff upper lip' attitude. It is not by chance that the Norwegian pilots in Britain during the Second World War were known as the easiest of all foreigners to handle. They were more British than the Poles, the French or even the Americans. Wing Commander David Scott-Malden specifically requested to command the Norwegian Spitfire squadrons in 1942. The cooperation between the very young but experienced Battle of Britain ace and the new and green Norwegian pilots was an immediate and lasting success. In 1943, 331 Squadron was the Royal Air Force's top scoring fighter squadron and I am extremely proud of my fellow countrymen for this achievement. Sadly, their success has largely been forgotten in Norway.

In 2012, the Norwegian veterans came back to their home base at North Weald one last time. They are few now, and sadly becoming less each year. The warm welcome they received at North Weald was felt by all of us that were there that special weekend. They have not yet been forgotten, and at North Weald Norwegians are still held in high regard. For aviation enthusiasts like myself, North Weald is a home away from home.

Needless to say, when the chance came to work on a book together with Chris, I jumped on it at once. It is, as one may say, tradition.

I first saw Arne Austeen's name on a memorial in the small town of Gjøvik, just a few minutes drive from my home in Eina. From that point on I have been researching his career with the RAF. His story is now, for the first time, told in English for this book. There are very few Norwegians that can top his career with the RAF.

There is a picture of Arne Austeen out on the icy lake of Mjøsa in 1940 flying a sailing plane. It made me stop and think – I was there, on the exact same spot seventy years later flying my Hawker Hurricane RC model plane. In contrast to Arne, I was not told a few days later, that Norway had been invaded by Germany. I didn't go home to pick up my uniform to go to war and not come back. Arne Austeen did.

Leif Lundsten is another local lad. Brought up in the municipality of Østre Toten, the young boy from the quiet and peaceful countryside escaped Norway and went to war in a Spitfire. He never returned home. Largely forgotten, his story is finally being told. I spoke to a childhood friend of his a few years ago and he said to me, 'Thank you for doing this for Leif.' To talk to someone using his first name like that, a real friend of a hero long gone, brought chills to my spine. I was moved by that short sentence and I felt much closer to Leif Lundsten.

Finn Eriksrud was just a boy when he escaped Norway and travelled around the world to finally become a Mosquito pilot for 333 Squadron at Leuchars. In the end he was the only surviving pilot of the original B-flight that flew Mosquitos. What he must have thought when all his colleagues kept disappearing – I can only imagine. The complete book about 333 Squadron's achievements in Scotland has yet to be written. His story told in this book is at least a start.

Kaj Birksted is the Danish hero of the air. Denmark did not form their own squadrons during the war, so Kaj joined the Norwegians instead. This decision was in direct opposition to his own government's plans, and at one point he was told that he should be shot for deserting. He was extremely successful flying for the RAF and in the end he became Wing Commander flying for the Norwegians. Kaj never stopped believing that his ideas were right, and for that he was eventually given his rightful place in Danish history as the true legend that he was.

All these young men were the absolute best of their generation. And now, due to their sacrifices many years ago, they have created a bond between our two nations that will never disappear. It is only right that we keep this friendship going as best as we can and to the best of our abilities. It's the perfect salute to all of them that have gone before.

Tor Idar Larsen
April, 2013

Hawker Hurricane. (*Brad Hurley*)

Prologue

The sound of a Rolls-Royce Merlin engine suddenly burst into life at the Royal Aircraft Establishment (RAE) at Farnborough in Hampshire. Its voice however, usually so clear and distinctive was interrupted by another, rumbling from a Daimler-Benz engine close by.

Workers at the Establishment turned their heads towards the sounds of the two aircraft. Group Captain Harry Broadhurst, a veteran fighter pilot, from nearby Frimley, with an assembly of 'brasshats' and Rolls-Royce experts gathered together in excited conversation about what they were about to witness.

The sight that followed must have been quite something for the RAE employees and residents of Farnborough at the time, as a Supermarine Spitfire Mk II and a Messerschmitt Bf109E was seen racing across the airfield before lifting off into the air.

Bob Stanford Tuck, a very capable flyer and fighter pilot belonging to 92 Squadron was sitting at the controls of the Spitfire. His soon to be opponent was Wing Commander George Stainforth, a very experienced pilot who had been part of setting up many air records in the 1930s. He had also been awarded the Air Force Cross for being the first man to exceed 400 mph.

From the cockpit of his Spitfire, Tuck looked across his elliptical wingtip to see Stainforth looking back handling the controls of the Bf109. They were now flying in line abreast, wingtip to wingtip, at 20,000 feet for the experts down below.

It was June 1940 and perhaps one of the strangest sights in the world at that time was to see Britain's most modern fighter aircraft flying in formation with a Luftwaffe fighter who had caused the RAF so much trouble in France. At this point, Fairey Battles of the Advanced Air Strike Force had been decimated by 109s in combat and the fighter boys equipped with Hawker Hurricanes out in France, had met their match. But a Luftwaffe pilot of JG76 by the name of Feldwebel Karl Hier was forced down after combat between Hornsburg and Bitche. His Messerschmitt Bf109E-3, known as 'White 1' force-landed at Goersdorf, near Woerth and the French captured the aircraft on 22 November

1939. 'White 1' was soon repaired and evaluated by the French at the Centre d'Essais en Vol at Orleans-Bricy. Hier's aircraft was then handed over to the RAF at Amiens in May 1940, where it was flown by Flying Officer Eric Brown of 1 Squadron in mock combat with a Hurricane and a Curtiss Hawk. Before too long, 'White 1' was subsequently transferred to Boscombe Down for initial flight tests and then given to the RAE at Farnborough for additional tests and evaluation on 14 May 1940. The Messerschmitt had been painted with RAF markings and at Farnborough it was given the serial number 'AE479'.

Soaring high above Farnborough, Tuck and Stainforth eased their sticks forward to begin a series of dives for the onlookers down below. The Spitfire and Messerschmitt dived neck and neck on several occasions, each time proving it to be a fairly even contest between the two fighters. A straight and level race at full speed was the next task for the two airmen. When Tuck and Stainforth put their machines to the limit, it seemed that the 109 had a slight speed advantage over the Spitfire.

Tuck and Stainforth then performed a series of turns and rolls, and as previously experienced in combat by the fighter boys scrapping with the Luftwaffe over the Channel, it was evident that the Spitfire was the more manoeuvrable aircraft of the two.

But the 109's greatest advantage was its ability to pull up out of a steep dive and climb away faster and at a steeper angle than the Spitfire and Hurricane was capable of. In combat Tuck had witnessed this capability first hand, as he recalled:

> This is the sort of thing that would happen: you'd work up behind a 109 at height, and just as you got set to blow him out of the sky he'd spot you, slam his stick fully forward and drop like a gannet, more or less vertically. If you tried to do the same, the moment your nose went down your engine would go 'pop-br-ang!' There'd be a puff of dark blue smoke and you'd lost all your power for several vital seconds.
>
> We'd guessed the reason, of course, and the boffins who'd gone over the captured 109 confirmed it. The Daimler-Benz engine had direct fuel injection, whereas the Merlin had a carburettor that couldn't cope with the negative 'G' imposed by this sudden transition from the horizontal to the vertical.[1]

The only response the RAF fighter pilots could give to this manoeuvre was to roll their aircraft over on to their backs and then dive after the enemy, but this took vital seconds, and the 109s would often slip away from their pursuers.

As a result of Stainforth and Tuck's demonstrations at the RAE, the Rolls-Royce experts soon found a solution to this problem by devising a float-less carburettor for the Merlin engine that functioned well under the most violent negative 'G'.

Again, it must have been quite a spectacular sight for those watching at Farnborough to see Tuck and Stainforth locked in a mock-dogfight over the RAE, after which they came in to land.

As previously instructed the two pilots then switched aircraft and carried out exactly the same comparison tests as before.

Finally sitting in the enemy's seat, Tuck observed that the 109's cockpit

Seemed even smaller than the Spit's, and the pilot's vision was decidedly poorer. The hood and windscreen were certainly far more robust, but they had a lot of thick, metal strutting – heavily studded, like girders – in front and on the sides, and these obviously obscured several sections of the sky.

After flying the aircraft for himself his concluding opinion was that the 109E was,

Without a doubt a most delightful little aeroplane – not as manoeuvrable as the Spit, mind you, nor as nice to handle near the ground. It had a tendency to a rather vicious stall, because, you see, it was even smaller than the Spit. But certainly it was slightly faster, and altogether it had a wonderful performance.[2]

White 1's evaluation at Farnborough was important and insightful for Rolls-Royce, the RAF, and ultimately the men that would be facing such machines in combat. On a personal level, the experience was also extremely beneficial for Tuck, who, just days after this flight, was back on the front line with 92 Squadron defending Britain.

Spitfire MH434. (*Ady Shaw*)

CHAPTER 1

The Woods-Scawens

Fifty-five York Road, a red-brick semi-detached house in Farnborough, is only a short distance away from the Royal Aircraft Establishment that evaluated the Messerschmitt 109 flown by Tuck, Stainforth, and later 74 Squadron's Adolph 'Sailor' Malan.

During the 1930s, 55 York Road was the home of two brothers, Patrick and Tony Woods-Scawen. The two boys were educated at Salesian College on Reading Road, which is located just around the corner from their old home. Patrick was the eldest of the two brothers, born in Karachi, India on 29 June 1916. Tony was also born in Karachi, on 18 February 1918. The Woods-Scawens returned to England in 1924, after Patrick and Tony's mother fell ill.

To begin with, the two brothers boarded at Salesian College. But when their mother passed away they moved into 55 York Road to live with their Aunt Nellie. When their education was complete, Patrick was employed as a storekeeper and Tony as a clerk. The jobs were steady enough but dissatisfactory for the adventurous spirits of the Woods-Scawen brothers. Living close to the Royal Aircraft Establishment in Farnborough it was almost impossible for the two boys to avoid falling in love with the idea of a flying career.

Both Patrick and Tony were known as playful characters and they were very popular amongst their peers. With both wit and charm the brothers soon won the affections of one young woman in particular, a pretty blonde called Una Lawrence also known as Bunny, or Bun-Bun to Patrick and Tony. It was almost impossible for the two boys to avoid falling in love with her.

Patrick was the first to join the Royal Air Force on a short service commission in October 1937. At the age of twenty-one, Patrick left 55 York Road behind and travelled to King's Cross where Bunny waved him off. He was destined for Prestwick in Ayrshire to begin his elementary flying training.

Tony was keen to follow in his big brother's footsteps but at this point it seemed that a career in the RAF was unlikely for him. With a spell of suspected TB, Tony missed a year of schooling with a patch on his lung and did not pass out with a School Certificate like Patrick did. The patch eventually cleared but his eyesight was left permanently impaired and he needed glasses when reading. With this against him it seemed that his chances of becoming a pilot in the RAF were slim. However in March 1938 he did join the air force on a short service commission. Tony's eyesight had not improved; instead he had sneakily passed the mandatory eye examination by memorising the eye-test card.

During this time Patrick was busy enjoying himself at Prestwick flying the Tiger Moth and socialising with his fellow students and the locals. On 9 January 1938 he was posted to No. 11 Flying Training School at Wittering and then moved to Shawbury in Shropshire. Patrick continued to correspond affectionately with Bunny, who had promised, perhaps nonchalantly, to marry him when he was promoted as a squadron leader. Patrick's letters to Bunny evidently exposed his love for her. In one particular letter he yearned for Bunny to send him a photograph of herself so that he could show her off to his pals. Bunny was reluctant at first but she eventually gave in and did send Patrick a photograph. She also sent one to Tony.

Patrick successfully completed his flying training and on 20 August he was posted to 84 Squadron at Debden. 'I have flown a Hurricane', he wrote to Bunny, 'so have reached the eighth heaven. The seventh, sixth and fifth are you. But my God, what an aeroplane!'[3]

Tony prepared for his training by acquiring special flying goggles with corrective lenses to improve his vision. Various tests loomed over him to begin with but he managed to scrape through them before being sent on to Woodley to begin his flying training. On 21 May 1938, Tony was posted to No. 6 Flying Training School at Netheravon and just like his brother he made the most of the pre-war social scene around him. By the end of the year, Tony was posted to 43 Squadron stationed at Tangmere, where he learnt to fly the Hawker Hurricane. The chaps in the squadron soon discovered Tony's questionable eyesight and nicknamed him 'Wombat' because apparently he looked a bit like a rabbit and was as blind as a bat, but Tony's infectious nature quickly won the approval of his colleagues. In a letter to Bunny, Tony tells how the experienced pilots in the Squadron, particularly Caesar Hull and Frank Carey, took him under their wings. 'For some strange reason, they have been giving me the benefit of all their terrific flying skill by taking me up for wizard dogfights and drilling me in aerobatics. I can now roll at 2-300 feet without being too scared, thanks to them, but I still get plenty frit on occasion.'[4]

Patrick was also given a nickname by the boys in 84 Squadron – he was dubbed 'Weasel' because of his sharp features and size. Unsurprisingly, Patrick became enormously popular and well known around the station.

After war was declared on Germany, Patrick was soon posted to France with the Squadron as part of the RAF Component in support of the British Expeditionary Force. The so-called 'Phoney War' was then in effect and it

Patrick Woods-Scawen. (*Tristan Woods-Scawen*)

proved a testing time for many of the pilots who felt bored and frustrated by the lack of action. Those squadrons based in France also endured a long, cold winter, with inadequate equipment and generally poor facilities. In the New Year, Patrick was given a welcome ten-days home-leave in mid-January, during which he drove to Tangmere with Bunny to visit Tony. It was a happy reunion for them all but perhaps difficult for Patrick who knew that he would soon have to tear himself away from Bunny and return to France.

The letters between the Woods-Scawen brothers and Bunny continued. When Patrick returned to France he reminded Bunny not to forget that they were going to marry when he was made a squadron leader. He was also fully aware of Tony and Bunny's endearing correspondence, which he playfully referred to in his writing, as did Tony. There was clearly an understanding of a shared fondness between the three of them but it did not affect their individual relationships as one might imagine. Exactly where did Bunny's true affections lie? It was a question that undoubtedly troubled both Patrick and Tony, but despite this quiet competition, the brothers did not let it affect their bond.

Hitler unleashed the unstoppable German blitzkrieg on 10 May 1940. At 0410 hours that morning Patrick and his colleagues were disturbed by the tremendous sound of numerous Luftwaffe engines overhead, combined with

Tony Woods-Scawen.
(*Tristan Woods-Scawen*)

the thumping sounds of anti-aircraft fire being pumped into the air. Within minutes six Hurricanes took off from base to engage the enemy bombers. Flight Lieutenant Bob Boothby led his section from A Flight with Pilot Officer David Mawhood and Flying Officer Ken Blair in tow. They engaged two Junkers Ju88s at 12,000 feet near Grammont. Boothby fired two lengthy bursts of ammunition into one of the bombers which went down pouring oil with a dead engine. Mawhood witnessed the Ju88's descent but in turn his Hurricane was struck by fire from the second Junkers and perspex splinters blinded him in one eye. Mawhood retaliated by firing four-second bursts into the enemy machine despite his injury. Blair also attacked this aircraft with a few bursts of his own and watched heavy smoke pour from its starboard engine as it went down. The Ju88 crew managed to bale out of their aircraft, but they were soon captured by Belgians and handed over to the British.

Flight Lieutenant Dickie Lee was leading his section of B Flight with Flying Officer Derek Allen and Pilot Officer Patrick Woods-Scawen flying tightly on his wing tips. The three of them encountered a formation of Hs 126s and made various attacks but the results were inconclusive. Within forty-minutes the six Hurricanes had engaged the enemy and returned to base to rearm and refuel. Patrick was back in the air at 0730 hours on a patrol with Dickie Lee and Flying Officer Allan Angus. A Ju88 was spotted at 15,000 feet between Armentieres and the Fort-de-Nieppe and the Hurricanes gave chase. The bomber took evasive action and dived down to the deck with the rear-gunner firing continuously at the trio. Lee reported firing short bursts from close range but saw no apparent results except for black smoke issuing from one of its engines. Lee's Hurricane was badly hit but he managed to get back to base without further incident. Angus also attacked the enemy aircraft and reported that after two bursts he 'saw the rear gunner disintegrate'. He also noticed that its starboard engine had stopped and he last saw it diving to the ground near Ghent. Angus then discovered that he was out of ammunition and that he had no oil pressure. His engine seized and he force-landed at Celles. Within a few hours Angus returned to the Squadron after hitching a ride back to Lille/Seclin. Patrick did not fire his guns on this occasion, but nine days later he would soon claim his fair share of enemy aircraft.

On Sunday 19 May at approximately 1000 hours, Patrick was out on the aerodrome when he noticed three Hurricanes above duelling with several enemy aircraft. Not one to miss the fight, Patrick raced to his aircraft and took off to join the action. He managed to shoot a Messerschmitt Bf109 down in flames, five miles east of Seclin, after a single burst of just two seconds. Patrick then climbed to 5,000 feet and then latched on to a second Bf109 which he attacked with several short bursts from 100 yards range. The 109 dived to the ground trailing black smoke. Two enemy fighters then opened fire on Patrick from behind and forced him to break away from the action. Patrick's ammunition boxes were empty so there was nothing more he could to but evade their attacks before landing safely back on his aerodrome.

Later in the day Patrick was back in the hostile air, this time leading Blue Section on patrol between Seclin and Lille/Marcq. At about 1550 hours Patrick caught sight of a single Bf109 travelling east. Suspecting a trap, Patrick ordered his section to cover him while he delivered a stern attack on the enemy fighter from 100 yards. He fired one burst lasting two seconds which subsequently caused the 109 to dive steeply, emitting smoke. Patrick watched the enemy aircraft crash-land in a field five miles west of Tournai. The engagement was witnessed by Pilot Officer Shrewsbury, who joined up with Patrick after the encounter to continue their patrol.

Soon enough Patrick picked out another enemy aircraft while patrolling Lille to Seclin at 8,000 feet. It was a Dornier Do17 which was flying slowly east at the same height as Patrick. Once again Patrick covered his back by suspecting a possible trap, so this time he climbed into the sun to get behind the Luftwaffe bomber. It was an intelligent move because in this new position (at about 10,000 feet) Patrick saw seven Bf109s nearby at his own height. He attacked the enemy fighters head-on, firing continuously from 600 yards until they passed by underneath his aircraft. Patrick noticed the leading 109 pouring smoke as it dived away. He then turned his Hurricane as quickly as he was able for another pass at the fighters but suddenly a cannon-shell hit his engine, which burst into flames. Patrick baled out of his aircraft (Hurricane P2547) as fast as he could and took to his parachute. He landed safely two miles south-west of Lille, despite being shot at twice by French soldiers on the way down. It is believed that Uffz Wemhoner of 5/JG26 was the pilot that shot him down.

During the Battle of France, Patrick and his comrades had demonstrated exceptional abilities in combat against unfavourable odds but it was not enough to stem the insurmountable German advance. The day after Patrick was shot down, the Squadron began to evacuate from France. No. 84 Squadron's diarist recorded the following: '20/5/40. Squadron Leader Peacock reported to take over from Squadron Leader Oliver, who left for England with Pilot Officer Woods-Scawen and Sergeant Pilot Deacon by air transport.'

The Squadron had suffered a great deal from the intense fighting in May. It had lost a great deal of aircraft but also, and more importantly, a great band of pilots who were either killed, wounded, or listed missing. Squadron Leader Peacock, who had only just arrived in France to assume Command of the Squadron, failed to return from a patrol on the 20th and two days later the Squadron arrived in Debden to reform.

On 25 June 1940, the *London Gazette* acknowledged Patrick's accomplishments in France by writing:

Pilot Officer Patrick Philip WOODS-SCAWEN (40452).
During May 1940, this officer destroyed six enemy aircraft, and assisted in the destruction of others. On one occasion, although heavily outnumbered, he attacked without hesitation a large formation of enemy aircraft, shooting down two of them. His own aircraft was hit by a cannon shell and he was slightly wounded, but succeeded in escaping by parachute and rejoined his unit. He has displayed great courage, endurance, and leadership.

The Woods-Scawen family together with Bunny were enormously proud of Patrick's exploits in France.

On 23 May, Squadron Leader Peter Townsend, DFC, arrived at Debden to take command of 85 Squadron with the task of bringing it back to operational efficiency. Townsend had previously served with 43 Squadron, where Patrick's younger brother Tony was now busy preparing for operations over Dunkirk. Of Tony, Townsend remarked that he was 'as brave as a lion and as blind as a bat'. During the weeks to come Townsend's assessment of Tony could not have been more accurate.

On 31 May, 43 Squadron, also known as 'The Fighting Cocks' began to carry out patrols over the Channel, with orders to protect shipping vessels coming back from Dunkirk. On its second patrol that morning, the Squadron reached their patrol line as instructed and swept the sky between Calais and Dunkirk. On approach to the smoky beaches of Dunkirk, where British troops were desperately being evacuated, large numbers of Bf109s were seen with Bf110s breaking out of cloud away to the west. The nine airborne Hurricanes of 43 Squadron dispersed in three sections and soon found themselves outnumbered by about six to one. Tony was flying in Blue Section with Squadron Leader George Lott leading. In a flash the Squadron was engulfed in a storm of Messerschmitts. For several long minutes Lott found himself evading 109 after 109 as they tried to latch on to his tail. Tony was also forced to evade the fighters but he did manage to fire a couple of steady bursts at one of the Messerschmitts, which knocked pieces off its port wing. Suddenly another 109 swept up beneath Tony's Hurricane and shot up his radiator. Glycol poured into his cockpit and the windscreen became smeared with oil. There was nothing for it but to get out of the fight and get back home. Tony returned to Tangmere and despite his damaged aircraft and a tricky landing he escaped unharmed.

In early June he wrote to Bunny and asked, 'Are you engaged or married or anything equally horrible yet? I won't be so enthusiastic about it if you go and do something silly like that.' He also mentioned the Squadron's recent patrols, writing in his boyish way: 'We have been having prodigious Hun-fun, but little else.'[5]

After the evacuation of British troops and shipping from Dunkirk, 43 Squadron was then ordered to fly patrols over the Amiens-Abbeville line to cover the remaining depleted forces being withdrawn.

During an evening patrol on 7 June, Tony was flying number two in Blue Section, led by Squadron Leader Lott on course for Amiens-Abbeville, but when they approached the French coast the Squadron caught sight of Bf109s and 110s, which they dived upon in line astern. Tony followed Lott down towards the enemy fighters but all of a sudden his Hurricane was hit from behind and his cockpit blazed with intense heat. With no time to spare, Tony pulled the cockpit hood back and evacuated his aircraft near Le Treport. After a safe descent, but now behind enemy lines, Tony gathered up his parachute and hid in a ditch. When all appeared clear Tony set off, eventually trekking some twenty-miles across country without being detected by the Germans. After some time, Tony fell in with a retreating motorised transport unit that took him to Rouen, but the bridge over the river had already been blown up. Tony found another way to cross the river by persuading a ferryman, whom he held at gun point, to get him across. A 43 Squadron Intelligence Report records that Tony's 'recollection of the journey is hazy as he was continuously being bombed and spent a lot of his time sheltering in cellars. At Le Mans he fell in with 73 Squadron and travelled by train to Caen and Cherbourg where he arrived six days after being shot down.'

Wearing a tin hat and an army major's jacket, Tony turned up in the Mess at Tangmere, with his parachute gathered in unruly folds under his arm. John Simpson, a pilot in 43 Squadron, wrote about Tony's return at the time, in a letter to his good friend Hector Bolitho:

> George (Squadron Leader Lott) and I were having a lunchtime drink in the
> hall when Tony walked in, wearing an army shirt and a tin hat. Under his
> arm was his same old parachute. On the 7th, when we lost him, he had
> baled out over the German lines. He landed all right and hid in a ditch.
> After it was dark, he crept out and he walked twenty miles, still hanging on
> to his parachute. He found a British patrol with whom he was eventually
> evacuated. But I wish you could have seen him walk into the mess, his face
> covered with smiles. He said to George, 'I am sorry I am late, sir.' All George
> did was to call Macey and say, 'Bring us a drink.' George asked Tony why he
> had lugged his parachute all the way home with him and Tony said, 'Well, I
> know that this one works and I might have to use it again.[6]

The continuous patrols had proven costly for 43 Squadron and a much needed rest was in order for the Fighting Cocks. Patrick, with 85 Squadron, was on the verge of returning to operational patrols when the first phase of the Battle of Britain opened on 10 July 1940.

After the fall of France, Hitler had desired peace with Britain, but failing to obtain it he then sought the neutralisation of the British so that he could be left undisturbed with his plans to conquer the east. But unlike France and the Low Countries, Germany's deadly Blitzkrieg tactics could not be enforced upon Britain with the Channel surrounding her shores. If Germany was to invade Britain then they had to secure air supremacy in order for their invasion barges to cross the Channel unmolested by the RAF.

The Battle of France had taken its toll on Fighter Command's Hurricanes and more importantly experienced pilots. Patrols flown over Dunkirk in May and June would also claim the lives of more pilots and aircraft, including the Spitfires. While the Luftwaffe prepared itself for the Battle for Britain, Fighter Command could take a much needed breather.

By 1 July 1940, Dowding had twenty-nine Hurricane squadrons with 347 operational aircraft available and nineteen squadrons of Spitfires with 199 aircraft available. In total that gave Fighter Command 546 aircraft with 912 pilots to fly them to fend off the might of Goring's vastly more numerous Luftwaffe. Despite the RAF's inferior numbers Dowding and Keith Park's organisational skills and battle tactics would prove superior to his enemies. Another crucial individual in building up Fighter Command's strength at this critical and desperate time was Lord Beaverbrook, whose talents for aircraft production were unmatched.

The Luftwaffe's initial attacks against Britain were against shipping convoys and ports, designed to disrupt British supplies and also to draw Fighter Commands Hurricanes and Spitfires up into the air where they could potentially be destroyed. No. 85 Squadron was actively involved in flying daily convoy patrols, operating from Debden's satellite landing grounds at Castle Camps and Martlesham Heath. The Squadron's efforts during this time were acknowledged in a telegram sent from Air Vice-Marshal Trafford Leigh-Mallory to Squadron Leader Peter Townsend:

> I am very pleased to see what an excellent month's flying 85 Squadron put in during July. I should like to congratulate you on the performance of your Squadron, both in attacking the enemy and in your training. I much admire the spirit and keenness shown by you and the other members of the Squadron.

The flying experience Patrick had acquired before war broke out, together with the combat experience he gained in France, was invaluable for a Battle of Britain fighter pilot. Many Luftwaffe pilots now opposing the RAF had already gained vital experience in the late 1930s, when the Luftwaffe's Condor Legion fought in the Spanish Civil War. Even before the Battle of France had begun many Luftwaffe pilots were already experienced flyers and fighters and the combat tactics they employed were far more evolved than those currently used by the RAF. Such were the calibre of men now coming for Britain, in a force which greatly outnumbered Dowding's Fighter Command. But in spite of the odds, the RAF quickly adapted to modern aerial tactics in what would be the greatest air battle fought in any theatre of the Second World War. British aircraft production would be steady but as the days passed by during the summer and autumn of 1940, Britain would always be found in desperate need of pilots. Experienced young men like Patrick would prove essential in opposing the Luftwaffe in combat.

Patrick's first claim of the Battle of Britain occurred on 29 July, during an afternoon convoy patrol off Felixstowe. As Blue 3 flying at 12,000 feet, Patrick sighted enemy aircraft travelling east at approximately 8,000 feet. He waggled his wings and informed Blue 1 over the radio but there was some sort of R/T failure because Blue 1 did not receive his message. Patrick broke away from his section and chased a Dornier Do17 out to sea. When in position Patrick performed a quarter attack out of the sun, then followed up with another long burst from his eight .303 machine guns. Initially the German bomber took no evasive action but suddenly it reduced in speed and skidded toward the sea with one wing lowered. Pieces fell away from its engine and centre section but Patrick was distracted from witnessing its fate due to four Bf109s, in line astern, turning towards the sun. By now Patrick was over occupied enemy

A Hawker Hurricane being serviced by mechanics in France. (*Peter Ayerst*)

territory and with no ammunition left and hungry 109s about, he made a dash for home.

The weight of the Luftwaffe's attacks increased in early August. On Thursday 8th the core of the day's battle raged over a convoy codenamed Peewit. Consisting of twenty merchant ships with nine naval escort vessels, Peewit set out on the previous evening's tide from the Medway and attempted to pass through the Dover Strait undetected at night. German radar on the Calais coast spotted the convoy which subsequently led to an attack by E-boats in the early morning hours. As the sun rose and the cloud base lifted the convoy became dangerously exposed to a heavy air assault, fronted by Junkers Ju87 dive-bombers. The convoy suffered repeated attacks throughout the morning which continued late into the afternoon.

At 1540 hours twelve Hurricanes of 43 Squadron were ordered off to protect the convoy which by then was positioned off the Isle of Wight. Flight Lieutenant Tom Dalton-Morgan was leading the Fighting Cocks into battle. Tony was leading Yellow Section in Hurricane P3214. As the Squadron approached St Catherine's Point, hordes of enemy aircraft were spotted. By

1600 hours over eighty Ju87s and sixty-eight Bf109s and Bf110s were making their way to Weymouth Bay. The ingenuity of British radar along the coast had exposed the enemy's approach so that two Hurricane squadrons were already in position to meet the attack. No. 43 Squadron was one of them, in company with 145 Squadron, led by John Peel. Some of the fighters were tasked with setting fire to the barrage balloons protecting the convoy so that the Ju87 Stukas could dive-bomb the ships with their notorious accuracy. High above the 87s were Bf109s and Bf110s circling like eagles. Tony climbed towards the 109s but his section was immediately engaged by Bf110s that dived on them from above and astern. Tony turned into three of them flying in line astern and led his section into a head-on counter attack. With the third and last 110 lined up in his gun sight, Tony thumbed the gun button on his control column, giving it a long burst. The closing speed between Tony's Hurricane and the 110 was tremendous and in seconds they zoomed passed one another. Tony snatched a brief look behind and saw white smoke trailing from the twin-engine fighter. Tony then scanned his surroundings and spotted a formation of Stuka's heading south on their way home. Tony engaged by diving through the formation which welcomed him with a hail of return fire. He managed to score strikes on one of the 87s which emitted clouds of smoke before breaking away to port. Tony then opened fire at a second Stuka, which also issued smoke as it dived away, narrowly avoiding a collision with another 87. Still diving through the formation, Tony lined up another Stuka in his sight and expended the remainder of his ammunition with a long burst. The Stuka poured black smoke as it dived towards the Channel. When Tony finally emerged from the Stuka swarm he was bounced by a fighter that had been waiting for him. Tony immediately took violent evasive action and in doing so caught a glimpse of his Stuka close to the sea pouring black smoke. Tony finally ducked into cloud and managed to lose his pursuer before returning to Tangmere.

During the scrap Tony's Hurricane had sustained visible battle damage so when he landed back at base his ground crew approached with caution, fearing the worst for the pilot inside. Tony emerged, apparently in one piece, much to the relief of his onlookers. He was slightly wounded however by shell splinters in his legs. Out of the twenty merchant ships in convoy Peewit, only four reached Swanage unscathed, six were badly damaged and had to sail for other ports, seven were sunk in the Channel and the rest were damaged. The Luftwaffe claimed twenty RAF fighters destroyed but in fact the RAF lost thirteen aircraft destroyed and five were damaged in the heavy day's fighting. The Luftwaffe fared worse from the convoy battle losing ten Stukas and twelve fighters destroyed with an additional four fighters and eight Stukas damaged. Two of Tony's colleagues, Pilot Officers Cruttenden and Oelofse had been shot down and killed by enemy fighters. His mentor Frank Carey had also been wounded in the arm after fighting with 110s.

That night Tony secured a few hours leave and returned to Farnborough to take care of his injuries and of course to see Bunny. Once at home Bunny helped him pick out the splinters which his medical officer had diagnosed as 'multiple foreign bodies in both legs'. Tony pressed Bunny to marry him instead. She promised she would marry him in a fortnight, half serious, just like the time she had promised to marry Patrick when he was made a squadron leader. Tony took the commitment seriously and booked a friend's cottage near Tangmere for their honeymoon. It was an impossible dilemma for Bunny who was clearly fond of both brothers, but with Tony being stationed closer to Farnborough than Patrick, she found it difficult to resist his charm.

At lunchtime on Monday 12 August Tony was back in the air leading Yellow Section in Hurricane R4108. During the patrol three Heinkel 111s were sighted flying at 15,000 feet off Portsmouth. Tony gave the order to attack and his section began to chase the bombers over the Channel. Tony selected his target and closed in. At 200 yards range his eight Brownings began to flash at the enemy machine. He fired three deflection bursts while closing to 50 yards range but his own aircraft was struck by return fire. With a damaged engine and oil tank, Tony had no choice but to break off the interception and return to Tangmere.

The next morning Tony was back in the air leading Yellow Section in Hurricane R4102. It was 13 August 1940, a significant day during the Battle of Britain because the Luftwaffe launched *Adler Tag*.

Adler Tag, or Eagle Day, was to be the start of intended mass attacks designed to knock out the RAF once and for all. At 0645 hours Tony and his colleagues ran into a large formation of KG 54 that was ordered to bomb the RAE at Farnborough and Odiham. There were thirty Junkers Ju88s in the lead of the formation, followed by another wave of 88s and He111s. Bf110s were also sighted flying above and behind the oncoming bombers. The Squadron approached the first wave of 88s head-on which caused the bombers to break formation. Tony attacked one bomber from astern with a long burst but he did not see any results and then broke away to engage the second formation. He then opened fire on another bomber which could have been a He111 or a Ju88. Tony was not sure which because of his poor eyesight. What he did see was black smoke streaming from the bomber's port engine and its starboard engine stop dead. The enemy aircraft continued to fly south, losing height rapidly. Another Hurricane began to attack the same bomber, so Tony left him to it and peeled away and made his way back towards the main formation. Again Tony attacked what he thought was a He111 or maybe a Ju88, he couldn't be sure. Either way his attack caused jet black smoke to pour from its port engine before it licked with vivid red flames. The bomber dived steeply and disappeared into cloud. Tony then attacked three stragglers but their return fire struck his engine. Initially Tony was tempted to bale out but he decided that he could probably force-land the aircraft instead. After selecting his spot, he took his Hurricane down and landed on Northend Farm, Milland near Midhurst at 0727 hours. As Tony scrambled away from his Hurricane it burst into flames. It had been an exhausting morning for Tony but by midday he was airborne once again. Such was the pace of battle.

After an evening patrol on 15 August, Tony reported the following:

> I was Yellow 1 in the rear section of 43 Squadron – flying at 15,000 ft when the enemy a/c [aircraft] were sighted. I remained up above them in the sun when our squadron engaged them. Seeing that the enemy fighters weren't going to play, I attached myself to 4 Heinkel 111[s] flying south at 17,000 ft where I was joined by Yellow 2 who had just engaged a JU 88. We attacked simultaneously just after crossing the coast at West Wittering, employing small deflection tactics at close range... The majority of my attacks were directed at the port aircraft which shortly afterwards crashed into the sea with a trail of thick white smoke issuing from it. (Yellow 2 witnessed this). I then attacked the opposite flank a/c together with my Number 2 and when I ran out of ammo the He111 was obviously damaged, the port engine issuing intermittent dense black smoke and flying in a see-saw fashion – though this might have been evasive action. The two rear gunners had long since ceased fire... I called up Yellow 2 telling him to return to base with me [as] we were uncomfortably far out to sea and I had no more ammo. We landed at base safely. On the whole the rear gunfire of the 111's was inaccurate.

Tony's last statement about inaccurate return fire seems ironic given the fact that the aircraft he was flying on this sortie, Hurricane R4107, code lettered 'FT-B' returned to Tangmere with two bullets in its main spar.

The following day the Squadron intercepted a raid destined for Tangmere during the afternoon. As usual Tony was leading Yellow Section when the Squadron engaged two large formations of Ju87 Stukas near Selsey Bill in a head-on attack. A melee ensued and Tony soon found he had become separated from his section. He then saw several Stukas flying low at 500 feet. Tony dived towards the last machine in the formation and opened fire with deadly accuracy. The Stuka dived steeply into a slight turn and soon crashed into the sea about two miles south-east of Bembridge. Another three-second burst from Tony's guns put another Stuka into the sea near the Sussex coast, but he discovered that his radiator had also been hit. Tony made way for home but on his way back he was attacked by four Bf109s that damaged his engine. Tony managed to dive away towards the Isle of Wight but he was forced to crash-land with his wheels up in a field near Parkhurst. The landing was difficult because he had to land in such a small space, but somehow he managed to grind to a halt but in doing so he was thrown forward on his straps and three of his front teeth were knocked out. Naturally dazed by the crash-landing, Tony was assisted to the ferry which crossed to Southampton. His Hurricane N2621 was a write-off.

That night Tony stayed in a hotel in Southampton where he drowned his sorrows with the locals. The following morning he telephoned the squadron adjutant and asked him to send someone to pick him up and pay his hotel bill. Tony was soon returned to Tangmere feeling the worse for wear, but as ever, he was greeted by his friends who were thrilled to see him back with the Squadron once again.

Tony's contribution to the RAF was deservedly recognised a few days later when he was awarded a DFC for his service. The citation to his DFC reads as follows:

Pilot Officer Charles Anthony WOODS-SCAWEN (40770).

This officer has taken part in all engagements carried out by his squadron since the commencement of hostilities. He has destroyed a total of six enemy aircraft, and severely damaged several others. In June 1940, Pilot Officer Woods-Scawen was shot down, landing some 25 miles within French territory, but succeeded in making his way back to his squadron. In spite of the fact that this pilot has been shot down six times, he has continued to fight with unabated courage and enthusiasm, and has shown outstanding qualities as a resourceful and determined leader.

News of Tony's award was another chest swelling moment for the Woods-Scawen family. Bunny was also proud of Tony, as she had been with Patrick at the announcement of his DFC.

Bunny made a special effort to travel to Tangmere to sew the purple and white medal ribbon onto Tony's uniform. That night Tony turned on the charm and Bunny finally agreed to marry him in all seriousness. Two nights later, Bunny went out with Patrick and when in the corner of a favourite night spot she began to cry. 'What's the matter, Bun-Bun?' Patrick inquired. Bunny told him of her decision to marry Tony, delivering a devastating blow for Patrick. Ever the gentlemen, he soon settled her down. 'That's all right, Bunny,' said Patrick. 'It can't be helped.' Patrick's love for both his brother and Bunny far outweighed his own disappointment. 'You'll starve on Tony's money,' said Patrick. 'Now that I'm a flying officer, I'll make you an allotment out of my pay.'[7.] The warm gesture had Bunny crying again.

Tony told his groundcrew that the award was just as much theirs as it was his, for all of the hard work they had put in around the clock keeping his aircraft serviceable. He even apologised to Flight Sergeant Parker for the number of aircraft he had lost or brought back damaged and divulged his secret about his bad eyesight. 'But for God's sake, Flight,' said Tony, 'don't breathe a word of this to anybody, or they'll whip me off ops.'[8]

On 18 August, the Luftwaffe intensified its attacks over Britain by heavily bombing RAF airfields on mass, including Biggin Hill, Croydon and Kenley, all of which were badly hit. Goring's Luftwaffe was not only trying to rid British fighters in the air but also on the ground. The day's violence would end with heavy losses to both sides. No. 43 Squadron claimed four enemy aircraft shot down and others damaged after intercepting a Stuka attack on Tangmere. Tony's mentor and friend Frank Carey was shot down by Messerschmitt 109s of JG 27 during this attack and he was forced to crash-land his Hurricane at Holme Street Farm, Pulborough. He was wounded in his right knee by a stray bullet and taken to hospital.

During the evening Patrick's friend in 85 Squadron, Dickie Lee, was also shot down and reported missing. He was last seen by Peter Townsend in pursuit of enemy aircraft 30 miles off the east coast, but Lee would never return from the pursuit and his Hurricane would never be found.

Patrick's next official claim during the Battle of Britain occurred on 26 August. At 1449 hours, twelve Hurricanes of 85 Squadron took off to patrol base before being vectored to the Maidstone area. Thirty minutes later the Squadron spotted a formation of Dorniers escorted by a daunting number of Bf109s near Eastchurch. Squadron Leader Townsend brought his pilots round in a wide turn, moving into echelon as they levelled out about 2 miles away from the bombers. Townsend throttled back to reduce closing speed as he led the squadron towards the Dorniers head-on. Townsend lined his opponent up in his sight and held his position, ignoring the streams of tracer darting overhead. He held his gun button for as long as he could until fearing collision he pushed the control column forward and broke away below. The head-on attack forced the leading section of the Dorniers to break formation and a general melee followed. Not far behind Patrick was leading Green Section into the attack. He fired a short burst at one of the bombers and then broke away below to avoid a collision. He then climbed back into the action and delivered another frontal attack on the main formation but he was travelling too fast and he overshot. The excess speed would not be wasted. Patrick climbed again and engaged about twelve Bf109s which were coming down in a shallow dive to protect the bombers. He fired a three-second burst into the belly of a 109 and claimed that 'it seemed to whip stall'. Patrick's Hurricane also stalled in the climb, so he dived away, unable to confirm any definite results of his attack, but he thought that it was probably destroyed. Patrick then swept in from dead astern and opened fire at one of the Dorniers which was being attacked by his colleagues, sergeants Walker-Smith and Howes. Patrick saw black smoke pour from the starboard engine in one big puff before it stopped. The Dornier then dived through clouds where it was engaged by other Hurricanes of the

Squadron. Patrick pulled back on the stick and climbed back up into the blue. He made a final attack on the large formation of Dorniers which had turned back across the Channel. Patrick expended the remainder of his ammunition and left the Dornier he had singled out streaming white smoke. Before heading back to base, Patrick followed the formation for a little while, called up the ground controller and passed on the formation's location and course.

Two days later Patrick was found patrolling with the Squadron at 18,000 feet. Shortly after 1600 hours the Squadron received an order to intercept 'Raid 15'. Townsend led his section towards Dungeness, with Hamilton's section on his right, Allard's on his left, and Patrick's Green Section under his tail. Soon enough twenty enemy fighters were spotted near Dungeness. No. 85 Squadron approached the enemy from the sun and engaged. An extract from Patrick's combat report continues:

> The EA [enemy aircraft] on sighting us all turned to the left I was able to give one EA a long burst from the quarter following to astern. The EA half rolled and I delivered another long burst from astern.

Black smoke and what appeared to be petrol from the wing tanks poured out of the 109 and it dived down vertically. Patrick dived after it for several thousand feet and broke off when it was apparently out of control. The 109 was believed to have crashed near Dungeness and this was confirmed by Maidstone Observer Corps who reported seeing a Messerschmitt 109 in the sea off Dymchurch at 1640 hours.

The Squadron claimed six Bf109s destroyed and one Bf110 damaged, with no losses in return. This action was also witnessed by none other than Winston Churchill, during his visit to the south-east coast defences.

No. 85 continued to fly and fight during continuous and exhausting patrols against the relentless Luftwaffe.

On 30 August Patrick destroyed a Messerschmitt 110 after firing several bursts into the enemy machine. The 110's starboard engine was put out of action and its port engine burst into flames. Patrick watched the enemy dive steeply into cloud until it was lost to sight, but shortly afterwards columns of smoke were seen on the ground near Dover.

Minutes after Patrick had shot down this 110, Tony was airborne with 43 Squadron, leading Red Section into attack near Tangmere. He dived after a Bf109 for several thousand feet using full boost and then opened fire at 250 yards range. The 109 emitted smoke, turned on to its back and dived vertically towards the sea. Tony was convinced that the pilot would not have been able to pull out of the dive, so he broke away in search of another target.

Saturday 31 August opened with fair weather and haze over the Thames Estuary and Dover Straits. All appeared calm until reports of enemy formations crossing the Channel began to fly in before 0800 hours. The day would flare into ferocious fighting.

During the afternoon the Luftwaffe raided Croydon, where 85 Squadron was stationed. Bombs began to fall on the east side of the airfield just as twelve Hurricanes were taking off. Leading the Squadron, Peter Townsend, felt a surge of anger at the attackers, when he turned around to see his Squadron emerging from a vast eruption of smoke and debris. His own aircraft was also affected by the blast when his engine suddenly faltered, faded, and then picked up again. Townsend remembered:

> Then I looked up; thousands of feet above, Me 110s were wheeling in the blue, with Me.109s swarming above. I thought the Me 110s had bombed. Yet some say a dozen Dorniers had attacked from lower down. If so, I never saw them. I was mad with rage at the Me 110s. 'After them, but look out for the 109s,' I called and the furious chase began.

Townsend, with all his might, climbed towards the 110s. He continued, 'The squadron were somewhere behind; that was enough. I did not give them a further thought. Only 'get those ill-mannered bastards' who had disturbed our lunch, smashed our airfield, invaded our sky.'[9.]

Townsend eventually caught up with the enemy over Tunbridge Wells. He shot down two Bf109s but while attacking a third from very close range his aircraft was shot up by a 110. Townsend felt a sudden shock as his left foot was knocked off the rudder-bar and he momentarily lost control of his Hurricane and went into a dive with petrol gushing into the cockpit. At first Townsend toyed with the notion of making a forced-landing but he was over a densely wooded area, so baled out at 1,400 feet and landed near Hawkhurst. Wounded, Townsend was taken to hospital to be treated. Later, the nose cap of a cannon shell was extracted from his left foot and his big toe was amputated.

Between 1340 and 1400 hours, ten of the twelve Hurricanes that had taken off from Croydon returned to base. Pilot Officer Pyers Worrall had been shot down by cannon shells and baled out of his aircraft with a wounded thigh. He was admitted to Croydon hospital, where Townsend was also treated.

With Townsend out of action the task of temporally leading the Squadron fell to Patrick and Sammy Allard.

The Squadron flew four more sorties before the day's end. Patrick led B Flight into battle and Allard fronted A Flight.

Just before 1745 hours the Squadron sighted enemy aircraft south of the Thames Estuary. Patrick estimated that there were about 30 bombers and 100 fighters, a mixed bag of Messerschmitt 109s and 110s. The Squadron attacked the bombers from its most favourable position, out of the sun. Patrick led Blue Section into the dangerous 'head-on attack', firing a short burst and quickly breaking away to avoid colliding with his foe. Tearing away from the bombers Patrick fastened his sights onto a Bf109 and thumbed his gun button. A five-second burst from his Brownings sent the fighter spinning away out of control. Patrick moved on to another 109 and carried out a quarter attack. The enemy fighter half-rolled and attempted to climb, but Patrick waited for it and gave it a long burst from astern. The 109 turned then dived out of sight pouring black smoke. Patrick reported that 'a Spitfire also gave me an inaccurate burst which was luckily too low'. At such high speeds in a sky full of erratic aircraft flying in all directions, misidentification was practically commonplace.

One of Patrick's comrades, a New Zealander, called William Hodgson, also fired a burst at the bombers head-on and then broke off to attack a Bf109 with two bursts. The 109 rolled over and went down in flames. Hodgson did not have time to revel in his success. His Hurricane was struck by a cannon shell which blew up his oil lines and glycol tank and set fire to his engine. With fears of being mutilated by fire or burnt to death, Hodgson began to prepare to bale out but when he was half-way out the cockpit he realised that he was over a densely populated area, near the Thames Haven oil storage tanks. Fully appreciating the danger his Hurricane could cause to the local population down below, Hodgson got back into his aircraft and decided to attempt a force-landing. For some very threatening moments, Hodgson skilfully kept the flames under control by side-slipping his aircraft. Despite low wires and other obstacles in his path, Hodgson finally made a wheels-up landing in a field at Fanton Chase, Shotgate. Unbelievably, Pilot Officer Hodgson was unharmed and his Hurricane 'VY-G' was said to be repairable. The selfless spirit demonstrated by Hodgson was later awarded with a DFC.†

It had been an exhausting day for Patrick and his peers but the action was not yet over. They had barely been back on the ground when they were once again scrambled off at 1917 hours to patrol Hawkinge.

An indication of the enemy's position was given by anti-aircraft fire thumping into the sky over Dover. The Squadron saw nine Bf109s flying at 15,000 feet, so they circled out to sea and when the fighters passed by to port the Squadron attacked, apparently catching the 109s by surprise. Patrick carried out a beam attack which forced a 109 to dive steeply. He then pursued it and fired another burst from astern. The enemy aircraft went down on fire with a wing-tank burning. Pilot Officer 'Zulu' Lewis had watched Patrick's attack from his own cockpit and later confirmed his 'kill' as destroyed. The Squadron landed back at Croydon between 2005 and 2022 hours.

---

† On 13 March 1941, William Hodgson, Sammy Allard and Francis Walker-Smith were tragically killed in a flying accident when the top nose panel of a Havoc aircraft they were travelling in detached and jammed the rudder. The aircraft went into a spin and crashed into the ground, killing all three of 85 Squadron's aces.

Fighter pilots scramble at Reims in 1940. (*Peter Ayerst*)

On Sunday 1 September 1940, eleven Hurricanes of 85 Squadron took off from Croydon to intercept a raid heading in the direction of Tunbridge Wells and Kenley. Just before 1400 hours a large number of enemy aircraft were spotted near Biggin Hill, flying at about 15,000 feet. At this point the Squadron was positioned about 5,000 feet below the enemy. The Squadron climbed as fast as it was able, but despite its best efforts, it was at a miserable disadvantage and the enemy fighters knew it and dived to engage.

Sammy Allard was able to avoid the fighters and went after a stray Dornier which he attacked as it made for Dungeness. He carried out three attacks before sending the bomber down belching smoke and oil from its engines. The rear-gunner baled out and the Dornier force-landed near a railway line at Lydd. Allard noticed that his oil pressure had dropped rapidly, so he landed at Lympne with a dead engine. Not long after, when his Hurricane was being repaired, the aerodrome was bombed and a mechanic working on Allard's aircraft at the time was killed and another mechanic was seriously injured.

The enemy fighters caught up with Flying Officer Arthur Gowers over Oxted and shot up his aircraft with cannon shells. Gowers baled out with severe burns to his hands and slight wounds to a hand and foot but he landed safely and was soon admitted to Caterham hospital. Gowers' Hurricane crashed near Merstham Tunnel.

Twenty-year-old Sergeant Glendon Booth was also shot down, a year to the day he was called up for service. Booth's aircraft was badly hit in combat with Bf109s over the Tunbridge Wells area. He baled out with burns and his parachute alight. Booth was further injured due to a heavy landing and was soon taken to Purley hospital to be treated. Sadly, Booth did not recover from his injuries and he later died on 7 February 1941.

Other pilots in the Squadron clawed back some retribution when Pilot Officer Charles English downed a Dornier, as did Sergeant Harold Howes, who also damaged a Bf109 that he interrupted from shooting at a Hurricane, and Sergeant Walter Evans claimed a Bf109 and Bf110 destroyed.

Out of the eleven Hurricanes that had originally set out on this patrol, only six returned to Croydon between 1427 and 1500 hours. Pilot Officer Lewis returned with battle damage after combat with Bf109s over Kenley and landed with his undercarriage retracted due to it being jammed.

It had been a gloomy day for the Squadron to say the least, and when darkness finally covered the aerodrome that night; two pilots were still unaccounted for. One was Sergeant Hugh Mortimer Ellis. The other was Flying Officer Patrick Woods-Scawen.

The next day Patrick's aircraft, Hurricane P3150, was found partly buried in the recreation ground at Kenley. The cockpit was empty, so Patrick for the time being was still listed as missing.

The news soon reached the Woods-Scawen family and of course Bunny, but Tony was unaware that his older brother had failed to return.

On Monday 2 September, the day Patrick's Hurricane was discovered; Tony was continuing the fight against the Luftwaffe with eleven other Hurricanes of 43 Squadron, led by Caesar Hull.

Tony was leading Yellow Section towards a formation of bombers headed for Maidstone, when a dogfight broke out between 18,000 and 20,000 feet. During the skirmish, at least two enemy fighters were shot down by the Squadron, but in return, Hurricane V7420, was set alight in combat with Bf109s over east Kent. This Hurricane belonged to Pilot Officer Tony Woods-Scawen, who attempted to crash-land at Fryland near Ivychurch at approximately 1330 hours. Two boys cycling near Ivychurch on Romney Marsh at the time had witnessed Tony's plight. 'I didn't actually see Woods-Scawen's Hurricane attacked,' remembered one of them, Len Green, many years later, 'But when I looked he had just come out of the plane and they seemed to fall together for a few seconds. The plane seemed to be alight and

No. 43 Squadron. L-R: Sgt James Buck, P/O Tony Woods-Scawen, Fl/Lt Caesar Hull, F/O Royce Wilkinson and Sgt Geoffrey Garton. (*Tristan Woods-Scawen*)

the pilot's parachute didn't seem to open fully and was flapping at about 2,000 feet or less. It all happened so quickly – it was over in a few seconds.'[10]

Close to the scene, an Anglican parson saw Tony bale out, dangerously low and not anything like 2,000 feet estimated later by Green. Whatever the height, it was far too low for Tony to evacuate his aircraft. By the time the parson reached him, Tony was dead. His body was carried into the nearby church and on 5 September, those most dear to Tony attended his funeral at Folkestone. The sadness only worsened the next day when Patrick's body was discovered in the unkempt, overgrown grounds of The Ivies, Kenley Lane. Like his younger brother, Patrick had baled out of his Hurricane, but his parachute had failed to open and he was killed on impact. Patrick's body was buried in the churchyard of St Mary's Parish Church, Caterham on the Hill.

In later years Peter Townsend referred to the eldest Woods-Scawen brother as 'little Patrick, who smiled with his eyes' and Tony 'as brave as a lion'. For all those who had the pleasure of knowing the Woods-Scawen boys it seemed impossible that such charming, gentle, good humoured and brave young men such as they could really be gone. Both Patrick and Tony had been enormously popular in their respective squadrons; they were fabulous morale boosters and proficient fighter pilots and leaders in the air and on the ground. Both Patrick and Tony had also left a lasting impression that would never fade on Bunny Lawrence's heart.

In June 1941, the boys widowed father, Bunny Lawrence, and their first cousin, Gerald Woods-Scawen, went to Buckingham Palace to collect Patrick and Tony's DFC medals from the King. Their Auntie Nellie was still too devastated by their deaths to go.

Gerald Woods-Scawen was a nineteen-year-old sergeant serving with 92 Squadron. Tragically for the Woods-Scawen family, he too was killed in action, when on 3 October 1941 his Spitfire was shot down.

Bunny later married when she was twenty-three years of age and had six children. She would never forget her cherished boys, Patrick and Tony Woods-Scawen, the two brothers, with one dream.

CHAPTER 2

Butch Barton

Robert Alexander Barton was born in Kamloops, British Columbia on 7 June 1916. His mother was of Scottish decent and his father was a Canadian civil engineer. As a young man Barton was educated in Vernon, which required a weekly journey by steamship to and from his home at Penticton. When he reached nineteen years of age Barton paid a visit to a recruiting office in Vancouver, where he was accepted into the RAF.

In January 1936, Barton made the long voyage to England to take up a short service commission. After completing his training at No. 9 Flying Training School in Thornaby, Barton joined 41 Squadron at Catterick, where he remained until he was posted to Church Fenton as a Flight Commander of 249 Squadron at its formation in May 1940.

When the Squadron moved south to Boscombe Down during August 1940, 'Butch' Barton's war really began.

At around 1700 hours on 15 August 1940, radar stations on the Hampshire and Sussex coasts reported the approach of enemy raiders. Spitfires and Hurricanes patrolling south-east of the Isle of Wight intercepted a number of enemy aircraft, but a mass formation of bombers broke through the line and made its way inland. Some of the bombers headed for the airfield at RNAS Worthy Down, and others targeted airfields at Middle Wallop and Odiham. During this time, 249 Squadron had been ordered to patrol Warmwell at 15,000 feet. It was a beautiful evening with a clear blue sky. The Squadron's A Flight did not see any enemy aircraft to engage throughout the patrol, but B Flight sighted eleven Junkers Ju88s escorted by a heavy number of Bf110s near Middle Wallop. Barton was leading Blue Section when he engaged the Messerschmitt Bf110s, in company with Spitfires of 609 Squadron.

It was approximately 1735 hours near the Ringwood area when Barton led his section into attack. He focused his sights on the rearmost section of the Messerschmitts, but soon discovered it was not going to be as straight forward as he had hoped, for the twin engine Messerschmitts were turned towards the approaching Hurricanes to engage his section in return.

Butch Barton with
249 Squadron mascot
Wilfred the duck. (*Tich
Palliser*)

Barton squeezed his gun button for two seconds, firing a 30-degree deflection burst at a 110 from his eight machine guns. Results quickly followed as smoke was seen emitting from one of its engines. Pilot Officer Bryan Meaker, flying as Blue 2, followed Barton into the attack but his aircraft went into a spin. Meaker managed to recover from the spin and in doing so he saw four Bf110s circling. Meaker selected one as his target and attacked from beam with a full deflection burst. His bullets struck a 110 which caused streams of white vapour to pour out from both its engines. Meaker followed it down to 500 feet and watched the enemy aircraft crash about ten miles north of Southampton.

Meanwhile Barton had lined another 110 up in his gun sight and let off two deflection bursts. Bullets entered the 110's fuselage behind the pilot and smoke poured from the aircraft's starboard engine. Barton followed the stricken Messerschmitt down and watched it crash about four miles north-west of Romsey.

Pilot Officer Terry Crossey, flying as Blue 3, also engaged a Bf110 that he caught following Pilot Officer Meaker. He also attacked another formation

Butch Barton portrait by
Ashley Marie Morrison.

but broke away when he thought that three enemy single-seater fighters were
on his tail. These fighters were most likely Spitfires or Hurricanes because the
Luftwaffe's only single-seater fighter at the time, the Bf109, was not involved
in this action. Such uncertainty was often a by-product of high speed combat.
A sky full of aircraft, diving, twisting and turning in all directions left little or
no time for a pilot to hang around to be conclusive. 'Get in and get out' was
a trusted rule in order for a fighter pilot to survive. Low on fuel, Crossey was
obliged to land at Harwell and two hours later he returned to base. Meaker
returned to Boscombe Down at 1755 hours and twenty-five minutes later
Flight Lieutenant Barton returned having fired 800 rounds in anger.

When the pilots of A Flight landed back at base they were a little surprised
to hear B Flight chatting excitedly amongst themselves about their various
combat experiences as they had not even seen one enemy aircraft during the
patrol. Pilot Officer Tom 'Ginger' Neil of A Flight joined the circle to listen
to their intriguing conversations. Not only had Blue Section seen combat but
Flying Officer Denis Parnall and Pilot Officer John Beazley of Green Section
had also been involved in the action. At the time he was not to know, but Pilot

Officer Neil would soon see a lot of action with the Squadron. By the end of the war he would claim twelve and four shared enemy aircraft destroyed, with additional 'probables' and 'damaged' enemy aircraft to his credit. The Canadian, Barton, had already started to show his calibre in combat.

The following day the Squadron would again be called into action when twelve Hurricanes, led by Flight Lieutenant Barton, were ordered off to patrol the area between Poole and Southampton at 1305 hours. During the patrol a formation of Bf109Es were sighted and Red Section, led by Flight Lieutenant James Nicolson, flew off to investigate. Suddenly, out of nowhere, Red Section was bounced from above and astern and Nicolson's Hurricane was hit and set ablaze. In a courageous flurry Nicolson remained with his burning aircraft and, ignoring his wounds and the intense heat, he remained in his cockpit to attack a Bf110 which appeared in front of him. Owing to the unbearable heat that followed Nicolson was then forced to bale out of his aircraft but as he floated down in his parachute he was shot at by a member of the Home Guard who mistook him for a German airman. Both attacks had left him severely wounded and he was taken to the Royal Southampton Hospital to be treated. A few days later from his hospital bed, Nicolson sent a report of the action to Squadron Leader John Grandy.

An extract of the report can be read below:

> I was proceeding with Red Section…when I noticed three enemy aircraft some distance away to the left. I informed Butch [Flt Lt Barton], who told me to go and investigate. As however the three unfortunates ran into twelve Spitfires long before I got in range, I turned round to rejoin Butch, climbing from 15,000 feet to 17,000 feet so that I could catch him when I saw him. As I approached Southampton I heard Yellow Leader shout 'Tally-ho, one mile to port' and immediately turned off to join the scrap, at the same time reaching for my map. As I was opening my map, I was struck in the cockpit by four successive cannon shells.

Nicolson's courage in remaining in a burning aircraft with cannon shell wounds to engage a Messerschmitt 110 was commended and he was later awarded the Victoria Cross. (In fact it was to be the only Victoria Cross awarded to Fighter Command in the Second World War.)

Pilot Officer Martyn King's aircraft was also damaged by a cannon shell and he too abandoned his cockpit but, horrifically, King's parachute failed him and he crashed down through a tall tree, fell onto the lawn of a house in Clifton Road, Shirley, and died in the arms of a man who lived nearby.

The third Hurricane in Red Section also received damage from the bounce but the pilot was able to safely return to base. It was a terrible day for the Squadron.

During the following week, enemy bombers continued to wreak havoc over the south of England. On 24 August a large raid of Junkers Ju88s attacked Portsmouth, killing and injuring many civilians and Royal Navy personnel. Meanwhile 249 Squadron was patrolling the Isle of Wight, with Butch Barton leading B Flight. At 1720 hours Blue Section sighted enemy aircraft at 19,000 feet heading south and they engaged the fighter escort. Barton soon found himself in a head-on attack, firing at a Messerschmitt 109 that was also shooting at him. The attack was over in a flash. Barton had only fired a quick burst from 150 yards range but when he turned away from the duel he saw the 109 diving towards the sea, emitting white vapour.

On 1 September, 249 Squadron moved to North Weald in Essex to relieve 56 Squadron. The next day the Squadron was brought to readiness at dawn and by 0720 hours ten Hurricanes were scrambled from North Weald to intercept a large formation of Dornier Do17s, escorted by approximately 100 Messerschmitt 109Es and 110s. The bombers had been ordered to attack RAF airfields. Out of the six squadrons sent off to meet the raiders only the Hurricanes of 249 Squadron and Spitfires of 72 Squadron made contact with the enemy. After patrolling Rochester at 15,000 feet, the Squadron, led by Squadron Leader John Grandy, sighted the enemy formation and engaged.

Barton's combat report illustrates his part of the action:

I selected a Dornier which had broken formation after our first attack and was flying eastwards on its own. I carried out an astern attack, firing about ten bursts at both engines and cockpit. No evasive tactics were adopted but there was a lot of return fire, some of which hit my aircraft. Pieces flew off the E/A and I noticed what appeared to be a weight on a piece of wire ejected from the aircraft, but this did not hit me. E/A gradually lost height. Plt Off Meaker also attacked this aircraft which crash-landed on Rochford aerodrome, having just caught fire. One occupant baled out at 100 feet and his parachute failed to open in time.

Bartron's wingman, Pilot Officer Bryan Meaker, wrote the following graphic description of the combat in his diary:

Attacked *en masse*, then dived away as fighters came down. Joined Butch again after a frantic tail-watching breakaway, and started after bombers again. Suddenly we see a Dornier coming towards us – running for home. We jump on it – Butch sits on its tail, pumping lead at it. I do quarter attacks. He doesn't like this, lumps fall off and smoke pours out. I am awake now and feeling hungry. Butch says, 'Don't waste any more ammunition on him; this guy's finished.' I say, 'OK Bud' and formate on the Dornier as he heads for Rochford. He is a wreck – rudders in ribbons and pieces falling off all the

Butch Barton
conversing with
Tom Neil in the
foreground. (*Tich
Palliser*)

time. One guy comes out at 100 feet. Parachute streams as he hits the ground
– bounces. Butch and I are very cocky, go home and shoot a line.[1]

The Dornier belonged to 9/KG3 and owing to the intense attack it belly-landed
at Rochford airfield. The German pilot was found wounded, the rear gunner
was dead and the other two crew members were injured but had survived the
attack.

In relation to Barton's character and capabilities, Wing Commander Tom
Neil, DFC*, AFC, Bronze Star, wrote the following of his comrade:

Butch Barton, in my view, was one of the best RAF fighter pilots of the Second
World War. Which was surprising, as he did not look or sound like a hero…
he was small, had little dress sense, could never be described as eloquent, and
his hand-writing looked like the trail of a fly with ink on its feet, crawling
across an empty page. Moreover, and to my personal distaste, he smoked
vile-smelling Canadian cigarettes called 'Sweet Caporals'… He was brave
and calculating in battle and, like many Canadians, was an excellent shot,
both with a twelve-bore shotgun and a Hurricane's eight Browning machine
guns. Always calm and fearless in the air he was a determined, self-effacing
leader.[2]

On 5 September, 249 Squadron was back in the thick of it when in conjunction with 46 Squadron the pilots intercepted a formation of enemy aircraft over the Thames Estuary. Flight Lieutenant Barton led his Section down to attack some Dorniers but his Hurricane (V6625) was hit by Dornier return fire and a Bf109E which had latched onto his tail with tenacity in its wings. Barton was left with no choice but to abandon his aircraft because his engine was on fire. He baled out and landed safely in a garden below. Retribution soon followed when Sergeant Henry Davidson attacked the 109 with a short burst at 200-yards range. The 109 dived and Davidson pursued it until at about 10,000 feet the German pilot pulled out of the dive and began to climb. Davidson let off a succession of short bursts, which caused the 109 to dive for the sea with smoke pouring from its engine.

After getting back on his feet, Barton was driven back to North Weald in an army car to be greeted by friendly jibes from his colleagues for allowing himself to get shot down by a bomber.

The following day Squadron Leader Grandy was shot down, presumably by a 109, which had caught him unaware. Grandy baled out of his aircraft but was wounded in the process. With the CO now recovering in hospital the task of leading the Squadron fell into the capable hands of Butch Barton.

During the afternoon of 11 September 249 Squadron was scrambled with an order to patrol the London Docks and Thames Estuary as enemy aircraft had been plotted in the Calais area. At about 1545 hours Barton led the Squadron into a head-on attack to meet 30 Heinkel He111s flying at 19,000 feet. Barton claimed one of the bombers as 'damaged' and witnessed four of the Heinkels break formation, pouring glycol. Pilot Officer Meaker, as ever, was close behind Barton but to avoid colliding with the oncoming bombers he broke away so violently that his Hurricane went into an inverted spin. He recovered several thousand feet below but he could not regain sight of the battle overhead. With little option, Meaker made his way back to base feeling peeved that he had missed out on the 'fun'.

Over the next few days the Squadron began to receive replacement pilots. The 14th saw the arrival of Pilot Officer Gerald Lewis, an experienced South African ace from 85 Squadron, who had been involved in the heavy fighting in France. Another pilot to arrive the same day was Sergeant Charles Palliser posted from 43 Squadron. Sergeant Palliser was soon christened 'Tich' by Pilot Officer Neil, as like Barton; he wasn't the tallest chap in the air force.

Sunday 15 September 1940, a day that would see the most intense aerial action of the Battle of Britain.

In the morning Flight Lieutenant Barton and Pilot Officer William Pattullo took off together to identify an unidentified aircraft, but nothing was seen and they were soon recalled to North Weald.

Shortly after they returned, at about 1130 hours twelve Hurricanes of 249 Squadron raced across the aerodrome at North Weald and began to climb towards the first major raid of the day. The Squadron, in company with 46 Squadron were vectored towards a formation of Dorniers near south London, which upon finding they attacked. Guns were fired and damage was inflicted on the bombers, but only Pilot Officer Meaker was able to claim one Dornier destroyed and Pilot Officer George Barclay claimed another as 'probable'.

Later in the afternoon the next order to scramble arrived and once again the fighter boys of 249 Squadron were hurrying towards their aircraft. A large raid of well over 100 bombers plus heavy fighter escort were crossing the Channel and all of No. 11 Group's squadrons were sent off to intercept the mass formations approaching Britain.

Over south London 249 Squadron met fifteen Dornier Do17s, followed by a formation of Heinkel 111s that were heading for the capital. Barton led the Squadron into the swarm and the bombers began to scatter. Pilot Officer Meaker attacked a Dornier with a short burst from his guns but immediately broke away to avoid heavy crossfire. Some 2,000 feet below the main action, Meaker sighted a Dornier diving from the clouds. A five-second burst from beam to quarter put the bomber's starboard engine and fuselage in flames. Meaker saw one of the bomber's crew bale out of the blazing furnace before he broke away.

Barton joined Meaker in attacking another Dornier, hitting its engine and fuselage with several bursts of machine gun fire. The bomber dived into cloud cover, with Barton and Meaker in hot pursuit. They watched the enemy machine smoking badly until it passed through cloud. Suddenly, Meaker broke away in a left-hand climbing turn to avoid the cannon shells of two Bf109s that were on his tail. He tightened the turn until he was able to get off a burst at one of the Messerschmitt fighters which was sighted slightly above him. Bullets hit the enemy's port wing and, clearly shaken, it dived into cloud. Meaker began to chase the two 109s until he lost sight of them. He then spotted two fighters coming straight for him. He held his fire, thinking the two aircraft were Spitfires, so he dodged under them, but then realised they were the same two yellow-nosed 109s as before. The Messerschmitts made off for France, leaving Meaker frustrated at being unable to catch them.

During this action Barton also claimed a second Dornier Do17 as probably destroyed, later reporting the following:

I carried out an attack on a Do17 from below and saw a great amount of material fly off front position of fuselage after a three-second burst. Aircraft dived down out of formation. Then attacked Dornier with Blue 2 [Plt Off Meaker] – smoke and oil pouring from engine and aircraft dived into cloud.

Back at dispersal Pilot Officer Tom Neil found 'a queue of pilots leading to the intelligence officer, everyone in a high state of excitement. It had been a fantastic fight, no one missing and a mounting tally of Huns: seven, eight, nine destroyed and about a similar number probable and damaged What a to-do! Crashed Huns burning on the ground everywhere; someone said that he had seen at least two. Plus mine in the sea of course!'[3]

Over the next couple of days, bad weather kept Luftwaffe activity down to a minimum, but the lull would be short lived.

After midday on 18 September Barton was leading the Squadron into a head-on attack against a force of Heinkel 111s, escorted by enemy fighters, over the Thames Estuary. Barton concentrated his fire on a Heinkel flying in the rear section and saw oil and puffs of smoke coming from its port engine. The bomber lagged behind its formation on its return to France and could only be claimed as 'damaged'.

On the 25 September, Pilot Officer Neil and Barton's good friend and trusted wingman, Pilot Officer Meaker, were informed that they had each been awarded the DFC.

Two days later the Squadron was airborne before 0900 hours. Barton led the Squadron through foggy conditions and rendezvoused with 46 Squadron. The Hurricanes began to patrol Wickford but they were soon vectored towards Maidstone where enemy aircraft had been detected. On approach, a defensive circle of Bf110s were spotted over Redhill and the Hurricane squadrons roared into action.

Barton led a diving attack out of the sun and fired a four-second burst at the nearest 110 from above. He saw pieces fall off the enemy's port engine, which streamed smoke. Barton was then forced to break away from the engagement as his own aircraft was hit and damaged by enemy fire. He landed safely at Gatwick at 0935 hours. The 110 that he attacked was seen to crash in the Redhill area by Pilot Officer Gerald Lewis.

Back at North Weald the Squadron learned that it had claimed an impressive eight Messerschmitts shot down, with an additional five probables. It was a brilliant feat but was later dampened by the sad news that one of the Squadron's very own had been killed in this action. Apparently wounded and out of ammunition, it was believed that Pilot Officer Percy Burton had deliberately rammed his Hurricane into a Bf110 that he was pursuing at low level.

Soon after, in Barton's absence, Pilot Officer Lewis led seven Hurricanes up to patrol Maidstone before sweeping the line between Hawkinge and Canterbury with 46 Squadron. A dogfight ensued with Bf109s and Lewis shot one down and damaged another. Pilot Officer Barclay also succeeded in shooting one of the fighters down, Pilot Officer Worrall damaged another and Wing Commander Victor Beamish reported a probable.

The Hurricanes returned to North Weald to be rearmed and refuelled and just before 1500 hours the strained pilots were called upon yet again for the third patrol of the day.

The Squadron met up with 46 Squadron in the Hornchurch area and engaged enemy aircraft over South London at about 1530 hours. Swarms of enemy fighters were seen escorting a formation of Ju88s. The Hurricanes attacked and enemy aircraft were soon downed and damaged, but in the melee, Pilot Officer Meaker was killed. While attacking five Ju88s his Hurricane was damaged by crossfire and he baled out, hit the tailplane of his aircraft and fell through the air with an unopened parachute. Meaker's loss was felt keenly by Barton and his colleagues.

In his diary Pilot Officer Barclay wrote, 'Poor old Pilot Officer Brian Meaker, DFC, got shot down and was killed near Battle. A great loss – he was one of the best.'[4]

Tom Neil was also saddened by the loss of Meaker:

In the hut we counted heads. George Barclay had gone – force-landed, we heard – also Bryan Meaker. Someone was saying that Bryan had been hit by return fire when attacking the first group of 88s ... Later still, we learned that he had baled out but, his parachute not opening, had been killed on reaching the ground. Bryan! The imperishable, imperturbable Bryan! It seemed impossible that he should have gone.

The statistics of the day were frightening; Burton and Meaker killed, Beazley wounded, Barton and Barclay shot down, all of us in one form or another deeply affected by events.[5]

Throughout October the Squadron continued to rise against the Luftwaffe, flying regular patrols and interception sorties. Towards the end of the month enemy activity decreased and the RAF was on the brink of a defensive victory that would keep Britain free from invasion and put Goring's Luftwaffe on the back foot.

On 20 October, Barton was awarded the DFC for his 'skill' and 'outstanding leadership'. He would later be decorated by the King at Duxford in January 1941.

On Thursday 25 October a dozen Hurricanes of 249 Squadron left North Weald at 1124 hours. Led by Flight Lieutenant Barton, the Squadron climbed to 25,000 feet with 46 Squadron to carry out their patrol. Bf109s of JG 26 were soon spotted making their way back to France. Combat followed.

Sergeant Bentley Beard was shot down and wounded but he baled out near Tunbridge Wells and was whisked off to hospital to be treated. Adjutant Henri Bouquillard, a Free French pilot, was also shot down by a Bf109 over North Kent, and seriously wounded; he made a forced-landing at Rochester before being admitted to the Royal Naval Hospital at Chatham.

Pilot Officer Tom Neil fired a short burst as a 109 overshot his Hurricane. A large piece broke away from the fighter it rolled on to its back and went down in a vertical dive.

As Blue 2, weaving behind the Squadron, Pilot Officer Worrall noticed some enemy fighters pass beneath his position. He opened fire at close range, totally surprising a Messerschmitt 109, which disintegrated in midair with a burning petrol tank.

Positioned up sun, was Pilot Officer Millington, who carried out an astern attack from slightly below a 109, which he attacked from close range near Hastings. Large pieces of metal broke off from the enemy machine before it dived steeply through clouds trailing a heavy amount of black smoke.

Barton did not make any claims during this patrol, but on 29 October he shot down a Bf109 whilst leading Red Section.

At about 1630 hours, the Squadron began to lift off from North Weald after being ordered to patrol base at 15,000 feet with 257 Squadron, but as the first sections were in the process of getting airborne, bomb carrying Bf109Es suddenly appeared over the aerodrome and attacked. Flying Officer Loft's aircraft was damaged by debris, but he was fortunate enough to be able to land safely. Sergeant Tich Palliser was also in the process of getting airborne when he heard a tremendous crack to his starboard side. He looked right and saw that a Hurricane had taken a direct hit from one of the Messerschmitts bombs. Suddenly Palliser's engine began to violently shake because part of his propeller had been knocked off by the blast.

Palliser recalled, 'I had to level out at naught feet and do a quick flat turn to port to enable me to land before my engine blew up. I landed in minutes beside the perimeter track, climbed out and ran back across the airfield.'

The Hurricane that had taken a direct hit belonged to 257 Squadron's Sergeant Alexander George 'Tubby' Girdwood. Horrified onlookers stood helpless as he burned to death in his cockpit.

On the ground nineteen people were killed and over forty were injured during the Messerschmitt attack.

Flight Lieutenant Barton led Red Section after the 109s as they made off due west. He attacked and damaged the rearmost enemy aircraft, then broke off to engage another. In all, Barton attacked six of the Messerschmitts causing one to stream glycol from its radiator and another to emit white smoke from a wing root. He shot one down, hitting the petrol tank behind the pilot. The pilot baled out of his aircraft which crashed on Malder-Goldhanger road. The pilot of 4/LG2 was wounded and taken to hospital, but he died from his injuries and shock the same day.

Flying as Red 2, Sergeant Michal Maciejowski, claimed another Bf109 and reported the following:

I followed Flt Lt Barton, as leader, attacking one of a formation of five at about 4,000 feet. Two of this formation separated and I pursued them. They dived into cloud and I cut through the clouds and found myself 50 yards behind both of them. I gave one of them five-to ten-seconds burst stern attack and it immediately burst into flames and fell to earth, where I saw it burning about 200 yards from the seashore, on land.

Maciejowski fired at the second fighter for another 5 seconds, but lost track of it due to cloud.

On 31 October 1940 the Battle of Britain was officially over, but Fighter Command, including 249 Squadron, would take the fight to the enemy across the Channel.

Just after midday on 7 November, Barton led the Squadron into combat and destroyed a Bf109. He reported the action as follows:

I attacked a single 109 at 8,000 feet. I fired several short bursts and glycol streamed back from his starboard radiator. E/A flew straight towards cloud and I had to break away as there were several other Me.109s above.

Four days later Barton claimed another aircraft destroyed with Pilot Officer McConnell. During a patrol over the Thames Estuary, they noticed an unusual aircraft which Barton described as 'a bomber of rather clumsy design with very dark green camouflage (almost black), and the roundels which looked like British ones from a distance were, in reality, white with the black German crosses inside'.

Both Barton and McConnell attacked the aircraft, which took evasive action, but ultimately to no avail.

The Squadron's Intelligence Report for this action offers additional details:

They [Barton and McConnell] both carried out attacks and the E/A took violent evasive action, climbing steeply, stalling and diving back towards the sea. F/Lt. Barton set the port wing fuel tank on fire. The pilot throttled back but the tank exploded and the fuselage caught fire. The E/A dived into the sea, broke up and sank and no trace of the crew was seen.

The enemy aircraft was thought to be a Ju86, but it may have been a FW58 of JG 51, which had been sent out to search for missing pilots.

On Thursday 14 November Pilot Officer Barclay was involved in a convoy patrol which he described in his diary:

We did a convoy patrol outside the Estuary today. Two 109s suddenly appeared at our own height about 18,000 feet. We split up and dived after them – one climbed away out of reach, the other dived and about six people followed it. I won the race to reach it first and approached from astern firing from 200 yards inwards. My throttle stuck fully open so I overhauled the 109 very rapidly at about 7,000 feet. I fired until I had to break away for fear of hitting the enemy aircraft, and then turned in again and did a quarter attack. As I fired glycol and black smoke came out – very satisfactory as I deliberately aimed at one radiator.

Other Hurricanes fired and the enemy aircraft turned inland and tried to force-land near Manston aerodrome. Just as he was at tree top height Sergeant Smyth shot at the enemy aircraft. It flew straight into some trees and crashed in flames.

On returning Butch tore a terrific strip off Sergeant Smyth about his unsportsmanship, etc, and we all heartily agreed.[6]

That same night frightening numbers of enemy bombers attacked Coventry, killing and injuring a large number of the population and causing awful destruction. The following day Barclay wrote that on 'Hearing of the bombing of Coventry last night we are inclined to think that perhaps Sergeant Smyth's action yesterday wasn't so bad after all.'

In early December, Barton was promoted to Acting Squadron Leader, and was officially given command of 249 Squadron.

During the afternoon of 29 December, Barton and Pilot Officer Wynn took off from base to conduct an offensive patrol. As the two pilots crossed the French coast they were fired upon by flak near Boulogne. They climbed into cloud and in doing so became separated. Alone, Barton followed the Boulogne road to Calais road and then flew on to St Inglevert airfield where he strafed what he believed was petrol tanks stacked in the west corner of the airfield's dispersal area. Barton soared through heavy ground fire without being hit and then made his way back to North Weald in his trusty Hurricane.

Barton's next aerial victory occurred on the afternoon of 4 February 1941, when with Sergeant Tich Palliser, he dived on a Bf110 from 10,000 feet and made a head-on attack. The enemy aircraft had been harassing a convoy at 2,000 feet, but its bombs fell wide of its target before Barton engaged. After an initial pass at the 110, Barton turned his aircraft around and delivered a second attack from astern as it entered cloud.

Sergeant Palliser followed the 110 and also fired various bursts. Both engines of the fighter were emitting black smoke. Barton pursued the aircraft as it climbed into cloud layer with oil streaming back onto Barton's windscreen. Palliser waited for it above the cloud, but as soon as it appeared it went down into cloud and disappeared from view, leaving two thick black trails of smoke behind.

Circling below the cloud layer was Pilot Officer Thompson who saw a large splash in the water to his right and went to investigate it with Barton. A large circle of foam and oil was seen and the Controller informed Barton that the convoy had seen a bomber crash into the sea.

The Hurricanes left the scene and returned towards the anti-aircraft fire thumping into the air over the convoy. Another Bf110 was spotted and Barton, using full boost, climbed and chased the enemy aircraft. He sprayed the 110 with his ammunition and its port engine stopped dead. The 110 went through cloud but Barton continued to attack, firing various bursts in a running fight. The 110 fired back at Barton in a head-on attack, but Barton drove it down to sea level and watched it crash into the water. The 110 submerged beneath the sea. Barton noticed the pilot floating and waving his arms at him.

Now the convoy was safe, Barton, Palliser and Thompson set course for North Weald and landed at 1455 hours.

A change was on the horizon for Butch Barton and his fellow fighter boys, but it would not be a welcomed one. The news soon arrived that the Squadron would be sent overseas, equipped with Hurricane Mk Is.

Tom Neil recalled his thoughts at the time:

> We were all struck dumb. Mark 1s! Oh, *no*! Not again! We were back again on the old, out-distanced, out-performed, out-everythinged Mark 1, and this time the tropicalised version, which was even slower and less combat-worthy than those we had flown in the Battle of Britain.[7]

After a spell of leave the pilots were instructed to report to Euston railway station on 8 May 1941 to journey to Liverpool, where they would board the carrier HMS *Furious*. At this stage the pilots did not know where they would be serving, but it was thought that the Middle East was more than likely to be their destination.

The Squadron reached Gibraltar on the 18th and throughout the night and early hours of the 19th, twenty-one Hurricanes were transferred to *Ark Royal* at Gib. Two days later Squadron Leader Barton led his Hurricanes off the carrier's flight deck and set course for Malta.

After landing on the island Tich Palliser recalled: 'Before we had our breath back, we were given the bad news that we, 249 Squadron, were to remain on Malta.'

With lack of kit, supplies and inferior aircraft the pilots were understandably displeased with their current predicament. The defence of Malta would be a tough campaign, but the Squadron's resilience and mettle would help them through it.

The day following their arrival, Squadron Leader Barton and Flight Lieutenant Neil organised the Squadron into two Flights. Barton would command B Flight and Neil A Flight.

On 3 June Barton would claim the Squadron's first victory in Malta when he intercepted an Italian SM79 which he caught flying from Sicily to Libya as an escort for Naval Vessels. Barton simply reported, 'SM79 shot down into the sea – on fire off Gozo – no crew known to have escaped.'

Barton returned to base to rearm and refuel his aircraft. He took off once again with a section of Hurricanes to search the scene for any survivors, but the SM79 crew had not survived.

On 8 June the Squadron took off in the dark early hours of the morning to intercept an enemy raid approaching the island. Barton continued to add to his tally, shooting down a Fiat BR20M in flames. Barton returned to Takali and again took off in search of survivors. Two Italians were rescued and taken prisoners, but the remainder of the crew had perished.

One of the survivors, Mar Guglielmo Mazzolenis, told his captors of Barton's attack:

> The Hurricane came in from the direction of the moon. [We] could see him quite well. His attack was very determined and the gunner was unable to return accurate fire, as the Hurricane was weaving across [our] tail. The first burst hit one engine which went up in flames, and from that moment the crew prepared to bale out.[8]

Towards the end of June the Squadron began to receive Hurricane Mk IIs, including several Mk IICs, which were armed with cannons. The new additions were welcomed with open arms by the pilots who were fed up of flying outdated Mk Is into combat against superior fighters.

On 17 July Barton fronted eight of these new Hurricanes when the Squadron engaged thirty Italian fighters that were acting as escort to a SM79 reconnaissance aircraft on approach to Malta. Barton shot a Macchi 200 down, a new arrival, Pilot Officer Graham Leggett downed a second and Flying Officer Davis damaged a third.

The following week, on 25 July, an Italian reconnaissance aircraft was detected in the morning as it approached the island, with the intention of photographing a convoy off the coast. Squadron Leader Barton led ten Hurricanes, together with 185 Squadron to shoot it down and engage its fighter escort. Six pilots of 185 Squadron were able to reach and attack the reconnaissance aircraft which was subsequently shot down. Meanwhile Barton claimed a Macchi 200 shot down into the sea.

On the last day of July, Barton was nastily wounded when he encountered engine failure on take-off and crash-landed his aircraft from 300 feet. His Hurricane (Z3492) ploughed through several stone walls and, trapped in the cockpit, Barton suffered second degree burns from battery acid, glycol and petrol. He was soon admitted to Mtarfa Hospital to receive treatment.

The next day Flight Lieutenant Tom Neil and Flying Officer Terry Crossey visited Butch in hospital and found him,

> Disfigured, shocked and trembling but profoundly thankful that things had
> turned out as well as they had. Few people had survived such an experience
> and with so much operational and other flying behind him, he felt that an
> engine failure of some sort was long overdue. And now it had happened, in
> Malta of all places, and he was still alive and kicking. Looking tiny and waif-
> like in his hospital bed, he was childishly relieved at his deliverance.[9]

While Barton recovered in hospital, the responsibility of leading 249 Squadron
fell on the capable shoulders of Tom Neil.

At the end of August Barton returned to the Squadron and on the 30th he
made his first flight since the crash in Hurricane Z2794 for the duration of ten
minutes. Two days later he returned to operations.

On 4 September Barton took off with seven other Hurricanes and led them
five miles off Cap Passero where they intercepted Italian fighters at 1546
hours. The Hurricanes dived on a formation of Macchis that were escorting
a Z506B seaplane. A fierce dogfight erupted at 1,000 feet above the sea and
Barton claimed one probable Macchi destroyed and one damaged. He later
remarked that it was the hardest fight of his career because the Italians put up
a very determined fight.

Two pilots, Sergeant Jim Kimberley and Pilot Officer George Smith attacked
the seaplane but in turn were shot down and killed by the Italian fighters.
Barton ordered the Squadron to disengage and head for base, later remarking
'We should have done better.'

During the morning of 19 October Barton took off with Sergeant Tich
Palliser to patrol the south of Lampedusa Island for enemy aerial activity.
The two pilots circled the area a few times with open cockpits, looking for
aircraft which would not be sighted. Barton signalled to Palliser to head back
for Malta, so the two of them turned for base.

Flying on a north-easterly course at 6,000 feet Palliser spotted a lone SM81
bomber-transport aircraft emerge from cloud 1,000 feet below them. Palliser
waggled his wings to get Barton's attention and pointed over his left shoulder.
Barton responded with a signal for them to turn steeply to port and the hunt
was on.

Palliser recalls what happened next:

> With full boost, the Mark II engine had us in firing range very quickly. Butch
> fired a burst in a quarter attack and the tracer field of twelve guns was
> something to see. I followed close to Butch, but diving under him, coming up
> under a lower target, and gave two three-second bursts, hitting the middle
> engine and the belly of what was a Savoya Trimoter Bomber, or possibly a

cargo plane. The sight of twenty-four lines of tracer bullets was awesome, and the aircraft caught fire and in no time at all it was a blazing mess in the sea.

Barton and Palliser then made off for base at full speed.

By the end of the month, Squadron Leader Barton was awarded a Bar to the DFC for his great success in the air and leadership. The citation for this award concluded that 'his excellent leadership inspires the pilots under his command'. There was no truer statement made than that for everyone in the Squadron respected and admired him for his courage and direction.

On 22 November Barton would claim his final victory of the war when he shot down a MC 202 eight miles north-east of Gozo, flying Hurricane Z3764. In total Barton had claimed an impressive twelve, five shared enemy aircraft destroyed and two probables, with additional others claimed as damaged.

From the Battle of Britain to combat in Malta, Butch Barton had earned a reputation that held him in high esteem amongst his friends and colleagues. He had displayed a great deal of courage and initiative both in the air and on the ground. Barton's leadership and fighting spirit was contagious, for he flew and fought relentlessly, with unquenchable determination, which undoubtedly inspired the men he led. So in December, when Barton left Malta to return to the UK, the Squadron would never quite be the same.

Tom Neil remembered:

Butch Barton slipped away one night to board a Sunderland in Kalafrana Bay bound for Gibraltar and home. There was no departing binge or palaver, he just went. Quietly. Without fuss. Disappearing as he had always fought, with unassuming distinction. I suspect he was glad to leave; he had been on the go since September 1939 and was beginning to believe that his luck would shortly run out.[10]

Barton left Malta on 8 December 1941 and thereafter served in various appointments until the end of the war. He was made an OBE on 14 June 1945 and retired from the RAF as a Wing Commander on 27 February 1959. Barton returned to Canada with his wife, Gwen, in 1965.

After a long war and career in the RAF, Barton preferred a quiet life in retirement, spending a lot of his time fishing in the rivers and lakes of British Columbia, where unsurprisingly, he gained quite a reputation for his fishing abilities.

Butch Barton died aged 94 on 2 September 2010, survived by his only son. During the morning of 15 September, (Battle of Britain Day), Barton's ashes were scattered on his favourite lake in British Columbia.

CHAPTER 3

Mungo

During the morning of 4 September 1939 at Hornchurch aerodrome, Pilot Officer John Freeborn of 74 Squadron looked up from his desk to see a slender, charming looking pilot officer standing in his doorway. The new arrival gave a magnificent salute and announced: 'My name is John Mungo Park, sir, and I've been posted to 74 Squadron.' Freeborn smiled. 'You don't call *me* sir, I'm only the Adjutant!' Freeborn got up from behind his desk and shook hands with Mungo, while introducing himself in return. 'I'm glad to meet you, John.' Mungo replied in his Liverpudlian accent, and that was the start of a lasting friendship.

John Colin Mungo Park was born in Wallasey, Cheshire on 25 March 1918 to Colin and Mamie Mungo Park. He was the third child in the family; his siblings were Alison and Geoffrey. Mungo's father, Colin, had signed up as a private with the 7th Battalion of the 7th Royal Sussex Regiment at the outbreak of the First World War and with just a few days to go before the Great War's end, he was killed. Mungo was only seven months old.

Despite the difficulties of raising three young children on her own, Mamie did a fine job. Young Mungo was a good student at school. He progressed through his school days to Liverpool Collage, where he also boarded. A keen athlete, a fine swimmer, rugby player and boxer, Mungo won an impressive number of trophies in his youth.

When Mungo finished college he moved to Bolton in 1934 with his family and began office work at Holden's Mill, Astley Bridge, where he studied textile manufacture. He also continued to excel in his sporting activities, becoming a member of the Bolton Rugby Club and Sharples Tennis Club.

It was while living in Bolton that Mungo's interest in aviation began to kindle. As a young lad he would often visit his neighbour, Mr Bird, who not only had a splendid collection of aviation books for him to read, but also his very own pilot's licence.

Mungo joined the RAF on a Short Service Commission in June 1937. He was posted to No. 10 Flying Training School at Ternhill for his initial training in August that same year, before moving on to the Anti Aircraft Co-operation Unit of the Fleet Air Arm at Lee on Solent.

John Mungo Park wearing his DFC. (*74 Squadron Association*)

In August 1938, Mungo was sent to the Fleet Requirements Unit, to Fly Fairey Swordfish from HMS *Argus*. When war was declared on Germany, Mungo was transferred back to the RAF and on 4 September, he arrived at Hornchurch in Essex, to be greeted by Pilot Officer John Freeborn.

No. 74 Squadron was already rich in history after its famed exploits during the First World War. Major Edward 'Mick' Mannock, VC, DSO and Two Bars, MC and Bar, is just one example of the calibre of airmen that the Squadron produced. The aggressive fighting spirit born from the Great War earned 74 Squadron the name 'Tiger Squadron'. Many years later, in 1936 the official Squadron badge was illustrated with a Tiger's head and the motto 'I Fear No Man' was endorsed. Being part of 74 Squadron inspired a great sense of pride amongst those who belonged to it and Mungo was just as pleased to be a part of it as anyone.

Before Mungo arrived at Hornchurch, the Squadron was flying Gloster Gauntlet biplanes, but in February 1939, Supermarine Spitfire Mk Is began to arrive at the station, which caused a great deal of excitement amongst the pilots and ground crew alike.

Like most fighter squadrons, 74 Squadron was comprised of pilots from different backgrounds with diverse personalities, but Mungo became very popular amongst all his colleagues.

In later years Wing Commander John Freeborn DFC and Bar referred to Mungo as 'the nicest person you could ever hope to meet'.

Another friend and 'Tiger', Harbourne Mackay Stephen said the following of Mungo:

> Mungo was my great friend. He had a wonderful sense of humour, tremendous courage and a delightful personality. And he could be wild! He possessed a certain *joie de vivre,* which was infectious. He came from the Fleet Air Arm to the RAF and when he first arrived on the squadron he immediately hit it off with Paddy Treacy who was B Flight commander at the beginning of the war. They were great chums. After Treacy went missing in France for the second time in May 1940, Mungo and I started flying together and we found we complemented each other very well in the air. Whenever we flew into a spot of trouble we would stick to each other and fight our way out together. We became known as 'The Deadly Twins'. There were other pairings on the squadron but none perhaps as successful as ours. We remained the closest friends, flying together almost daily until we were parted in February 1941.

Once the excitement of the declaration of war announcement had simmered down, the reality of the 'Phoney War' really began to kick in around the aerodrome and it seemed to the pilots that the only war being waged was against boredom and relative inactivity. During this calm before the storm, Mungo took it upon himself to arrange a low flying competition at Rochford whilst their Commanding Officer and Flight Commanders were away on business. Mungo had attracted three other pilots to participate in this competition by starting a kitty. In order to win the kitty, the pilots had to take off, fly a circuit and then make a low pass over the middle of the aerodrome. The pilot judged by the others to have flown the lowest would win. Ever the competitor, Mungo would make sure that he would secure this victory and sure enough no one questioned his achievement when his aircraft's propeller began chewing up the aerodromes turf. Everyone watching gasped in horror but somehow Mungo managed to pilot his Spitfire to safety. After climbing out of his cockpit he grimaced at the bent propeller blades. Fortunately for Mungo, his riggers hammered them back into shape and he avoided an official reprimand. The riggers were paid in return for their hard work by blowing the kitty in a local pub.

In May 1940 Hitler invaded Norway and soon after Luxembourg, Belgium and Holland fell to his devastating Panzer Divisions. During this time Mungo flew with the Squadron escorting convoys. One memorable patrol occurred during the second week of May, when 74 Squadron Spitfires escorted HMS *Venomous* as she carried the Dutch Royal Family to safer shores. Towards the end of May, the retreating troops of the British Expeditionary Force began to flee to the beaches at Dunkirk and things suddenly turned serious for the Tigers.

On 21 May, 74 Squadron's A Flight had been ordered to patrol over Dover at 20,000 feet, with Sailor Malan leading.

Adolph 'Sailor' Malan, a South African from Wellington, Western Cape, would not only become a Squadron hero, but also an RAF legend. Malan, nicknamed 'Sailor' due to his past at sea with the ship *General Botha* and the Union Castle Steamship Line, would prove to be a prolific leader, tactician, and 'ace' fighter pilot. By the end of the war Malan had risen to the rank of Group Captain and was credited with an impressive tally of twenty-seven and seven shared enemy aircraft destroyed, two and one shared unconfirmed destroyed, three probables, and sixteen damaged.

When A Flight broke cloud at about 17,000 feet on 21 May, they noticed anti-aircraft fire bursting into the air over Calais. Flying as Red 1, Malan turned towards the commotion with Pilot Officers John Freeborn and Bertie Aubert on his wingtips.

As the Tigers neared Dunkirk in line astern Malan suddenly warned his men of enemy bandits ahead. In a flash he was going like the clappers after a Heinkel He111 to starboard, with his wingmen Freeborn and Aubert in close pursuit. Yellow Section, led by Tinky Measures, broke off towards a second bomber that had been sighted.

Malan had built up so much speed that he ended up overshooting the Heinkel, which had started side-slipping to evade his attack. Malan made the most of his terrific speed and wheeled his Spitfire around for a second pass. From close range, the South African thumbed his gun button on the Spitfire's control column and raked the Heinkel with a solid burst from his eight machine guns. The stricken bomber made no attempt to dive into nearby cloud cover, so Malan gave it another accurate burst which forced the bomber's undercarriage to drop. Malan eased the stick back towards his stomach and climbed his responsive aircraft back up into the blue, with Freeborn and Aubert sticking to him like glue.

While scanning the sky, Malan soon spotted exactly what he was looking for – more bandits. This time they were Junkers Ju88s. Red Section set course for the Luftwaffe bombers, ducking in and out of cloud like Tigers stalking an unknowing prey in the grass. As they neared the 88s, five were counted until Malan spotted a sixth flying some 1,000 yards to the left of the main formation. Malan tried to reach the others over the radio, but it was out of action. Using hand signals, Malan ordered Aubert off after the sixth Junkers, while he and Freeborn went after the others. Malan selected his target and opened fire.

74 'Tiger' Squadron at Manston during the Battle of Britain. L-R: Willie Nelson, Piers Kelly, Peter Stevenson, Don Cobden, Dennis Smith, Sailor Malan, John Mungo Park, John Freeborn, Douglas Hastings, Thomas Kirk, Ernie Mayne, Bill Skinner. (*74 Squadron Association*)

Freeborn recalled the engagement:

I was feeling terrible. I didn't know what the matter was with me. We bumped into some 88s and I followed Malan in... I was right behind [him]. He put the Ju88's port engine right out and then its tail burst into flames. I still felt terrible, I couldn't breathe, I couldn't do anything. Then I looked down at my instruments and found that I didn't have my oxygen on! So as soon as I turned it on, I was back to my old self. I attacked one of the 88's giving it a good long burst, raking it from nose to tail.

Malan and Freeborn returned to base feeling pleased with their success, but the American, Pilot Officer Bertie Aubert, was nowhere to be seen. A few days later, Aubert returned to the Squadron and filled in the blanks about his absence. After he had shot down the Ju88 that he engaged on the 21st, he was left short on fuel, so he made an emergency landing at Calais. Aubert was missing for two days until he was able to hitch a ride back to England

via a Blenheim. On the same day Aubert returned, he was lost on a patrol
flying Spitfire N3243. Once again he was reported missing, last seen by Malan
diving after Ju88s 20 miles south of Dunkirk, but this time Aubert did not
return.

The Tigers continued to fly patrols over Dunkirk and with Malan at the
helm, they added to Fighter Command's success against the enemy.

Mungo struck up a great and lasting friendship with Malan, and as much
as Malan treated him as an equal, Mungo, like all the Tigers, still respected
him as a great leader. To First World War Tiger 'ace' Ira Jones, Mungo said the
following of Malan

What I like about Sailor is his quiet, firm manner and his cold courage.
He is gifted with uncanny eyesight and is a 'natural' fighter pilot. When he
calls over the R/T, 'Let 'em have it! Let 'em have it! There's no messing. The
bastards are for it, particularly the one he has in his own reflector sight.
Mannock and Malan have made 74.

During the morning of 24th May, Flying Officer Mungo Park saw action at
0800 hours, one mile inland near Gravelines. A Henschel Hs 126 was sighted
at 400 feet and Blue Section of B Flight engaged. Mungo's report describes the
attack:

I was Blue 2 on Offensive Patrol with 74 Squadron, Calais – Dunkirk at
2000 feet off the coast when I heard Blue 3 give "Bandits". I then sighted
E/A at 400 feet and followed Blue 1. After Blue 1 broke away I gave E/A a
five-second burst from 300 yards and saw incendiary entering E/A fuselage.
Gave a second burst of 6 seconds and broke away. I then saw E/A crash,
in the back garden of a cottage, in flames. E/A used quick right and left
turns at ground level to avoid fighters. E/A camouflage was normal and
excellent at low altitude. Black Crosses with white edging were seen on top
of Mainplanes.

Later that afternoon Mungo was slightly wounded in his arm during combat
over Dunkirk and his Spitfire was damaged just before he engaged a Heinkel
He111. Despite his predicament, Mungo managed to skilfully fly his aircraft
back across the Channel before landing at Rochford.

Mungo reported:

I was flying as Blue 2 with 74 Squadron, 24th May, 1940, on Offensive
Patrol, Dunkirk – Calais – Boulogne at 500 feet off the coast. I observed A.A.
fire at 12,000 feet and immediately climbed line astern. The Leader gave
echelon starboard and I followed him in to the attack. At about 350 yards

range and before I had opened fire, I was hit by Me.109 doing a beam attack and was wounded in the left forearm and hit in the tank. Before breaking away I noticed smoke pouring from the starboard engine of Blue Leader's target (He111) I was then able to return to base.

Mungo's next recorded action occurred on 10 July 1940, the opening day of the Battle of Britain. In the early morning hours the Squadron took off from Hornchurch and landed at Manston to await their orders.

The tense waiting game was underway at dispersal, but the Tigers would not have to suffer long before the call came for 74 Squadron to scramble.

With great haste Mungo joined his comrades in racing towards their purring Spitfires to get airborne.

The weather was terribly inconvenient for flying, with showers and dark clouds hanging over the south of England. The Squadron climbed away from Manston towards the Deal-Dunkirk area where they had been instructed to look out for enemy aircraft.

The reports were accurate. Large formations of enemy aircraft, made up of Dornier Do17s, Messerschmitt Bf109s and Messerschmitt Bf110s were soon sighted by the small force of Spitfires. The sight was intimidating for the Tigers who felt ridiculously outnumbered, but despite the odds, they turned into the enemy armadas to attack. The sky erupted into action. Tinky Measures pumped some ammunition into a Bf110 and a Do17, but could only call them damaged. In the terrific melee of turning aircraft he also witnessed two enemy aircraft collide before escaping the chaos. Peter St John managed to damage a Bf109, Brian Draper let off a burst at a Do17 and Peter Stevenson crippled two Bf110s. The only confirmed enemy aircraft to be destroyed by the Squadron during their first patrol of the Battle of Britain fell to the guns of Mungo Park. During the fight, Mungo had lined a Dornier Do17 up in his sights, squeezed the gun button and watched the bomber's starboard engine burst into flames. The Dornier turned lazily on to its back and dived into the sea. It was an exhausting affair, but the Tigers had performed rather well for their first patrol of the Battle. The only pilot to have real cause for concern was New Zealander, Donald Cobden, when his Spitfire was riddled with bullet holes as he was attacking a Dornier. He employed the assistance of his aircraft's emergency boost and broke away from the scene in a steep climbing turn before landing back at Manston.

When the Squadron returned to Manston, the ground crews quickly got to work, ensuring the pilots Spitfires would be refuelled, rearmed and serviceable for the next patrol.

By mid-morning the Squadron was back in the air. On this patrol the Tigers spotted a single reconnaissance Dornier Do17 with a heavy escort of thirty Bf109s. The six Spitfires, flying at 20,000 feet engaged, but the enemy fighters did their jobs well and the Dornier slipped away across the Channel. Pilot Officer John Freeborn succeeded in destroying one of the fighters over the Thames Estuary from close range. Freeborn remembered, 'I was so close to the leader of this formation of 109s that I could see everything that hit him when I opened fire. He turned straight over on his back and dropped into the sea.'

Peter Stevenson damaged one and destroyed another. Cobden, St John and Draper each damaged a Messerschmitt, concluding a busy morning for the Squadron.

John Freeborn later commented on the nature of such patrols:

Once we entered the fray we were on our own. We concentrated on the German we were after and as such we were our own masters. In a one to one situation I was confident that I could always come out on top, added to which was the thought that I could fight without endangering anybody else's life – my number two for example who would be in the sky somewhere looking after himself – and so on. One thing that did astound us all was the fact that despite losses, the Luftwaffe could continually send such numbers of aircraft against us.[1]

Throughout the rest of July and early August Mungo flew constant patrols with the Squadron. On 11 August the Tigers flew into combat on four occasions between dawn and 1400 hours. Most of the action took place against enemy aircraft that were detailed to bomb shipping and East coast ports. By the day's end 74 Squadron claimed twenty-three enemy aircraft destroyed, one probable and fourteen damaged. Later that evening a telegram arrived for Malan's Tigers from the Chief of Air Staff: 'A magnificent day's fighting 74... This is the way to keep the measure of the Boche. Mannock started it and you keep it up.'

Winston Churchill also commended the Tiger's success that evening with a visit to Hornchurch, where he offered his personal congratulations to the busy pilots and ground crews alike.

Mungo's first scrap of the day took place when he was leading Blue Section high over Dover at 0800 hours.

Cruising at 23,000 feet, he caught sight of a Bf109 crossing his 'bows at 300 yards range'. Mungo turned his aircraft towards the fighter and let off a three-second deflection burst which forced the 109 into a fast dive streaming glycol. Another unseen 109 dropped down onto Mungo's tail, so he turned his Spitfire away from the first fighter, half rolled to shake the second of his tail and watched his attacker diving towards the French coast. Mungo lined the fighter up in his sights and let off a short burst. He observed his de Wilde incendiaries striking the 109's fuselage before breaking away from the French coast. In his official report Mungo only claimed one Messerschmitt 109 as damaged.

Just before midday Mungo returned to battle, this time 30 miles east of Harwich. During the patrol the Tigers located a large swarm of Bf110s flying at about 4,000 feet. Mungo attacked one of the twin-engine fighters from slightly above at 150 yards range using deflection. Black smoke poured out of its engine and Mungo watched it dive into the sea.

Mungo found himself at 2,000 feet, so he began to climb back towards the fighters. He latched onto another Bf110 and opened fire 300 yards range. He gave the fighter a lengthy burst which caused black smoke to gush from one of its engines. The enemy aircraft was last seen diving towards the sea, but Mungo did not hang about to watch its fate.

Back at base Mungo claimed the first 110 as 'unconfirmed destroyed' and the second as a probable. The 110 that crashed into the sea was flown by Hmpt Kogler of 1/ZG26. Both Kogler and his gunner were wounded but they were soon picked up and spent the remainder of the war as PoWs.

At approximately 1400 hours, Mungo was again in the air leading Blue Section on patrol off Margate. There was heavy cloud base at 4,000 feet, where Bf109s were spotted ducking in and out of cloud. Mungo attacked from astern with a five-second burst. His bullets struck the enemy fighter and black smoke began to pour from its engine. Mungo watched the 109 burst into flames as it entered cloud before diving into the sea below. Mungo reported that his aircraft was carrying a cine camera gun film that was not yet developed and that Flying Officer Willie Nelson (a Canadian Tiger) had also seen the 109 diving towards the sea.

On 12 August the Tigers were given a break from flying patrols, but their devoted ground crews spent the day with their sleeves rolled up servicing the Squadron's battle-worn Spitfires.

The following day was *Adler Tag* and Mungo and his fellow pilots were back in the thick of it.

In the early morning hours, twelve Spitfires of 74 Squadron got airborne and when they reached the Thames Estuary they found enemy aircraft down below their position at 4,000 feet. Mungo reported:

> I was Blue 2 in the Squadron when we encountered approximately forty enemy bombers. I attacked one Do17, opened at 300 yards, closing to 250 yards from dead astern. I fired all my ammunition at the Do. And I saw large pieces falling from it, and the starboard engine was smoking. Since the enemy aircraft was still heading West at a low altitude, I think it unlikely that it would have reached home again.

The next day 74 Squadron was withdrawn from the front line and sent to Wittering to rest and recuperate. The break from combat was well deserved and much needed but for some of the pilots languishing away from the action at Wittering was frustrating. After a spell at Wittering the Squadron moved to Kirton in Lindsay and then on 9 September they were sent to Coltishall.

Mungo was now a Flight Lieutenant and he assumed command of 74 Squadron's B Flight. At this time the Tiger's Commanding Officer, Sailor Malan, led A Flight, but Mungo was often called upon to lead the whole Squadron in the air.

The pilots found Coltishall to be a dismal place to reside, but the posting did allow them to get back into the fight, which by now had moved over London, with the Luftwaffe doing its damndest to bomb the capital into submission.

The Tigers shared Coltishall with Douglas Bader's 242 Squadron. Together they became components of the Big Wing – a concept dreamed up by Bader and Trafford Leigh-Mallory.

The idea behind the Big Wing was to use a handful of squadrons to attack the enemy *en masse* rather than to send individual squadrons up to nibble away at large enemy formations. The concept was contested by Air Vice Marshal Keith Park, who believed it was impractical as a defensive tactic. Many of the pilots involved felt the same way, but for now it was the Tiger's ticket back into the fray.

On 11 September, Malan led the Squadron to Duxford where they would be participating in Bader's Big Wing for the day.

During the afternoon large formations of enemy aircraft began to build up over the Pas de Calais, and soon enough the Luftwaffe crossed the Channel on route for the City of London.

To intercept the raids, the Big Wing was ordered off. No. 19 Squadron was at the Wing's spearhead, followed by 611 Squadron at the centre, with Malan leading 74 Squadron at the rear.

The Tigers were flying in three-fours in section line astern. Mungo was leading Blue Section when Malan ordered them to attack a formation of Junkers Ju88s which had been identified.

After the 'Tally ho!' was given Mungo carried out a beam attack, firing a short burst at one of the 88s. He saw pieces of the aircraft fall away before breaking off and climbing to 20,000 feet. Mungo checked the arena and caught sight of seven He111s, which he attacked from above. Mungo reported setting its starboard engine on fire and seeing it go down in a steep dive, before he broke off and returned to base.

The Squadron took off from Duxford later that evening and returned to Coltishall with a tally of one Dornier destroyed (by John Freeborn) and ten probables.

Three days later Mungo was back in the air leading Blue Section at 23,000 feet. During the patrol his keen eyes caught sight of a Bf110, so he quickly ordered an attack from line astern, 10 miles north of Happisburgh.

Mungo reported, 'I closed to 200 yards range and opened fire for a four-second burst at starboard engine, black smoke poured out from engine [and] E/A went down in steep diving turns.'

Mungo's number two then had a crack at the same aircraft; he scored hits and then broke away.

Mungo continued the attack with three short bursts of deflection shots and saw its starboard engine catch fire. The enemy aircraft dived steeply into cloud and Blue Section broke away from the engagement.

Throughout the attack Mungo had experienced intense return fire from the 110. When he landed and had climbed out of his Spitfire he saw that he had sustained three hits: There was a hole in his aircraft's spinner, another in the air intake and one more in the port wing.

In mid-October, 74 Squadron left Coltishall and returned to the front line when they were posted to Biggin Hill in Kent.

The Tigers knew they were back in the thick of it as soon as they landed, for all around them bomb craters littered the aerodrome and ground crews quickly set about to refuelling their Spitfires.

Biggin Hill was the most heavily attacked aerodrome in Fighter Command during the Battle of Britain, and Mungo could well believe it.

While at Biggin Hill the Tigers would be sharing the station with 92 Squadron, and staying in a house called Holly Cottage outside of the aerodrome's perimeter.

Malan's hard-drilled, well-disciplined Tigers would soon discover that their neighbouring colleagues of 92 Squadron were their absolute antitheists. The Squadron proved to be prolific in combat, but their behaviour on the ground lacked discipline and order. Fast cars, late night parties and boisterous behaviour became 92 Squadron's trademarks, but despite their lax attitude to RAF protocol, they were a band of brothers, who achieved great success in the air.

Drinking well into the night was not a practise the Tigers indulged in, but they did find other ways to relieve themselves of battle stress. Once a week, when the boys were released from flying duty, they would go pheasant shooting with 12-bore rifles. John Freeborn recalled one afternoon where they had been shooting pheasants that were penned in a lovely garden nearby their station. Mungo drew the short straw and ended up climbing over the fence to collect their spoils. When Mungo was in the process of throwing the dead birds over the fence, the game keeper interrupted him.

'What do you think you're doing!?' He demanded. Slightly embarrassed, Mungo replied. 'Oh, we just wanted a pheasant, if the owner wouldn't mind?'

'Do you know who the owner is?' The game keeper asked. Mungo looked at his pals on the other side of the fence. All of them were laughing. 'No, but I'm sure he's wealthy enough to have a game keeper and a pen like this.' Mungo quipped. 'His name is Winston Churchill. So I'll be having your name!'

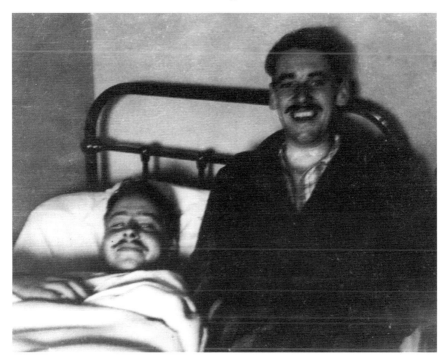

John Freeborn and Mungo Park after being pulled from the Battle of Britain and sent to Wittering to rest with the Squadron. (74 *Squadron Association*)

The pilots went silent and then Peter St John called out. 'Don't tell him Mungo! Don't tell him your name!' 'Archbishop of Canterbury will do Mungo!' The game keeper decided to let Mungo off the hook and opened the gate, but asked for the pheasants back in return. The Tigers made a run for it. 'Sod off!' Freeborn shouted back.

Later that evening the birds were cooked at a local pub and thoroughly enjoyed by the boys.

On 20 October 1940, Mungo was back at his best. He filed the following report after engaging Messerschmitt Bf109s in conjunction with 66 Squadron:

I was Blue Leader 74 Squadron ... We intercepted a 30 plus raid in Maidstone area at 29,000 feet. The enemy aircraft were slightly below us and we dived from 500 feet above. They immediately dived away and then half of them zoomed up. I followed them up and fired a short burst of 4 seconds at the last of them. He immediately spun and I followed him down for about 4,000 feet when his tail unit broke away. I had to break off the engagement as I was being fired at from behind and do not know whether the pilot baled out or not.

The German pilot did manage to evacuate his aircraft but his parachute caught fire and he was killed.

Harbourne Stephen flying as Mungo's number two also enjoyed aerial success when he attacked a section of four 109s as they dived towards Dungeness. At 9,000 feet, Stephen caught up to them and opened fire at a fighter on the far left of the section. His lethal burst tore into the tail and the cockpit area of the enemy aircraft. He observed the Messerschmitt's cockpit hood fly off before he broke off from the remaining three fighters that were then climbing towards him. Stephen evaded their attacks and pounced upon another 109, giving it a long burst, which forced the German pilot to evacuate his aircraft, before it crashed into a nearby wood.

Sergeant Clive Hilken was flying as Blue Section's 'tail end Charlie', vigorously weaving to and fro behind Mungo and Stephen. When he fell behind, he decided to fly straight and level for a moment to catch up with his section, but the decision was costly and his aircraft was suddenly hit. Hilken recalled

> The explosion shook the aircraft. From the bottom of the cockpit smoke came up and the aircraft was uncontrollable. I baled out at what must have been 20,000 feet. My flying boots, however, remained in the cockpit. I hadn't unhitched my oxygen tube and the rubber stretched and gave way without pulling my mask off, giving me what turned out to be a beautiful black eye to add to the many bits of cannon shell which I received in my left hand and right arm, face and body.

Hilken's Spitfire crashed at Cowden while he drifted down in to an orchard near Tonbridge in Kent. Two nearby Land Army girls quickly came to his aid and he was taken to hospital where the shrapnel was removed from his body. Hilken would return to the Squadron in early 1941.

Two days later Mungo was Blue Leader, with orders to patrol Maidstone at 15,000 feet. When the Tigers arrived in the area they received further instructions to climb to 30,000 feet. Mungo led the climb and then levelled out. New orders came through to drop down to 27,000 feet at about 1420 hours.

Mungo sighted enemy aircraft 1,000 feet below their new position flying southwest. They were identified as Messerschmitt Bf109s. Mungo gave the 'Tally Ho!' and dived down to attack. The enemy fighters must have seen the Spitfires because just as Mungo's thumb hovered over his gun button, the enemy half rolled. Mungo followed his target down and held his fire until they reached about 9,000 feet. Mungo pressed the trigger down for 2 seconds and watched the 109 dive steeply with black smoke trailing in its wake.

Momentarily Mungo had to break off to wipe ice from his windscreen, but he returned to engage, again firing a two-second burst. The 109 went down to 2,000 feet and Mungo followed before he lost it to haze and low cloud.

Mungo turned for home, while clearing more ice from his windscreen. He later reported that gunners had seen the 109 crash into the sea near Hastings.

As well as being a popular figure amongst his fellow airmen, Mungo was also well regarded by those who kept the pilots flying, the often unsung ground crews. No. 74 Squadron armourer, Arthur Westerhoff, worked on Mungo's aircraft on a number of occasions and got to know him quite well. Arthur recalled,

Mungo Park was a brilliant pilot and one of the Few. He was the quiet type and a real gentleman. Sometimes he would visit the aircraft on such times when the Squadron was on sixty-minutes readiness. He would arrive with another pilot in a small sports car and give all the crew a flat box of 100 Player's cigarettes. I suppose it was to show his appreciation. The rigger would fill up his car with 100 Octane fuel and on leaving we would give him a salute and he would flash that wonderful smile that he had. He always seemed to be enjoying whatever he did.

Arthur also remembers seeing Bob Stanford Tuck and Sailor Malan around Biggin Hill.

They were both great pilots and leaders of men. Sometimes I fill up when I think about them. I must also mention John Freeborn, whose aircraft I worked on, because although he never made it to Commanding Officer of 74 Squadron, he was their equal.

To most people Malan was known as Sailor, but to the ground crews he was called Maxi. This was due to his first name – Adolph – we couldn't possibly call him that. One incident comes to mind while at Biggin Hill when Malan instructed his rigger to remove the Squadron letters from his aircraft and replace them with his initials. On a sortie the following day his initials were spotted by one of the German aces who immediately directed the whole of his flight against Malan. The brilliant pilot that he was, recognised his mistake and using up all his ammunition headed back to base. He then instructed his rigger to put back the Squadron letters of 'ZP' to his aircraft.

During the early months of the Battle of Britain the two armament corporals on 74 Squadron were Ron Stone and Cheeseman. One corporal was to be awarded the BEM for the brilliant work carried out during those hectic months. For Malan this was going to be a difficult decision to make, so he sent for the two corporals and told them that if there had been two medals he would have given them one each, but unfortunately there was only one. Malan took a coin out of his pocket and then tossed the coin. Corporal Cheeseman had the BEM.

Again at Biggin Hill we often got nuisance raids from German aircraft

A Supermarine Spitfire of 74 Squadron code lettered 'ZP-J'. (*Author*)

L-R: Wood, Mungo and Freeborn standing in front of a de Havilland Puss Moth. Mungo's dog Ben sits on the Puss Moth's wing and Wood's two dogs Sam and Pat are below. (*74 Squadron Association*)

almost every day. One day a lone raider approached the station and Malan was at his aircraft. The engine was quickly started and Malan didn't worry about wind direction to get airborne. He returned a short time later doing a victory role over the airfield to a great cheer from the boys. This was Malan at his peak and why we admired him so much. A true leader.

Later we had Mark V Spitfires with four Brownings and two 20 mm Hispano cannons. Bernie Stebbings and I were fitting one of the cannons and could not get it to drop past one of the spars on to the mounting. We had tried for several hours without success, so we took a file and with two strokes it dropped on to the mounting. It was fitted, we fired it off and it returned to the hanger were the two marks were spotted and reported. The mainplane had to be changed. Stebbings and I were put on a technical charge. Malan took the charge and we were marched in. After trying to talk ourselves out of it, Malan said, "What you have done could have endangered someone's life, it was entirely wrong. I appreciate the hours you are putting in and I am proud of you and all the Squadron. Don't let it happen again or you will be in big trouble." The charge was dismissed and we were marched out. Left left, left right, left.

While at RAF Manston Malan and all of the pilots bought us a couple of barrels of beer and the Squadron had a party. We were billeted in the village primary school and the party was held in a large hut opposite. The tables were lined with cakes, large custard pies, jelly and the likes.

Malan, Freeborn, Mungo Park and other pilots attended and the party got off to a good swing. Once a good deal of beer had been consumed the pilots departed. This was to allow the lads to let off a bit of steam and enjoy the rest of the night. After the beer ran out some inebriated airman decided to drop a large custard pie on his mate's head to liven up the party. This resulted into a huge bun fight until all the tables were cleared. Steam was let off and a good night was had by one and all. The next day we feared that Malan would have something to say about the sheer waste of food during days of rationing. I believe that word got back to Malan that the lads had had a great time and enjoyed themselves. They had appreciated the generosity of the pilots and let off steam. Malan would not want to spoil any of that and we were let off the hook.

During the height of the Battle of Britain at Biggin Hill, a score board was kept in the armament section of 74 Squadron. This showed the number of aircraft a pilot had shot down. Another board was kept in this section which showed who had scored the most with the girls in Bromley and surrounding districts. I am sure Maxi Malan would have never objected to that.

During the morning of 28 October, the Tigers were sent up to patrol Biggin Hill at 30,000 feet. At 0900 hours enemy aircraft were sighted flying at 22,000

Alan Ricalton (left) and Mungo (right) with Bill Skinner in the back seat. Manston, 1940.

feet in their vicinity. Mungo and his section turned towards two Bf109s that had become detached from the main body of aircraft and attacked. Mungo thumbed his gun button but something felt wrong. Only three of his eight machine guns were firing. With only three guns firing .303 bullets, Mungo didn't have much chance of doing much damage to his target, so he pulled up right behind the 109 at close range and expending the rest of his ammunition.

The up close and personal approach still did little damage to the 109. A couple of bits fell away from the enemy's tail unit, but Mungo had to break off feeling frustrated with his faulty guns.

Mungo's wingman attacked the second 109 and watched it go down with black smoke trailing from it, but its demise was inconclusive.

The following day Mungo took out his frustration on two Bf109s that had the misfortune of crossing his sights.

During an evening patrol over Biggin Hill, thirty-plus 109s were engaged by the Squadron east of Grinstead at 24,000 feet. Mungo, flying as 'Dysoe Leader' led the Tigers in to attack after climbing to 26,000 feet. Mungo half rolled his Spitfire and latched on to a 109 flying in a section of six. He fired two short bursts and the enemy fighter burst into flames.

Mungo continued to dive and found another 109 at 18,000 feet. A two-second burst was enough to cause glycol to pour out of the enemy machine. It went down into a vertical dive and Mungo followed it, giving it two more bursts. Pieces fell away from the 109 which was 'still going down very fast with black smoke pouring out and well over the vertical.' Mungo broke off the pursuit at 2,000 feet due to the amount of speed he had built up in the dive. He pulled out at 800 feet and lost sight of the descending 109 as it disappeared into thick ground haze.

Mungo's two victories were to be the last for the Tigers in the Battle of Britain which closed on 31 October 1940. But the fighting would not let up over the Channel.

On the morning of 2 November, 74 Squadron found itself amongst sixty-plus Messerschmitt 109s over the Isle of Sheppey. Four enemy aircraft were claimed by the Tigers. Mungo claimed one as damaged after firing at a diving 109 at 10,000 feet. He fired two three-second bursts and then was distracted by his windscreen icing up. He wiped it clean and managed to fire off a final burst at 200-yards range before it iced up once again, forcing him to return to base. The 109 was last seen flying low over the sea emitting white smoke.

Three days later Mungo learnt that he had been awarded a Distinguished Flying Cross for his service. His good friend and wingman H. M. Stephen was also awarded a Bar to his DFC.

On 15 November the *London Gazette* published the following:

Acting Flight Lieutenant John Colin MUNGO PARK (40008), 74 Squadron.

In October 1940, this officer was on patrol with his squadron at 30,000 feet when a formation of enemy aircraft were sighted. Flight Lieutenant Mungo-Park attacked a Messerschmitt 109 but had to break off the engagement as his windscreen became iced up. He cleaned this and again attacked the enemy aircraft and caused it to crash into the sea. He has personally destroyed eight hostile aircraft and has at all times displayed great courage and coolness in action.

On 14 November, Mungo led the Squadron in Malan's absence of leave into a swarm of fifty Junkers Ju87 Stukas and their Bf109 escorts with 66 Squadron in tow. In the eventful melee that ensued, the Tigers claimed fourteen Stukas destroyed, one 109 destroyed and an additional number of probables and damaged. Mungo had shot down two of the Stukas claimed.

Near the end of the month, 74, 92 and 66 Squadrons had collected an impressive record of enemy aircraft destroyed between them. On 29 November, the tally at Biggin Hill stood at 599 aerial victories. Bets were soon placed as a sweep-stake went around the station betting on who would get the station's 600th victory and when. The pilot who achieved the 600th would take the kitty.

Squadron Leader
Adolph 'Sailor'
Malan in 1942.
(*74 Squadron
Association*)

The next day brought a low mist over the aerodrome. It was cold and cloudy and many of the pilots assumed that not much flying would be had while these conditions lasted. Then all of a sudden the subdued station burst into life with the sounds of two Rolls-Royce Merlin engines. Those nearby looked out at the aerodrome and saw two Spitfires racing across the runway. When the Station Commander found out that the two pilots climbing away from Biggin were none other than Mungo and Stephen, he remarked, 'Of all the bloody cheek!' A small convoy of cars and motor bikes led by Malan screamed off towards the Operations Room to follow the two Tigers over the R/T. Mungo or Stephen called the Controller informing him that they were out on a voluntary patrol. A bemused 11 Group responded to the Controller. 'Vector those two idiots to Deal. There's a convoy moving up-Channel which might tempt Jerry-even in this weather!'

The two Spitfires broke through the haze and appeared in a clear patch of sky. Mungo and Stephen spotted eight Bf109s at around 30,000 feet, they climbed 4,000 feet higher than the enemy formation and engaged the tail end Charlie.

Mungo's combat report describes the action from his perspective and also offers a couple of his personal insights into the performance of the Spitfire. After his previous experiences with his cockpit icing up at high altitude it also seems that he finally found a solution to tackle the problem:

> I was 'Knockout' Blue Leader sent to patrol convoy off Deal, I was informed by operations that many 'Snappers' (Bf109s) were in the close vicinity, and I climbed to 29,000 feet and sighted 8-plus raid coming in from the south towards convoy, we climbed to 34,000 feet and engaged the 'weaver'. I opened fire with a two-second burst at 150 yards approximately, and enemy aircraft immediately dived. I broke off as I was overshooting and Blue 2 (H. M. Stephen) went in to attack...The E/A then half rolled, and I followed him down giving a further two-second burst at 100 yards and saw the hood of the E/A fly off. I broke away to avoid being hit by same and Blue 2 attacked again, the E/A was over the vertical when I last saw him, going through cloud. I noticed particularly that the performance of Spitfire II at that height, and with only two aircraft in company was manoeuvrable and also quite as fast as an Me.109 and I found no difficulty in following E/A. My aircraft was fitted with a half sheet of NO-MIST, which in my opinion is excellent, the lower half of the armour plated windscreen froze completely, but the top half, which was treated with NO-MIST, was completely clear, and I was able to fire successfully with no trouble. It would be an advantage if every aircraft was fitted with a complete sheet as soon as possible.

The 109 crashed near Dungeness and the German pilot died fifteen hours later. He was thereafter buried with full military honours.

The 600th enemy aircraft destroyed by Mungo and Stephen made Biggin Hill the first station in Fighter Command to reach such a figure.

Some accounts of the 600th victory credit H. M. Stephen as the pilot to have actually shot the 109 down and suggest Stephen took the sweep-stake. John Freeborn believed that Stephen had actually arranged for the Controllers to tip him off so that he could get off early to secure the 600th victory, but that when the call came Mungo was detailed to take off with him. John was also adamant that it was Mungo that shot the 109 down, but that he was too much of a gentleman to say otherwise. From Mungo's combat report, it suggests that he felt the 109 was a shared victory but whatever transpired between the pilots after is a bit of a mystery.

H. M. Stephen's recollection is as follows:

> The previous evening Mungo had come up to me in the Mess, taken me to one side and told me quietly that the next German aircraft to be shot down by one of the Biggin Hill Wing would be its 600th of the war. Malan had

also been told, and he had sanctioned an attempt by Mungo with another
– me – to claim the valuable prize, valuable not only in terms of Squadron
pride and achievement but also money, for a sweepstake had been organized
amongst air and ground crew. Everyone knew that the 600th was not very
far away, and that chance of a lottery was too good to miss. Armed with that
information, we set off for the airfield to sleep. At around 0600 hours a call
came through from the Controller asking whether we could get off, given
the conditions we had awoken to. Mungo took the call and I remember
him saying that we were Tigers, a bit of fog couldn't deter us, of course
we could get off, and where was the enemy? I didn't feel too put out about
Mungo's supreme confidence, given the fact that we were pretty experienced
in working as a team. We donned our flying gear and, with a man on each
wing, were guided out to the runway's end. We took off as a pair, wing tips
literally overlapping, and climbed. Operating in such a way was second
nature to us. Malan had the whole Squadron capable of such tight formation
flying and it really gave us all a great kick to be able to do it. Not only did it
increase our confidence and faith in our colleagues, but it gave us a boost to
know that they had complete confidence in you as well.[2]

In relation to the attack on the Messerschmitt, Stephen continued:

I got in a decisive shot which spelt the end for the 109. Mungo fired as well
and caused more damage. We broke off and returned to Biggin, where the
weather had cleared and enabled us to get down safely, to be greeted by an
enthusiastic group of pilots from 66 and 92. And I claimed a welcome £35 as
my share of the prize money!

Stephen also dispelled any myths about pilots competing with one another
over victories, remarking that he has never known how many aircraft he had
actually shot down:

I don't really care how many I shot down. Much has been written about
the competition between individuals in their quest to be top scorer. Such
competition in my experience did not exist. We all did our job, which was to
destroy as many of the enemy as we could. If the opportunity presented itself
then we took it as an individual, a section, or a squadron. That opportunity
either arrived or we went out and searched for it, There were also occasions
when discretion became the better part of valour and we pulled away from
the chance of engaging the enemy because it was patently obvious that we
would come off the worse. We were not in there for personal glory but as
part of a team and in 74's case a very well disciplined team.[3]

In late 1940, Mungo was one of the few pilots selected by Fighter Command to have his portrait drawn by wartime artist Cuthbert Orde. His portrait was also painted by Eric Kennington during the Battle of Britain.

In early 1941 the RAF began to focus its energies on offensive sweeps into France. Hugh Dowding and Keith Park had proven to be superior commanders and tacticians in comparison to their German opposites. Britain was no longer threatened by invasion plans and Fighter Command had won air superiority. In November 1940 Dowding stepped down from his position and Air Chief Marshal Sholto Douglas was appointed as Fighter Command's Commander in Chief. Leigh Mallory also succeeded Park as Air Officer Commanding 11 Group, to oversee Fighter Command's offensive strategies into France. These fighter sweeps were codenamed *Rhubarbs*, and were designed for RAF fighters to fly over enemy territory with the purpose of attracting Luftwaffe fighters up into the air where they could be destroyed.

The New Year also brought changes to the Tigers when Mungo's dear friend H. M. Stephen left with a posting to No. 59 Operational Training Unit.

On 10 March, Sailor Malan also left their ranks after a commendable four years of service to become one of Fighter Command's first Wing Leaders. Malan's experience, fine leadership and terrific combat record earned him the role of Officer Commanding Flying, of the Biggin Hill Wing, while Mungo's determined spirit and cool-headed leadership secured him Command of 74 Squadron. Mungo's appointment was well received by the Tigers, but some felt that longer serving members of the Squadron were better suited, including John Freeborn who had led the Squadron on numerous occasions. In fact, Freeborn flew more operational hours during the Battle of Britain than any other RAF pilot.

In May 1941, the Squadron was posted to Gravesend where it began to be re-equipped with Spitfire Mk Vs. The new marks carried two 20-mm cannons as well as four .303 machine guns, making its punch that much better than their previous Mk IIs.

On 6 June John Freeborn also left the Squadron with a posting to No. 57 Operational Training Unit at Hawarden. Surmising his time with the Tigers, Freeborn recalled: 'It was war time. We didn't enjoy the war but we fought it to the best of our ability and we were very good at it. I was relieved to be away from the fighting. [Squadron] 74 was one of the best fighter squadrons in the air force, I was glad to be a member of it and I did what I had to do.'

On 17 June, the Tigers soon learnt the dangers of flying offensive sorties. During the Battle of Britain the pilots felt comforted knowing that if they were forced to bale out they would be landing over home land and waters, but over enemy territory, fears of becoming PoWs now troubled their minds.

During a late afternoon sweep, Squadron Leader Mungo Park led the Tigers over the Channel with 92 Squadron flying in front. Just after crossing

Mungo Park in the cockpit of his Spitfire conversing with H. M. Stephen at Biggin Hill. (*74 Squadron Association*)

the French coast he saw a schwarm of Messerschmitt Bf109Fs approaching the rear section of 92 Squadron's Spitfires. Mungo immediately dived down with Red Section to intercept the fighters. As he opened fire he noticed approximately sixteen more 109s on his port side at about the same height as him. Mungo continued to dive towards a 109 and when in range he gave it a two-second burst of cannon and machine gun fire which caused the enemy's tail plane to completely disintegrate. Mungo saw the 109 fall away out of control but was suddenly attacked from behind.

> I received hits down the fuselage and a cannon shell in the engine, I climbed as best as I could and was just crossing the French coast…when three pink A.A. shells burst slightly below and giving my direction, in less than a minute five Me.109's arrived, the leader, not realising my slow speed overshot and I gave him the rest of my cannon shells from 50-250 yards, where upon he burst into flames.

Mungo took his Spitfire down in aileron turns, while blasting quick bursts of machine gun fire at other enemy aircraft on his way. Fortunately for Mungo, the enemy fighters left him alone at 15,000 feet over the Channel. 'My engine was very rough and stopped at 6,000 feet about two miles off Folkestone. I glided across coast and crash landed near Hawkinge aerodrome through lack of glycol.'

Mungo's skill, along with his growing tally and leadership, soon brought him the news that he had been awarded a Bar to his DFC.

On the evening of 27 June 1941, Mungo climbed into Spitfire Vb X4668, which was a presentation aircraft paid for by the people of Hinckley in Leicestershire and named *Burbage* after one of the nearby towns. It would be the last time Mungo would climb into the cockpit of an aircraft.

Mungo took off from Gravesend, leading eleven of 74 Squadron's Spitfires to Biggin Hill, where they would take off again at 2150 hours on a *Circus* operation to escort a formation of bombers on a raid over northern France. 19 and 266 Squadrons were also airborne on this run, but when the Tigers crossed the French coast they became separated from the other squadrons. Two formations of Bf109s pounced on the Tigers with a hard-hitting attack.

Clive Hilken was subjected to fly as the Squadron's 'tail end Charlie' due to his wingman failing to take off from Biggin Hill with engine trouble. Hilken recalled:

Thump! Thump! Thump! Cannon shells whipped into my plane. I pulled round to port and yelled into the radio but it was dead and I could see that my Spitfire was spewing out a white trail of glycol but I couldn't see the attackers. I can only presume they came out of the sun, hit me and went on to take out Sandeman and our CO. My elevator was stuck and a piece of metal in my ankle was causing it to bleed at full speed. I baled out only to find my parachute pack waving about by my side. I pulled it in and undid the strap fasteners, sowing the chute out for a yard or two before it caught up and opened. It took me down to France, hospital and a PoW camp.

Pilot Officer Sandeman, a Kiwi Tiger, was also taken prisoner after being shot down.

The Luftwaffe formations which had ambushed the Tigers were led by two very experienced Luftwaffe pilots, Hptm. Rolph Pingel (who was shot down and taken prisoner on 10 July 1941) and Hptm. Wilhelm Balthaser (who was killed on 3 July).

On the ground below the action, in the Belgian coastal town of De Panne, just north of Dunkirk, teenager Joseph Recour was playing tennis with friends when they noticed a solitary Spitfire coming down, tailing smoke before it crashed. The young boys quickly got on their bicycles and pedalled as fast as they could in the direction of the crash site, which was about two miles away. Joseph and his friends found the Spitfire wreckage near the railway station

The wreckage of Mungo Park's Spitfire X4667 'ZP-E', named 'Burbage'. (*74 Squadron Association*)

at Adinkerke. They were unable to get close to the Spitfire as Germans had already arrived to guard it. Joseph remembers clearly seeing the body of the pilot lying beside it.

The exact circumstances that led to Mungo being shot down in the air are unknown, but at the crash site German soldiers took photographic evidence of the scene. From these photographs it is known that Mungo did not bale out of his Spitfire. When the Germans arrived at the site they found Mungo hanging from his straps in the cockpit before removing him from the wreckage and laying him on the ground nearby.

Mungo was buried in the cemetery at Adinkerke (in the company of German soldiers from the First World War) where his body still rests. Some of the locals visited Mungo's grave and laid flowers, an act which was expressly forbidden by the Germans.

Squadron Leader John Mungo Park DFC and Bar, was the first and only Commanding Officer of 74 Squadron that was ever lost in action.

On 9 July 1941 Mungo was posthumously awarded a Bar to his DFC. The citation read:

> In June 1941 he was attacked by six Me.109s while over the French coast. He succeeded in shooting down two of them and although his own aircraft was badly damaged he flew back to this country, making a skilful forced landing. His courage and leadership have contributed materially to the successes achieved by his squadron.

Mungo's untimely loss was keenly felt by the Squadron and later by those Tigers who had moved on to other units. Arthur Westerhoff also noticed the CO's absence, as he recalled:

> Mungo Park took off on a sortie from RAF Gravesend and never returned. We were never given any operational information about a pilot, and if they didn't return we presumed they had been shot down. If they had baled out without problems they would return to the Squadron. We missed Mungo Park, he was popular with the crews. In those days no tears were shed and the war was still on.

A few days after Mungo's death the Squadron Adjutant, Flight Lieutenant Powell wrote a letter to Mungo's mother Mamie:

> I've known Mungo since my arrival on the Squadron in March 1940. Since he took over command I've been his Adjutant. I love him like my own son. I've never met a nicer man and his loss has been a real shock to me as too for the rest of the Squadron. There is not one in the Squadron down to the lowest rank who didn't like John and admire him. What we admired most was his modesty. In spite of all the publicity he received about his outstanding record it didn't go to his head. He stayed himself.
>
> For all his heroics in the air, for all his Tiger fighting spirit, for all his determination, Mungo was a modest, private man, greatly liked by his 74 Squadron colleagues. Whenever he could when on leave he returned to his home town of Bolton but if he was asked to perform some civic function whilst there, he did so but reluctantly, for he disliked being in the limelight. He was in many ways the archetypal young RAF Battle of Britain pilot – handsome, dashing, good humoured, unassuming on the ground – but fearless, skilful, tactically aware, determined, even ruthless in the air when confronting the enemy.

Some seventy years after the Battle of Britain was waged, fellow Tiger and friend John Freeborn would smile when thinking of Mungo appearing in the doorway at Hornchurch all those years ago and flashing a marvellous salute at him. John also treasured a memory of handing Mungo his tattered, blood stained flying helmet that he had borrowed before being shot up by 109s. When John returned from hospital Mungo exclaimed 'Freeborn, next time, wear your own bloody helmet!'

It is clearly evident that everyone that had the pleasure of knowing Mungo spoke of him with the greatest of respect and highest esteem. He would forever be sorely missed not only by his colleagues but especially by his family and friends back home.

Mungo Park was indeed one of the Few, one of the aces, and one of the greatest Tigers in RAF history who ultimately gave everything he had in the service of his country.

CHAPTER 4

Allan Wright

On a glorious summer's day in 2010, a trim, unassuming man in his nineties was tending to his beautiful garden somewhere deep in the Devon countryside. Behind him, stood a lovely white house, which he had designed and built with his own hands. The man was clearly in his element, surrounded by flowers bursting with colour, with the hot sunshine beaming down from a blue cloudless sky. Wiping the sweat from his brow, the man looked up as his wife Barbara called from the house for him to come inside for a much needed drink. The man obliged and entered his home for a welcomed break. Once inside the house, which was full of charm and character, the man walked passed a framed picture of an impressive looking young man drawn by wartime artist Cuthbert Orde.

The living room, adorned with family photographs of children and grandchildren, make him proud as he sits to rest. Nearby is another room, smaller in size and quietly reminding the man of a summer that was a far cry from the peace he enjoys today. Soon after his break the man enters this room and gazes at one of the few Spitfire paintings hanging on the walls. The painting depicts a 92 Squadron Spitfire swooping low over a narrow road. A young lady has stopped riding her bicycle to look up at the Spitfire overhead. Group Captain Allan Wright, DFC*, AFC, smiles. The painting reminds him of days gone by, in 1940, when he was a Spitfire pilot of an elite squadron, swooping low above his girlfriend Barbara, as she rode her bicycle down the same country roads. They were such memorable days in an unforgettable glorious summer.

Allan Richard Wright was born to Elise and Arthur Wright on 20 February 1920 in Teignmouth, Devon. Allan was the second eldest of four boys, and one sister. Their father had served in the Royal Flying Corps, so the family had lived in a variety of places, including England, Ireland and Egypt, due to Arthur's postings. Allan's education began at Blackfriars School Laxton Northants, before he entered St Edmund's Collage Ware Herts in 1934. Allan proved to be an intelligent student who excelled in his studies. He was entered for his Higher School Certificate two years earlier than was usual for his age

Tony Bartley far right next to Paddy Green and Bob Holland centre. (*Allan Wright*)

and he passed. As well as being a bright young man, Allan was also a fine athlete. He was a good sprinter, excellent at Long Jump and an efficient Rugby player. During his college days Allan was also a member of the shooting team. He developed into a skilled marksman and won several prizes for his accuracy.

Following in his father's footsteps, Allan elected for a career in aviation. He entered RAF Collage Cranwell on 28 April 1938 and was assigned to C-Squadron. For Allan, the two-year course was cut short by six months due to the outbreak of war. On 22 October 1939 Allan Wright was commissioned as a Pilot Officer and on the 30th he was posted to the newly re-formed 92 Squadron at Tangmere, Sussex.

Pilot Officer Wright would soon discover that 92 Squadron was a Night Fighter squadron, in the process of being equipped with Bristol Blenheims. The Squadron's Commanding Officer was Roger Bushell, who would later be coldly murdered by the Gestapo for his role as Big X in 'The Great Escape'.

92 Squadron's new beginnings turned out to be a miserable affair leading up to the New Year. The weather was often poor and their twin-engine Blenheims were mostly unreliable, but there was a light at the end of the tunnel.

In March 1940, the Squadron re-equipped with Supermarine Spitfire Mark Is, much to the ecstasy of the pilots and ground crews alike.

The Spitfire was the most modern fighter in the RAF at this time and highly sought after by almost every, if not all, fighter pilots in Fighter Command during 1940. The RAF's first monoplane fighter, the Hawker Hurricane was a brilliant and robust aircraft but when the Spitfire came into service it was soon overlooked. Many pilots who flew the Hurricane in combat have testified of its fine capabilities, commenting that it was a stable gun platform, it could take a lot of punishment and it was far easier to maintain than the Spitfire, yet undeniably the Spitfire won the popularity contest overall.

Warrant Officer David Denchfield, who flew with 610 Squadron, said the following:

> I had a great regard for the Hurricane, both mechanically and the men who flew it. Luckily I had no choice; I was posted to a Spitfire unit. I thought the Spit was superb to fly in – it was responsive and agile. We had great respect for the Luftwaffe. They had some excellent aeroplanes, and were highly trained, and of course many had far more experience than us. We learned about their planes the hard way, firstly in France, and this information was filtered back to those of us who had yet to meet them. Then of course came first-hand knowledge, and from that came the realisation that the bombers were good, but beatable, but to beware of the Junkers 88. The 109s were our greatest worry. It was mostly a question of who saw who first. Of course we had confidence in our own aeroplanes, especially once involved in close combat where the agility of our planes was superior. But heaven help you if you were bounced.

Squadron Leader Geoffrey Wellum, DFC, who joined 92 Squadron as an eighteen-year-old pilot officer on 22 May 1940, remarked:

> Regarding the Spitfire – I would not have wanted to go to war in any other aeroplane. I always thought that if I could see my antagonist then I could out-fly him in a Spitfire. The German pilots were well trained in a very good aeroplane, particularly the Messerschmitt 109. The 109's were always something to be, if not worried about, then very aware of their capabilities.

Wellum, who instantly became known as 'The Boy', amongst his colleagues, not only thought very highly of his aircraft but also of Pilot Officer Wright; 'Allan was a wonderful man, a Christian and a great friend'.

Wright's first impression of this new fighter was one of trepidation,

> I remember that we were near London – Croydon. And I can remember this line-up of Spitfires and thinking, "My goodness, that's going to be

something," because there's no dual. You sat in the cockpit a long time, with a chap over your shoulder showing you everything, and saying how they behaved, but you didn't know how it was going to behave until you actually flew it.[1]

Wright continued,

The Spitfire was a very powerful aircraft, oh yes…You've got fifteen hundred horsepower just six feet away from you, in the front there…We felt very privileged, actually, to begin to fly the Spitfire in our case, rather than the Hurricane, because a Spitfire has obviously cleaner lines and will obviously go faster, and therefore it's going to be a better – so we thought, and probably rightly – fighter…I certainly wouldn't have liked to have had to cope with 109s flying a Hurricane.[2]

During the ensuing weeks Squadron Leader Bushell had the boys practising interceptions, formation flying and mock formation attacks on a Blenheim, which was flown by 92 Squadron's Sergeant Michael Barraclough. By 8 April, they had all flown solo on Spitfires.

A report dated 1 November 1939 – 1 May 1940, recorded details of the Squadron's flying hours. Pilot Officer Wright had flown 151.55 hours, 69.05 of those were on Spitfires.

In May, the Squadron was declared 'Operational', which meant that the short period of training was now over and things began to get serious. On 9 May, Flight Commander Bob Stanford Tuck, who had recently been posted to 92 Squadron from 65 Squadron at Hornchurch, led seven Spitfires to Northolt. The pilots were Allan Wright, Paddy Green, Pat Learmond, Tony Bartley, Tich Havercroft and Bob Holland. They landed at Northolt just before midday and were sent immediately to their dispersal points around the aerodrome. One section of three were put at 'readiness', another section were made 'available' and one aircraft and pilot was spare. Later in the day Roger Bushell led the rest of the Squadron to Northolt, making the unit complete for operational duties.

On 16 May, Blue Section, which consisted of Bob Tuck, Allan Wright and Bob Holland were chosen by their CO to fly from Northolt to Hendon for a special assignment. Once the three of them had landed they were told that they would be escorting Winston Churchill to Paris for a meeting with the French prime minister.

After a smooth flight across the Channel, the three Spitfires touched down at Le Bourget airport. That night they slept at the Airport Hotel at Le Bourget and returned to Northolt the following morning at 1000 hours. During the afternoon a telegram arrived at the station from Churchill, who personally thanked the officers involved in escorting him to France.

As previously mentioned, 22 May saw the arrival of Pilot Officer Geoffrey Wellum. In his excellent book *First Light* he wrote of his introduction to the Squadron:

> That evening in the Mess all is new to me and exciting. I am with a fighter squadron as one of its pilots…I am surrounded by fighter pilots, self-assured in one respect but conscious of the fact that they have yet to prove themselves worthy of that title. Their chance is very near and they are aware of it…I feel unimportant and out of things but that is only to be expected. I am a new boy, a bit of an outsider. They are a team that formed the squadron and worked up together and who are now being drawn closer together by the imminence of their first action.
>
> Mac (Herbert McGowan, Squadron Adjutant) introduces me to Pat Learmond, 'the best aerobatic pilot in the squadron and ex-Cranwell', and Pat in turn introduces me to the others, one of whom is a quietly spoken, wavy haired young man. His name is Allan and I'm told later his surname is Wright. He seems quieter than the rest and appears to be totally in control of himself and the situation. He stays talking for quite a while before he excuses himself. He is also ex-Cranwell and I feel that Allan is going to be a helpful friend to have around.[3]

The chance to prove themselves as fighter pilots arrived on Thursday 23 May 1940. At 0500 hours, twelve Spitfires took off from Northolt and flew to Hornchurch, where they waited at readiness until 1045 hours, when the Squadron was ordered off to patrol the French coast.

The first sweep between Boulogne and Dunkirk proved uneventful, but at 1130 hours, when the Squadron made a second pass over Dunkirk, chaos erupted out of the blue. 'Here they come, eight o'clock!' cried Barraclough over the R/T. His words had barely filtered through the other pilots' headsets when horror struck. Pat Learmond's Spitfire P9370 suddenly exploded into a ball of fire and plunged towards the ground.

There was panic in the sky. Aircraft turned and twisted in all directions. In mere seconds all those months of training in formation flying and numbered attacks went up in smoke. The Squadron scattered and individual dogfights ensued in a confused melee.

By 1245 hours, the last Spitfire returning from the battle zone touched down at Hornchurch. The Squadron's tally was two enemy aircraft destroyed by Bob Tuck and Gus Edwards and four probables claimed by Paddy Green, Paul Klipsch, Michael Barraclough, and Gus Edwards.

Excited chatter began to gush out at Hornchurch, as the pilots recounted their actions over Dunkirk to Mac McGowan and their ground crews. Tuck and Tony Bartley's banter ended with a wager: the one with the most bullet holes in his aircraft after each sortie would buy the other's beer that night.

During combat Bartley had seen Pat's aircraft:

> I saw the blazing wreck of a Spitfire as I darted seawards over the beach. It was Pat Learmond's – the squadron's first war casualty. I made Hornchurch with only a few gallons to spare, and as I climbed out of my cockpit, my head ached from the smell of cordite and my heart was hammer-pounding.[4]

Later, when things had settled down, the pilots discussed the loss of Pat Learmond. He was just twenty years of age, a brilliant pilot, a cheerful character, but shot down in a flash by an unseen enemy. It was a very sad way to start their war and no one felt his death more deeply than Allan Wright, who, with his girlfriend Barbara, was extremely close friends with Pat.

That evening the Squadron was sent up once again to patrol the French coast. When the fighter boys reached Boulogne another frantic battle broke out. Wright was quickly learning first-hand that aerial combat was a scene of total confusion as aircraft screamed across the sky in all directions.

Ju87 Stukas could be seen bombing Boulogne harbour, but Wright, flying Spitfire N3250 'GR-S', followed his Section up towards a substantial amount of Bf110s that were already being engaged by other members of 92 above. Wright reported:

> I joined in the lower part of the dog fight, and fired a number of deflection shots with little result. The pilot's cockpit of one, however, burst apart, and the E/A went down in a spiral. I followed another which was diving with white smoke coming from its starboard engine.

Wright pursued this Bf110 as it dived towards the deck. When the enemy aircraft reached 500 feet it pulled out of its dive and set course for Germany. Wright followed, flying just above the tree tops for about 20 miles, giving it short bursts, which caused 'flaming material' to fall from the enemy machine. When his ammunition boxes ran empty, there was nothing left for Wright to do but break off the chase and return to base.

The Squadron's first day in combat had proven to be a fierce and exhausting affair. The pilots had done well for themselves in shooting down and damaging enemy aircraft, but they had also suffered losses to their own ranks. Paddy Green didn't return to Hornchurch that evening, instead he landed his damaged Spitfire at Hawkinge and was soon admitted to Shorncliffe Hospital. Green had sustained a compound fracture in his thigh during combat over Boulogne. The Squadron's popular CO, Roger Bushell was also reported missing and Paul Klipsch went down with his aircraft in France. A young boy, who happened to be the local undertakers son found Klipsch's crash-site. A priest was soon called to the scene. Klipsch's body was finally buried in the village churchyard of Wierre-Effroy, Pas de Calais.

In a television documentary called *The Last Few*, Wright commented on Pat's death:

> I was having a bath the next night and I really realised that Pat was not going to... that I wasn't going to see him at all. It really got to me and I wept, I must say. It's the only time as a grown-up that I've ever cried. But after that, well, the best German is a dead one.

Although that statement reads cold, it must be remembered that at the time, having lost a close friend to the enemy in such a brutal way, emotions were naturally running high for the young man amidst a ferocious air war.

Many pilots did not visualise shooting down another human being. Wright explained:

> It was another aeroplane that you were fighting. You weren't fighting another person... it didn't occur to me, certainly in those early stages what happens to the person in it, whether he was dead already, or whether he was going to be dead when he hit the sea, or whatever it was.

Throughout the night of the 23 May, the devoted ground crews worked hard to patch up and repair the Squadron's Spitfires. The following morning eight of them were serviceable for the pilots' next patrol.

Wright reflected upon that first day in combat:

> It's rather amusing, really. Not having been to war at all, not having had an enemy to be nasty to, when we went up the first time to fly around Dunkirk, our briefing was very poor, I don't know why they didn't give us a proper briefing, telling us that we were retreating and that we had to try and hold the enemy back from attacking our ground troops. All we were told, was that our ground troops were at Dunkirk, and that we'd recognise Dunkirk because there was a great plume of smoke coming up from it, because they'd pretty well burned the place down. So it was very easy to find, so we just were told to go there, patrol up and down, you'll doubtless see some Me.109s, and when you see them, shoot them down. As simple as that. And that's how it happened. In fact, the first ones I saw, I was with the squadron in formation, and when I looked over my right, I saw some aeroplanes with swastikas on, or crosses, they were, from that position, flying below there. And I called up and I said, "Oh, I can see some aircraft down there with crosses on." And my leader said, "That's the bloody enemy, you fool." And then he said, "Down we go."[5]

Group Captain Allan Wright, DFC, AFC, holding his Spitfire's gunsight that was damaged by enemy fire in combat with Bf109s. (*Author*)

With Bushell missing and Paddy Green out of action, Bob Tuck assumed temporary command of the Squadron. Tuck's first task was filling Green's position of flight commander. He stopped by his old Squadron (65) at Hornchurch and recruited his good friend Brian Kingcome.

Kingcome had no problem fitting in to the Squadron. He instantly became a popular figure among the boys and would eventually become a great leader in the air. In early 1941, Kingcome was given command of 92. Of Wright, Kingcome remarked that he was 'extremely bright and professional' and a 'determined and successful pilot.'

On Friday 24 May, eight Spitfires took off from Hornchurch at 0805 hours to patrol the French coast. After thirty-five minutes of scanning the sky, the Squadron finally sighted large formations of enemy aircraft flying at 11,000 feet. The Squadron began their approach in a shallow, curving dive and then attacked the bombers from behind. Tony Bartley's section reached the bombers first and Bob Tuck watched an impressive attack from Bartley, as he recalled:

> He went down the starboard side of the stream, shooting them up one wing, and I distinctly saw him leapfrog over one 'vic', under the next, then up over

the third – and so on. He did the whole side of the formation like that, and he tumbled at least one – maybe two – as flamers at that single pass. It was just about the cheekiest bit of flying I'd seen.[6.]

Tuck then led his section down to engage the port side of the formation. He hosed the rearmost Dornier's port engine, wing-root and fuselage with a decent burst from his eight guns. The enemy aircraft broke away from the main body of aircraft, with pieces falling off it. Tuck's attention was rudely demanded by enemy gunners on his right who blasted away at his Spitfire. Bullets invaded Tuck's cockpit around his feet and a sheering pain was felt on the inside of his right thigh. Despite the pain, Tuck followed the machine he had previously attacked which by now was spewing black liquid, while banking sharply to one side. Tuck flew below the Dornier and raked its duck-egg blue belly with two long bursts of ammunition. Two of the Dornier's crew took to their parachutes as Tuck broke away. The Dornier's port side erupted in flames and it turned over almost on to its back, before plunging down vertically towards the deck.

The heavy crossfire from the Dorniers caused problems for other pilots of 92 as well. Gus Edwards's aircraft was struck by several bullets but he was saved from certain death thanks to his armoured windscreen. Flying Officer Peter Cazenove's Spitfire was also stricken by lethal crossfire and he was forced to crash-land on the beach below. Before he went down he called up his colleagues on the R/T, 'Put me down for two Do17s and tell the family I'll be home in a couple of days.' Cazenove successfully landed his aircraft on the dunes near Dunkirk. He then climbed out of the cockpit and walked along the beach, where he came across a burnt out shell of a Spitfire. The intense fire had barely left anything recognisable other than a blackened, twisted buckle from the pilot's parachute harness. In Bob Tuck's biography, Larry Foster names the aircraft as Pat Learmond's, but Tony Bartley later wrote that it was Paul Klipsch's Spitfire and that Cazenove had cut the buckle off to return to Klipsch's parents when he returned.

Two days later Flying Officer Cazenove was captured by the Germans and ended up in Stalag Luft 3 as a prisoner of war.[7]

Back at Hornchurch the ground crews watched attentively as Tuck landed his damaged Spitfire. After lifting himself out of the cockpit he saw that his leg had a small tear near his right trouser pocket. He felt inside and pulled out a buckled penny amongst his loose change. The coin had stopped one bullet but something else had lodged in the back of his thigh. Tuck explained his part of the scrap to Wright and Bartley while the medical officer inspected his wound.

A surgeon later removed a piece of metal from Tuck's thigh. It wasn't a bullet or a piece of shrapnel, but a small duralumin nut from a rudder pedal. It must have been knocked off by one of the bullets that penetrated his cockpit. 'A few inches higher,' the surgeon remarked, 'and they'd have had to transfer you to the W.A.A.F.'

Aside from Tuck's injury, the loss of Cazenove and some damaged Spitfires the Squadron had fared well. The tally for the day was two Dornier Do17s destroyed and seven probables.

On 25 May, nine pilots of the Squadron made their way to dispersal to wait for further orders. The waiting period before being scrambled into action was, for many of the airmen, worse than the actual fighting. It was an unavoidable time that caused the pilots to feel nervous, apprehensive, anxious and even frightened. 'The Boy' Wellum described the waiting as purgatory, as they waited for the call to scramble. Whenever the telephone would ring, adrenaline would pump around the pilots' systems, but sometimes the call would be a trivial matter, and then the pilots would have to settle themselves back down. It was an exhausting process and one that never got any easier. To distract their minds, some of the pilots would read, or play cards, or if they were able, to sleep. Wright remembered: 'I couldn't settle down to a book, I just couldn't. I think the reason being that if you got into a book and you're suddenly called out, it takes a few seconds or a minute or so to readjust to reality. I thought that might slow me up.'

The telephone quickly became a hated device to the pilots and many of them, even in later years, would still jump at the sound of it ringing.

The first serious message to arrive that morning called for two aircraft to take off and intercept an unidentified aircraft flying over the Thames Estuary. Bob Tuck and Tich Havercroft went off and found the aircraft was a friendly Avro Anson on a navigational flight.

At 1130 hours the phone rang again. This time all nine pilots were ordered to scramble. With hearts thumping away beneath their Mae Wests, the pilots ran towards their Spitfires to get airborne as quickly as possible. Minutes later nine Spitfires were racing across Hornchurch. Once airborne the Squadron formed up into three sections. Brian Kingcome led Red Section, with Bartley and Williams in tow. Blue Section was led by Tuck, followed by Holland and Wright. Yellow Section consisted of Edwards, Eyles and Bryson.

The Squadron levelled out at 13,000 feet and began to patrol the French coast. The enemy's position was soon given away when Anti-Aircraft shells began bursting into the air near Calais. The Squadron sighted two Dorniers flying 5,000 feet above their position and began to climb towards them. The bombers must have been aware of the nine hungry Spitfires below because they suddenly spilt up. Red and Blue sections went after the Dornier that was heading north of their position and Yellow Section pursued the aircraft travelling south. For once, the Squadron had time to prepare for its attack without interruptions from fighter escort or enemy crossfire.

The six remaining Spitfires approached the Dornier from the rear and attacked it one after the other. The enemy aircraft had no chance and it crashed into the sea.

Leading Yellow Section, Gus Edwards attacked the other Dornier and unloaded 2,800 rounds on the bomber. Edwards broke away to evade enemy return fire and became separated from his section. Dangerously low on fuel, Edwards made his way back across the Channel and landed at Hawkinge.

When the others returned to Hornchurch they were soon informed that Squadron Leader Philip James Sanders had been appointed to command 92 Squadron. Tony Bartley commented on 'Judy' Sanders' position saying that he...

... started to exercise his authority as our new CO but it was an unenviable task. We were cock-a-hoop with our substantial victories which had established us as one of the top-scoring fighter squadrons over Dunkirk...We just couldn't respect any other leaders than those we had had: Roger Bushell and Bob Tuck. We were a 'bolshie' bunch of bastards, our tails riding high.[8]

Later that same afternoon the Squadron was ordered to Duxford in Cambridgeshire to rest and re-equip. The fighter boys were thrilled to find a village pub near their new station called the 'Red Lion'. It naturally became a regular haunt for the Squadron.

On Sunday 2 June, the Squadron fought its last battle over the Dunkirk beaches. In the morning Wright and his colleagues flew to their forward base at Marlesham Heath in preparation for an offensive wing operation to Calais with two other squadrons.

During this sortie the Squadron sighted six Heinkel 111s flying at approximately 12,000 feet in the direction of Dunkirk. Squadron Leader Sanders was leading Green Section which he kept up-sun from the enemy before attacking.

Blue Section carried out a formation attack on the rear vic of the bombers. Wright was flying as Blue 3, but in the fast dive towards the Heinkels, he held his fire thinking that the bombers might be RAF Blenheims. Wright returned for a better look and realised that they were indeed Heinkels after all. He turned his Spitfire to attack, but before he could fire he was put off by four Bf109s diving out of the sun towards him. Wright attacked one of the enemy fighters and saw its engine catch fire at 1,000 feet before it dived towards the ground. He then heard a loud crash from behind; he turned to see what was there and found another 109 on his tail. Wright took immediate evasive action by turning his aircraft. He was about 5 miles south east of Dunkirk and unhappily discovered that he was out of ammunition. With some difficulty and sixteen bullet holes in his aircraft, Wright managed to shake his attacker off by pretending to attack him in return. The 109 broke away and Wright was free to return to base.

Wright was not the only one to have difficulty in recognising aircraft on this patrol. Bob Holland mistook four Bf109s for Spitfires and alarmingly he formatted on them. Holland realised his error when the 109s attacked, but impressively he managed to shoot one out of the sky and escape the others.

The sortie lasted for about two hours making it the first successful 'Big Wing' operation of the war. No. 92 Squadron took pride in being the squadron to front it. The pilots finally returned to Martlesham Heath with eighteen claims of enemy aircraft destroyed and damaged.

It was during this first week in June that Bob Tuck was chosen to travel to the RAE at Farnborough to carry out a series of tests on the first captured Messerschmitt Bf109 that had fallen into British hands. The experience proved extremely useful for Tuck on a personal level because after handling the controls of the 109 he could then visualise what the enemy fighter pilots were doing in combat.

In early June the Squadron moved to Hornchurch in Essex, where 54, 65 and 74 Squadrons were based. After they had arrived Allan Wright decided to explore the Essex countryside on a temperamental motorcycle that he and Bill Williams used to get around. While out exploring, Wright came off the bike and badly injured his shoulder. When the Squadron fitters examined the motorcycle they found that the frame was bent and the wheels had never been properly aligned. Wright was given ten days sick leave to recover from his accident.

The first week of June also saw the departure of 92 Squadron's Adjutant Mac McGowan. A Norwegian from Fredriksted, called Tom Wiese was posted to the Squadron to take over the Intelligence Officer duties.

On Tuesday 18 June a signal arrived ordering the Squadron to move to Pembrey in South Wales. The pilots received the news with great disappointment, for the quiet Welsh countryside was too far away from the action.

On arrival at Pembrey, the fighter boys flew in so low that they hedge hopped and beat up the area with their nimble Spitfires. Within minutes the police and RAF station phone lines were jammed with complaints from the local inhabitants. Tony Bartley recalled:

Farmers, doctors, parsons, lawyers, local councillors and police flooded the telephone lines to the Station, demanding an explanation for our demoniacal flying. I rolled my Spitfire around our new CO, Judy Sanders, my engine cut dead, and I force-landed in a bog which I had mistaken for a field.[9]

When Bartley waded out of the mud he was promptly arrested by the Home Guard due to his suspicious appearance. He was wearing red Daks trousers and an old Stoic tie. After a couple of telephone conversations, Bartley was driven back to base by Tom Wiese.

The following days brought relative inactivity for the Squadron, although local flights were conducted so the pilots could get a good idea of the area surrounding their new station. Wright's shoulder was still too damaged for flying, so he was given a further week's leave to recover. A day before he was due to return to flying duty, Wright took up the Squadron's Magister with Bill Williams to test his reactions in flight. In typical 92 Squadron fashion, they made a mundane task enjoyable by playing a game of 'chicken'. They took it in turns to dive the aircraft towards the ground, the first one to grab hold of the stick and pull up lost. The fun abruptly ended when they almost left it too late to pull out of the dive. The Magister's port wingtip scraped the ground and they had to force-land near St-Athan. Other than a brief moment of panic, Wright's shoulder seemed to be in working order, so he reported for duty on 27 June.

Although the pilots were frustrated to be away from the fighting, it was also a welcome break from the action over Dunkirk. But the novelty soon wore off. Towards the end of June, Bartley wrote to his father:

> We were really glad to get our rest. Some of us couldn't eat or sleep much after Dunkirk, but now we are ripe, ready and itching to get back to the action again. If I live through this war, I doubt I shall ever be able to settle down to a conventional life. As soon as our wheels touch ground, wine, women and song seems to be the next order of the day.[10]

In early July 1940 the Squadron flew daytime patrols over Cardiff, Swansea and Pembroke. Most of these patrols were uneventful although sometimes a lone enemy aircraft was intercepted. The heavy fighting was being waged in the south of England and over the Channel. Unhappily the Squadron also began night flying which usually commenced at dusk if the call arrived. Night flying in a Spitfire was not ideal and the pilots began to feel very dismayed with the task.

On 18 July, Wright took off in Spitfire N3287 and flew it to Hornchurch where it was due for a prop modification. After waiting around at the aerodrome, Wright decided to take some 'unofficial' leave. He took off for Booker Airfield, which was close to where his girlfriend Barbara lived. A few hours later Wright returned to Pembrey.

On Wednesday 14 August, Wright took off with Bill Williams and Peter Eyles on an evening patrol to Weston-Super-Mare. Wright led Green Section up to 15,000 feet and then received further instructions to fly over to Hullavington, where a Heinkel 111 was seen at 5,000 feet.

Wright lined the intruder up in his reflector sight and fired a short deflection burst at 400 yards' range. His bullets struck home but the Heinkel managed to escape into cloud cover. Wright stalked the bomber from below and waited for it to reappear in a clear patch of cloud. When the Heinkel re-emerged he fired a long burst from below and followed it up into astern, again from 400 yards range. Again the bomber disappeared into cloud and this time Wright lost track of it and discovered his Section had split up.

Bill Williams found the Heinkel over Bristol and carried out a beam attack, followed by a quarter attack before he too lost it in cloud.

The Heinkel 111P belonged to III/KG27 and it force-landed by the side of a road at Charterhouse, Somerset. The aircraft was credited to Wright and Williams as a shared enemy aircraft destroyed.

Williams also shot down another He111 that he engaged head-on as it approached Bristol. By 1845 hours, Wright, Williams and Eyles had all returned to base.

When the Spitfires landed the dedicated ground crews immediately got to the task of re-fuelling and rearming the aircraft so they were ready for the next patrol. Looking back many years later Wright regretted that he didn't really outwardly show his appreciation to his crew:

> I should have paid more attention to my crew, but I'm afraid I didn't. You know, I expected the machine to be ready and when I got out, the first thing was to be debriefed. I didn't take myself off to the huts or tents where they would be and find them and talk to them. I didn't make friends with them, but I'm sorry about that now.

Wright's next claim against the enemy was to be a first for 92 Squadron because it occurred at night.

At this time pilots in the Squadron had expressed their great displeasure at flying at night-time in a Spitfire. The Spitfire's long nose made taxiing a bit tricky in daylight, let alone in the darkness and besides the lack of visibility, another problem that made night flying a difficult task was the Spitfire's exhausts which would flare out in front making it near impossible for a pilot's eyes to adjust to the darkness. The night patrols were proving unfruitful so many of the boys felt it a great waste of their time.

However, on 29 August Allan Wright took off from Bibury under a moonlit sky in Spitfire R6596 'QJ-S'. Flying as Blue 1 on a lone night patrol, Wright was vectored towards a bandit flying near Bristol.

Alone in the dark Wright maintained his course until eventually he began to hear a German crew chatting away over the R/T. The chatter increased and grew louder, giving Wright the feeling that he was eerily close to the enemy. All of a sudden, Wright spotted a Heinkel 111 at 20,000 feet, exposed in the beams of a Searchlight Battery far below. Wright readied himself and moved into a favourable position to attack the bomber. All he could really see was the glow from the Heinkel's exhausts and so when at 250 yards range, Wright thumbed his gun button, firing two accurate bursts from his machine guns between the enemy's engines. Then all of a sudden Wright was momentarily blinded by two bright flashes, which at first he thought was enemy return fire. In fact it was anti-aircraft fire being fired into the air from down below. Although a little too close for comfort, the danger of being struck by ground fire soon passed when the Searchlight beams lost track of the Heinkel, leaving Wright to close in once again from around 100 yards to 40 yards. At this favourable distance Wright continuing to make attacks from below and astern. The difficulty at being this close to the bomber was trying to keep his aircraft from overshooting the Heinkel, but Wright managed to stay behind it and saw his De Wilde ammunition bursting into the enemy's glowing engines. Finally the bandit decreased its speed as each engine was put out of action by Wright's eight sparkling guns. A bright flash of flame erupted from the Heinkel and Wright watched it diving towards the ground. At 13,000 feet, Wright broke away from the scene and returned to Bibury.

After landing back at base at 2305 hours, Wright taxied his Spitfire across the small, rough airfield under the moonlit sky, feeling absolutely elated with his success.

He switched off his Spitfires engine and climbed out of his cockpit and began to make his way towards a bunch of morose looking colleagues. Much to Allan's surprise his superb victory was greeted by groans and grimaces from his pals. The reason for this behaviour was that Flight Lieutenant Brian Kingcome was on the verge of convincing 10 Group that night defence was unproductive, hazardous and a waste of 92's time. The boys were all extremely keen to get back to the South East, where the Battle for Britain was still raging and the burden of night flying would be lifted. Wright's victory just might foil Kingcome's case. Feeling a bit deflated Wright took himself off to bed. The Heinkel he had shot down crashed in the village of Hale near Fordingbridge.

On Saturday 7 September, the Squadron's misery ended when a signal arrived ordering them to Biggin Hill in Kent. They were to replace 79 Squadron which had taken a pounding and needed to be withdrawn from the front line. That night the Squadron celebrated the news at the Stepney Hotel.

At 1500 hours on Sunday 8 September, fifteen Spitfires took off from Pembrey for Biggin Hill. Regarding the Squadron's arrival, Pilot Officer Geoff Wellum wrote the following:

The Squadron has just landed at Biggin Hill. Here at our new home the fighting is the hardest of anywhere in the skies over England. If any aerodrome is in the forefront of the battle and right in the front line, it's Biggin. Situated on a plateau, it is known throughout Fighter Command as 'Biggin on the Bump'. The whole place has an air of total war and mortal combat. Broken Spitfires and Hurricanes, hangers in ruins, filled-in bomb craters everywhere and so much general bomb damage that one is left in no doubt whatsoever that all is total war.[11.]

At 1630 hours on their first day at Biggin, twelve pilots were ordered to patrol Canterbury at 26,000 feet. Kingcome was the first to see the hordes of enemy aircraft in the vicinity when he spotted enemy bombers being attacked by another squadron of Spitfires. He climbed to tackle twelve yellow nosed Bf109s circling above. He let off a snap shot at one of the enemy fighters, watched it dive away trailing smoke and then was in turn engaged by other 109s. Kingcome dived and managed to evade the enemy's attacks. During the fracas Allan Wright and Bill Watling were attacked by 109s and had to return to Biggin. Watling's Spitfire was badly hit and caught fire. His aircraft spun out of control and Watling's hands were badly burnt by the flames licking at him from the engine and into the cockpit. Wright's aircraft 'QJ-S' was severely damaged but he escaped unscathed. Sammy Saunders's Spitfire was hit by a 20 mm cannon shell, which exploded and wounded his leg with shrapnel. Saunders crash-landed on a farm at Midley near Rye in Sussex. It was a humbling affair for 92 Squadron. They had not known fighting like it up until this point. The waves and masses of enemy formations were utterly startling for Wright and his comrades. Biggin was so heavily pounded by the Luftwaffe during the Battle of Britain that pilots quipped that it was safer to be up in the air.

Being a deeply religious young man, Allan Wright found comfort through prayer during those hectic days. Wright recalled:

> I know that God will do with me what he will, and so I hoped that he would pull me through. So, during the Battle of Britain, I must say that every night I would ask, and I daren't ask to come right through, I'd just ask for tomorrow and I'd say 'give me tomorrow', and then when tomorrow came, that night I was still there asking for the next day.

Allan also found himself praying for victory during the war but after one evening prayer he visualised a German pilot across the Channel asking for the same thing, and wondered to himself how that could be so. From then on he didn't ask for victory, just for tomorrow.

On 11 September the Squadron was scrambled at 1520 hours to engage enemy aircraft over Dungeness. Twenty minutes into the flight, Wright became separated from the rest of the Squadron. He decided to climb to 25,000 feet and positioned himself over Croydon. After about thirty minutes, Wright saw a very large formation of enemy aircraft approaching London from the direction of Ramsgate. Wright checked for enemy fighters. The bombers

Bf109 E, Black 11 belonging to III./JG 2 during an escort mission over southern England. In order to make recognition easier during combat, many of the German units had their aircraft painted with yellow noses and wingtips. (*EN Archive*)

appeared to be unescorted, so Wright engaged. He carried out a head-on and quarter attack at the leading formation, but was forced to dive away as Bf109s came into the vicinity. He saw one of the bombers break away from the main formation with smoke coming out of its engine. Wright pulled back on the control column and climbed his Spitfire to 20,000 feet towards the sun. He turned and saw the bombers heading towards Dungeness. He was unable to catch them up but before he returned to base he attacked a Heinkel 111 from astern and head-on with three other Spitfires of 66 Squadron. The bomber crashed intact beside another in flames on the Dungeness peninsular.

The Squadron were again called into action that evening when eight Spitfires were ordered to escort bombers over the Channel and then link up with Spitfires of 66 Squadron to patrol over base. The two Squadrons did not meet, so 92 Squadron was vectored towards Ramsgate to patrol. When over Ashford at about 1815 hours Bf109s were sighted above their position (20,000 feet) and the Squadron split up to attack. Wright managed to reach the same height as one of the Messerschmitt's but he could not catch it up. Despite the distance, Wright fired a four second burst from 500 yards range.

The German pilot immediately put his aircraft into a dive and Wright observed 'some smoke' before he lost it going towards Folkestone. Wright broke off and landed back at Biggin Hill at 1930 hours.

Flying Officer James Paterson and Pilot Officer Gus Edwards did not return to base that evening. Paterson, a New Zealander, was shot down by 109s over Folkestone and was forced to bale out when his Spitfire burst into flames. Paterson evacuated his aircraft and delayed pulling the ripcord on his parachute until the slipstream extinguished the flames that were burning his clothes. He landed safely but was then rushed off to hospital to be treated for burns to his face and neck. Edwards was reported missing, but he was later found dead in his Spitfire (P9464) in a wood at Evegate Manor Farm, Smeeth.

On 14 September, the Squadron's intelligence officer, Flying Officer Tom Wiese wrote the following report:

> Thirteen aircraft of 92 Squadron were sent off from Biggin Hill at 1800 hours to patrol Canterbury at 15,000 feet.
>
> They were first given a Vector 140 and then later 80, and told to climb to 18,000 feet. Coming out of the sun they saw a formation of forty Me.109s coming in the opposite direction.
>
> The Squadron turned round and started climbing but had already been sighted by the enemy aircraft [that] started attacking them in pairs, coming out of the sun. Number 92 Squadron split up and dived into cloud and only a few of our fighters managed to make contact after coming out of cloud. However P/O Wright was attacked by four Me.109s turning on to his tail as he was climbing so he did the best turn he could without stalling and got in a two second burst as they passed. He saw his tracer going into one of them. Spun away and lost sight of the enemy aircraft.
>
> F/Lt. Kingcome when climbing towards the Me.109s saw another Squadron of Spitfires below being attacked by Me.109s who apparently did not notice them so he turned and dived into the Me.109s. He attacked one enemy aircraft and gave it a two-second burst 3/4 deflection and it turned away in a spiral glide. He later attacked another giving a two-second burst full deflection. It pulled away vertically on to its back and fell away.
>
> Eleven of our aircraft returned to Biggin Hill at about 1935 hours. One of our pilots Sgt Mann landed wounded in the back by an armour piercing incendiary which had passed through the armour plating behind the pilot's seat.
>
> One aircraft landed at West Malling through lack of fuel and one aircraft crashed near Faversham, the pilot, P/O R. W. McGowan was taken to Faversham Cottage Hospital slightly injured.

Wiese also recorded that Wright had fired 210 rounds of ammunition after out turning the 109s as previously described.

In Wright's combat report he made a point of criticising their take off time,

> I saw about thirty M.E.109s 3,000 feet above our formation and travelling in the opposite direction. We were at 18,000 feet. The sun was behind us and had we been 7,000 feet higher we should have surprised them. An earlier take off and climb over Base would have made this possible. As it was they saw us and having passed over us into the sun began their attacks by peeling off in twos.

Before Wright returned to base he turned southwards and patrolled over the coast to see if he could catch any raiders on their return. The sky appeared clear, so he returned to Biggin.

During the afternoon of 15 September, the Squadron scrambled to meet a great armada of enemy aircraft approaching the Kent countryside. The pilots claimed five He111s destroyed, two Do17s destroyed, two Do17s probably destroyed, two more damaged, and a Bf109 probably destroyed. The Squadron's talented pianist, Pilot Officer Bob Holland, was shot down in Spitfire R6606. He baled out by inverting his aircraft and fell out but at an unfavourable height. He landed heavily in a haystack at Goudhurst in Kent. His cheek and chin were cut and he damaged his jaw and loosened some teeth. Holland was later admitted to the E.M.S. Hospital at East Grinstead and was treated by Dr Archibald McIndoe.

At 1715 hours eleven Spitfires took off to join 66 Squadron for a patrol over Gravesend. No enemy aircraft were contacted and the Squadron returned to base. The last pilot to return to Biggin that evening was Allan Wright. He had taken off at 1035 hours bound for Hawkinge, from where he operated alone at high altitudes to spot enemy aircraft and report on incoming raids. Wright remembered,

> That just happened to be the first time that I'd done what they called a "Jim Crowe", where a Spitfire was sent up from the south coast and his job was to have an actual eye report on the enemy who was coming. It wasn't your job to attack them, it was to report on them. You would be one of the first people to see the enemy forming up in battle, no question. You would be the first to actually see them, they'd be seen on radar but that's not the same thing. I happened to be the first one given that job. I was attacked by the two 109s who were leading the formation so I wasn't able to stay there any longer to give any further information. What happened after that, I don't know. It was going to be in rotation, anyway, so I wouldn't be asked to do it again. It was very unpopular, because you always want to fight with your mates, you wouldn't want to have to do this solo job.[12]

A few miles from Biggin Hill's aerodrome there was a lovely country pub called The White Hart. This pub soon became 92 Squadron's local haunt and many nights were spent drinking until closing time, but even then the boys wouldn't be stopped.

No. 92 Squadron historian and author Michael Robinson wrote the following in his book *Best of the Few*:

> As lax as country pub hours were, closing time would eventually arrive, which presented them with two options. The first being returning to their billets... where they would lay awake, unable to sleep even on the point of physical exhaustion. Their minds reliving the roller coaster of emotions, fear, elation, sorrow, relief, experienced in the air that day. Anticipating how the next day may end, the incessant bark of the anti-aircraft guns, and the un-synchronised drone of enemy bombers engines heading towards that orange glow on the horizon, London, would also deprive them of any sleep. The second option was to accept the regular invitation to move the party the short distance to The Red House, a Georgian mansion owned by Sir Hector MacNeal, whose twin daughters Sheila and Moira were among the regulars at the "The White Hart". They were beautiful and infinitely generous young ladies, the epitome of a companion for a dashing young fighter pilot. Their relationship with 92's pilots varied from confidante, to shoulder to cry on, to companion and they were soon affectionately known as 92's "Godmothers".[13]

At lunchtime on 19 September, Pilot Officers Allan Wright and Howard Hill were instructed to intercept raid X27. Wright and Hill took off from Biggin Hill as Red 1 and Red 2 at 1222 hours. Five minutes later they intercepted a Junkers Ju88 at 8,000 feet and gave chase.

On sighting the two Spitfires the Junkers pilot took evasive action and dived down to 4,000 feet. Both Wright and Hill fired a succession of bursts at the bomber. Wright fired two two-second bursts from abeam at 400 yards and several short bursts at 300 yards with some deflection. Wright concluded his attack with a seven-second burst using full deflection until his guns fell silent. Wright followed the enemy aircraft for ten minutes. The Junker's speed decreased but it continued to use evasive action until it disappeared into a large bank of cloud. Wright landed back at base at 1300 hours having fired 2,800 rounds.

Later the damaged aircraft was seen by the Maidstone Observer Corps passing over Dover, travelling south east at about 900 feet with smoke pouring out from both engines and tail.

Wright reported:

After using up all my ammunition I repeatedly called up Biggin Hill for Pipsqueak zero, so that the controller could have a direct plot of the bomber from my own Pipsqueak, as both Red 2 and Green 1 and 2 were in the air trying to find the bomber. Biggin Hill could not hear me and I later remembered that I had no Pipsqueak crystal as there are insufficient on the Station for the whole Squadron.

The following day Pilot Officer Howard Hill was killed in action. His Spitfire (X4417) was found crashed and burned out in the corner of a field in West Hougham in Kent. It is believed that Hill was killed by cannon and machine gun fire after being bounced from behind and above.

Another of Wright's colleagues, Peter Eyles was also reported missing with Spitfire N3248. It is assumed that he went down with his aircraft over the Channel.

The Squadron's CO, Judy Sanders, was also put out of action on the 20th when he was admitted to hospital with burns. After returning from an exhausting patrol, Sanders, while walking towards Tom Wiese, lit up a cigarette and was immediately engulfed in flames. Sanders burnt his hands when he dabbed out the flames on his fuel covered uniform.

The daily patrols were exhausting and naturally stressful for the pilots stationed at Biggin Hill. In the air they were always outnumbered and on the ground they were often bombed. It was living hell. Tony Bartley recalled:

> Some days, we could only field five serviceable aircraft out of twelve. We fought all day, and played most of the night. We lived for the present and dismissed our future. The battle would be won, of course. We had no doubts about that. Meanwhile, the casualties mounted, but no one grieved as we knew it was inevitable. I found myself secretly watching the others, searching their faces for who would be next, and I thought I saw them looking at me the same way. But we never revealed our thoughts about fear. They were locked up as tight as the straps on our parachutes.[14]

With regards to combat stress Geoff Wellum remarked: 'We did not realise quite what it was although we obviously felt very tired. The answer we thought was to live life to the full, grit your teeth and carry on.'

For some of the pilots in the Squadron drinking was the only way to relax and block out the traumatic events that they were constantly experiencing or seeing around them. They did indeed 'fight hard and play hard', which inevitably caused the Squadron's reputation to be known as undisciplined with 'playboy' fighter pilots. Allan Wright, however, kept himself aloof from this lifestyle. Whenever he was given a day's pass or leave he would fly to see Barbara and spend time with her. Allan was very much seen as a 'serious' and 'quiet' member of the Squadron, but in no way was he thought of as the odd one out. He was highly respected by everyone in the Squadron and was very much a good friend to all of 92 Squadron's colourful characters.

Tony Bartley recalled one occasion where Biggin was being bombed at dinner time:

> Johnnie Bryson suggested, 'Let's all get out of here, and watch the bombing from the White Hart at Brasted. Far more fun.' Wimpy Wade wouldn't be hurried over his dessert, and Allan Wright declined. He was more interested in processing the war photographs he took, and reading, we figured. He took the war quietly, in his stride, unworried. We couldn't level with him. He liked a party, but only one a week. The rest of us liked one every night. Having taken over Bob Tuck's flight, Al had a lot of responsibility. We secretly admired him because we knew that we needed the alcoholic tranquilliser and stimulant in order to keep going, all the time, while he relied on his sober self-control, and a philosophy all his own.[15]

On 26 September Wright led Green Section on a patrol over Tenterden at 1600 hours where they caught a Dornier 215 ducking in and out of cloud. Wright fired a three second burst before it darted into ten-tenths cloud at 6,000 feet. The Section then spotted a Heinkel 111 also using the cloud to its advantage over Hailsham. Wright managed to get quite close without being seen by the Luftwaffe crew by flying through the tops of the clouds. He fired a two-second burst at close range before he lost it in the clouds. Wright landed and explained the action to Tom Wiese, who informed Allan that the Observer Corps had confirmed that a He111 had crashed at Hailsham shortly after he delivered his attack.

The following morning Wright was flying as Green 1 with eight other Spitfires. The Squadron sighted a formation of Dorniers over Sevenoaks and engaged them head-on at 0925 hours. Wright picked out a bomber to his port, lined it up in his sight and then fired a four second burst from head on to beam at close range. Wright turned up and away and noticed two bombers falling out of formation. He also spotted a few 109s turning to attack but they were too far away to cause any real concern. A short while later Wright attacked another enemy aircraft, this time a Heinkel 111. He fired several bursts into the enemy machine from above and quarter. Wright later reported that 'other friendly fighters joined in and he went down with smoke from his engines'.

Later in the day Allan was informed that he had been promoted to Acting Flight Lieutenant with immediate effect. After he had received the good news, Wright took off once again from Biggin, this time as Blue 1 on an afternoon patrol with the Squadron. Approximately fifteen Ju88s were seen flying at 18,000 feet with fifty-plus Bf109s acting as fighter escort.

Wright reported:

The 109's forbore to attack in force and the Squadron attacked en masse from below, beam and head on. I fired several bursts from below starboard and saw pieces come off one of the 88's. I broke away and saw an 88 break away from the formation. I followed and attacked with about four other Spitfires. In a few minutes it burst into flames and dived into the ground by the oblong lake near Gatwick and exploded. I climbed up again and met the Ju88's returning, only about seven of them, with many Hurricanes a few Spitfires and about thirty Me.109's in attendance. I got in four good bursts at 300 to 250 yards from below starboard and saw pieces come from one Ju88 and the starboard engine of another caught fire as I finished my ammunition.

The day's fighting did not come without a cost to the Squadron. Kiwi, Flight Lieutenant James Paterson was shot down in flames by Bf109s. Some of his colleagues saw him struggling to get out of his cockpit, but he never did. His aircraft crashed and burned out at Sparepenny Lane, Farningham. Sergeant Trevor Oldfield was also shot down and killed by enemy fighters. His aircraft exploded on impact at Fullers House, Hesketh Park, Dartford. Flight Sergeant Charles Sydney had only been with 92 Squadron for seventeen days when he was shot down by the enemy and killed in Spitfire R6767 QJ-N. Sydney's aircraft crashed at Kingston-on-Thames at 0940 hours.

On 30 September Allan returned to base during the afternoon after being away from the station on a thirty-six hour pass. Wright recalled:

I was walking back to our dispersal; I became aware of a dull roar from the south. Almost immediately the air raid warning sounded. Those around hesitated, then began running towards the nearby shelter. I looked up for enemy bombers, instead I saw a single aircraft high above, dark against the clouds; spiralling down, trailing black smoke. I stood transfixed, "would he, could he, pull out at the last moment? No".

A black pall of smoke billowed up from behind the trees, poor bastard. Thinking to myself, "This is no place for me". I shouted to a passing airman, "Anything serviceable?" He shouted, "Over there!". "Come on then!" I replied. There was a parachute on the tailplane, as was the custom for a pilot at readiness, a parachute was essential, apart from the obvious reason, because in the aircraft it became part of the seat, without it one could not see over the instrument panel. The airman held in the switch on the starter trolley. The engine turned, fired, 'chocks away', zig zagging to get to get into wind, I could not get in the air quick enough. Two Spitfires from 72 Squadron were also staggering upwards at full throttle, to get into the melee of Hurricanes, Spitfires, and 109s. One of the Hurricanes dived past me glycol streaming from it, and a Spitfire seemingly unaware that a 109 was behind him. "Spitfire, Spitfire, look out, 109 on your tail!" I shouted over the R/T. Out of range, I fired two short bursts at the stalking 109, and frightened him off. He climbed away into the sun, but by cutting the corner, I was able to catch up.[16.]

Wright fired a second burst which struck the enemy fighter and caused a large amount of glycol coolant to pour out into the air. The German pilot put his aircraft into a dive and Wright fired another burst from underneath. Black smoke issued from the 109's engine, and Wright had to throttle back to avoid overshooting his prey. The 109 lost power and slowed trailing smoke. Another Spitfire appeared on the scene. Wright later learnt that it was Flight Lieutenant Villar of 72 Squadron. Together they searched the sky for more activity, but finding none, they returned to base.

Wright climbed out of his Spitfire and soon saw Tom Wiese approaching to collect his report. Much to Allan's displeasure, Wiese would not allow him to claim the 109 as 'destroyed' because he did not see it hit the ground. Even Villar's confirmation was not enough, so the Messerschmitt was put down as a probable. Allan walked away feeling annoyed and muttering to himself, 'It could never have got home across the Channel having lost all its oil and coolant.'

The action had taken place at 12,000 feet over Redhill at 1400 hours. Wright had fired a total of 2,540 rounds.

Later that afternoon the Squadron was scrambled again. Twelve Spitfires climbed away from the aerodrome destined for the Dungeness area where large swarms of Bf109s were flying at about 27,000 feet. Kingcome ordered the Squadron into line astern when he spotted a formation of bombers flying south-east 10,000 feet below. Kingcome called 'Tally Ho!' over the R/T, then the Squadron peeled off and dived towards the bombers.

Flight Lieutenant Wright was leading B Flight in his usual aircraft X4069 'QJ-S'. He dived down to bounce the bombers, travelling at about 400 mph and closing. Wright selected the leading bomber and opened fire with a three-second burst from above. In a flash Wright's Spitfire had passed through a narrow space between the formations. He pulled back on the stick and brought his Spitfire's nose up towards the sun. The 109s lurking above made another attack on the bombers too risky, so Wright climbed up to 20,000 feet.

He then noticed a loose formation of seven 109s behind the main gaggle and slightly above his position. Wright attacked the nearest fighter from the beam. The 109 broke away from the others and dived for home; Wright followed and fired another succession of bursts until his guns fell silent. The 109 was trailing white smoke.

Bob Stanford Tuck. (*Michael Robinson*)

Wright picks up the story:

It occurred to me that as I was now out of ammo I could take this opportunity to find out how long a 109 could fly without coolant, and confound Tom Wiese. I check my watch, just before five, and followed the 109 at a respectful distance in case his friends came after me. The clouds had cleared from below and he continued down at a fairly steep angle, crossing the coast at Brighton at about 200 feet. He was still smoking, perhaps he could go on forever, the smoke stopped, he was really low, but still going. Then he must have clipped a wave with his wing because he cartwheeled and settled in the spray. I nearly forgot to check my watch, he had lasted seven minutes. An air of smugness filled the cockpit, BANG, and so did the smell of cordite. The Spit reared up like a frightened horse, and banked over to the left. In that moment I knew I had been bounced.[17.]

Wright grabbed the control column and allowed his aircraft to continue round in a steep turn. He spotted two 109s and immediately wanted to lift his wing and level out, but the aircraft wasn't responsive to his touch.

His Spitfire turned round and over and dived vertically towards the sea. Wright feared that he was rapidly approaching his end, but he continued to wrestle with the stick and rudder, until finally he was level with the coast.

> I began to assess the situation, there was a gaping hole in the right side and in the wing root, a bullet had smashed the oil pressure gauge, above all my right leg hurt. The engine sounded fine, I looked for my map, which I had tucked behind fixtures on the right wall of the cockpit, it was slashed to pieces. A left-turn inland seemed the best option, I could see that my right trouser leg was dark with blood and my right boot felt squelchy.

After a great deal of difficulty Wright managed to land his damaged aircraft at Shoreham airfield. He was then helped out of his cockpit by two young men and thereafter taken to Southlands Hospital. Shrapnel was extracted from his thigh, bottom and elbow. Much to his displeasure, Allan, would have to miss out on the fighting for awhile until he was again fit for flying duty. On 22 October, Wright was awarded a DFC for his gallantry in the air.

Towards the end of that same month, a Canadian named Johnny Kent took command of 92 Squadron. Before war was declared, Kent, had served in 19 Squadron and then moved on as a Test-Pilot at the RAE at Farnborough. On 29 July 1940, he was posted as A Flight Commander to 303 Squadron (a Polish squadron), which he helped form in to an efficient fighting unit. A day before Squadron Leader Kent arrived at Biggin Hill he was awarded a DFC for his success in combat and for proving himself 'a born leader'.

Kent recalled his arrival:

> The mess sergeant pointed out the offices of my new squadron who were all sitting together at one table so I joined them without telling them who I was. My first impressions were not favourable and their general attitude and lack of manners indicated a lack of control and discipline. I began to realise that I was probably going to have my hands full – and how right I was.[18.]

Tony Bartley remembered that prior to Kent's posting; Fight Command had sent a psychologist down to Biggin to check on the pilots 'habits'. For three days the psychologist observed the Squadron and, according to Bartley, concluded that they should be left to their own devices so long as they continued to shoot down enemy aircraft. Their 'habits', in effect, was just their way of coping.

Kent was determined to enforce discipline into the Squadron, but old habits die hard. Bartley recalled:

> We didn't take much more notice of John than we had of our two previous CO's and he spent most of his time in the office when he wasn't flying, which

suited us fine. No one had done any of the squadron paper work in two months, and unanswered correspondence and unfilled forms were piled high.[19]

Bartley recalled one morning where Squadron Leader Kent summoned his senior NCO's and pilots to his office for a roasting.

> "First, the station warrant officer tells me that the squadron airmen won't obey any orders except from their own officers and NCO's…" Kent turned to his officers. "You are the most conceited and insubordinate bunch of bastards it's ever been my misfortune to meet in my service career. You dress like bums, you steal air force petrol for your cars, you drink like fishes, you don't sleep and you've made a night club out of your billet, where your girlfriends spend the night."[20]

Kent's initial impression of the Squadron was an understatement. He was definitely going to have his hands full.

While all of this was going on at Biggin, Allan Wright was still recovering in hospital, feeling frustrated to be away from his friends and out of action. November passed by without much incident for Wright but in early December he was back in the thick of it.

During the afternoon of Thursday 5 December, Wright was chosen to lead the Squadron on patrol towards Dover. Wright took off in a cannon-armed Spitfire (Mk I R6908 'QJ-T') and led the Squadron into the air. Spitfires of 74 Squadron soon followed.

After about thirty minutes in to the patrol, Wright's R/T failed, so he handed over leadership to Tony Bartley. The Squadron climbed to 20,000 feet and then made its way towards the ack-ack bursts over Dover, where enemy aircraft were sighted and engaged.

Wright reported:

> We ran into about six or seven 109's in loose formation at about 20,000 feet and a little above us, without any warning from ground station. Individually we chased them towards France. Whilst returning I climbed to 15,000 feet and at least three sections of 109s in threes and fours passed over my head towards France without attacking me. When I was again over Dover I joined up with 74 Squadron at 20,000 feet.

Flight Lieutenant John Freeborn, DFC, was leading 74 Squadron on this patrol in Spitfire Mk IIa P7366, when, like Wright, he encountered R/T failure and handed over leadership to Yellow 1. Just after the change over, the Tigers sighted six Bf109s and attacked. Freeborn attacked the leading enemy fighter and shot it down into the sea. He then attacked another 109 from astern. He fired a short burst which damaged the 109's cooling system. It then appears that Allan Wright then attacked the very same 109, as Freeborn reported that the aircraft he damaged was then attacked by a 'cannon firing Spitfire'.

To begin with, Wright fried a short burst of cannon and machine gun fire, at the enemy machine but scored no hits.[21.] Then the 109 dived steeply and Wright rolled after him, overtaking 'another Spitfire which had been level with [him]'. This was most likely Freeborn's aircraft. Wright attacked for a second time, this time switching to machine guns and firing a long burst from astern which pelted the enemy's fuselage and port radiator. The 109 slowed up slightly with black smoke and glycol streaming into the air. Wright broke away from the engagement to avoid other enemy fighters and did not see the 109 he attacked crash into the sea, but Freeborn did.

Due to the plethora of RAF claims and confused nature of some of the actions, it has proven difficult to single out the Bf109 that was shared shot down by Wright and Freeborn. However the 109 loses from this afternoon engagement are as follows:

Stabsschwarm JG26 Messerschmitt Bf109E-4/B (5816). Belly-landed on beach at Wissant damaged in combat with Spitfires of Squadrons 74 and 92 and Number 421 Flight over the Channel off Folkestone during escort sortie for Jabo attack on Hawkinge by II.(S)/LG2 3.10 p.m. FF Oberlt Walter Horten *(Geschwader TO)* unhurt. Aircraft Black − + − 30% damaged but repairable.

1./JG26 Messerschmitt Bf109E-7 (5968). Shot down in combat with Spitfires of Squadrons 74 and 92 and Number 421 Flight south-east of Dover during escort sortie for Jabo attack on Hawkinge by II.(S)/LG2 1510. FF Lt Hans Heinemann missing. Aircraft White 4 + 100% write-off.

3./JG26 Messerschmitt Bf109E-4/B (6324). Crash-landed at Wissant damaged in combat with Spitfires of Squadrons 74 and 92 and Number 421 Flight over the Channel off Folkestone 1510. FF Oberfw Robert Menge badly wounded in left arm and shoulder − admitted to hospital in Calais. Aircraft 40% damaged but repairable.

4.(S)/LG2 Messerschmitt Bf109E-4/B (5563). Failed to return from Jabo attack on Hawkinge and believed crashed in the Channel off Cap Gris Nez following combat with Spitfires of Squadrons 74 and 92 and Number 421 Flight 3.10 p.m. FF Oberlt Heinz Vogeler *(Staffelkapitän)* missing. Aircraft ▲ + White C 100% write-off.

In mid-January 1941 the Squadron moved to Manston to operate for a short time, returning to Biggin Hill on 20 February.

In March, Allan Wright continued to chip away at the Luftwaffe, when on 13th, he damaged two Bf109s in combat while flying a Spitfire Mk Vb (R6293). Wright's next claim occurred on 16 May when he shared in the destruction of a Bf109 over the Channel off Dungeness. During this action he was flying Spitfire R6923 'QJ-S'.

On Saturday 14 June the Squadron took off from Biggin on an early morning sweep to St Omer/Fort Rouge. Neville Duke recalled the sweep well:

> It was a perfect summer day in England, clear and cloudless. I was Number 2 to my flight commander Allan Wright – I was nearly always his Number 2 – a grand little fellow with wiry, fair hair, short and stocky, blue eyes and a ready smile. I rather let him down this day. How it happened, I don't quite know. I remember the first indication I had that we were engaged was something going down vertically, going like a bomb out of a clear, cloudless sky- the sun glinting on a yellow nose. Gone in a flash. But I knew what it had been – a 109.[22]

Wright was flying as Blue 1, leading the left hand four of the Squadron's three sections. He recalled diving from 20,000 feet to 7,000 feet over Boulogne, before patrolling for seven minutes at 8,000 feet over three aerodromes. Wright reported that during a steep turn Duke lost him and was unable to inform him because of R/T failure. At the same time Blue 3 and 4 were left behind and mistakenly took two Bf109s to be Wright and Duke. Allan soon realised that he was on his own. He chased one Messerschmitt fighter but realised it was too high and it slipped away with relative ease. Later, Wright turned his Spitfire and saw a light blue nosed aircraft following him and firing. At first he thought it was Duke firing at something close by, so he continued to patrol, but he soon discovered it was a Bf109F attacking him, but it was too late and his aircraft was hit. Wright reported:

> I had only been hit with seven bullets but unfortunately two had disconnected my starboard aileron from its controls and jammed it up at an angle. It took me about thirty seconds to recover control and beat it for home as fast as I could. The extraordinary aileron control also affected the fore-and-aft movements of the aircraft, causing it to climb then dive whenever I tried to ease the nose up. Luckily no other enemy aircraft attacked me and I was able to get back to the English coast using some fog patches as cover over the sea. Lympe was the first aerodrome I came to, so I attempted to land there. The aircraft would not fly level at less than 145 mph but I put the wheels down intending to try the flaps. I did this well, banked over against the dud aileron,

but had to put the flaps up again rapidly as only one worked, rolling me over onto the opposite bank. I knew that my starboard wheel was probably punctured because of a bullet hole very close to it, so I put the wheels up again and flew the aircraft onto the ground at 140 mph. The aircraft bumped once then settled down and remained straight, although trying to tip up. From a casual inspection the engine and fuselage appeared undamaged, however, one bullet, an incendiary, had pierced one of the cannon magazines and had jammed it.

Meanwhile, Wright's number two, Neville Duke, had duelled with 109s, turning in tight circles and getting off some snap shots before his ammunition had run dry. He pulled out of the combat area and joined up with a colleague, Don Kingaby in line abreast, before they returned back to base.

Duke remembered leaving Wright during the sweep to frighten off a 109 that he saw on another Spitfire's tail.

> Allan Wright had been shot up pretty badly. He did not see me leave him, and fool that I was I never told him that I was leaving. He had looked behind and seen a machine where I should have been and thought I was still there. But I wasn't. Next thing, tracer was whistling and whirling past him and he was shot up badly. He got away OK, and with a damaged aileron, had to crash-land at Lympne at 140 mph. I deserved a good ticking-off for leaving Allan; but he realised that I had learned my lesson and confined himself to a few carefully selected words. And I never forgot those two lessons: don't break away from your leader without telling him and don't waste your ammunition.[23]

Allan's reaction to Duke's self-confessed error speaks volumes about his character. Not only was he reasonable and calm about the matter but he took into account Duke's inexperience in comparison to his own and recognised his potential to learn. It would later become evident that Duke would learn many valuable lessons by flying off Wright's wingtips. Duke would later become a squadron leader with an impressive tally to his credit of 26 and 2 shared enemy aircraft destroyed, 1 probable, 6 damaged, 2 shared destroyed on the ground, 1 shared probably destroyed on the ground. After the war he would become a famous test pilot and also break the world air speed record.

On 17 June at 1930 hours Wright was leading Blue Section at about 29,000 feet, operating as top cover to the Squadron. When about half way back from the target to Le Touquet, Wright saw a Bf109F flying at about 5,000 feet below. Wright radioed the CO and then went down to attack.

> I attacked from slightly beneath, overtaking fast. Unfortunately this put him near the sun and it was difficult for me to see my reflector sight. I gave him

[a] one-second burst and broke away above. He did an extremely fast half roll and went down, apparently out of control, in a series of half spins and spirals.

The 109 was seen emitting white puffs of smoke from its engine as it went down. Wright broke off the attack, noticing that two enemy fighters were diving from behind. Wright climbed and saw another 109 which he shot at vertically above him. At this point Wright was at 14,000 feet about 4 miles inside Le Touquet and alone. He looked upsun and saw twelve aircraft, mostly 109s, milling around about 5,000 feet above his position. Wright broke for home and flew at about 100 feet across the Channel towards Folkestone before finally landing at Biggin Hill.

The next evening Duke wrote in his diary:

> Show in the afternoon, 6 o'clock. Top cover for Blenheims bombing troops in a wood near Calais. Two 109s dived on Allan and self but did not engage us. Got a good view of one's silver wings and belly and enormous black crosses, as he whizzed past and then one went above and shot behind me.[24]

During the afternoon of 25 June, Flight Lieutenant Wright strapped himself in to Spitfire W3265 for a patrol over Gravelines. Wright took off as Blue 1, leading the left hand three on Wing Commander Sailor Malan. A patrol was carried out at 28,000 feet between St Omer and Gravelines before Malan began to chase two Bf109Fs. Wright reported:

> I was on the inside of the turn and was able to get closer. They evidently saw us as they both dived steeply and then the rearmost one half rolled and dived vertically. I followed the leader who was taking evasive action and I did not seem to be gaining so I fired two bursts with machine guns and cannons at 400 yards. He then pulled up, finally climbing vertically. I gained on him at this stage and got in a long burst of machine gun fire at 100 to 40 yards. He suddenly streamed glycol from port radiator and then we both spun.

When Wright got out of the spin he managed to fire off another short burst at the 109 that was still spinning downwards. When the 109 descended to about 10,000 feet, Flying Officer Geoff Wellum saw it flick over on to its back and dive vertically. Wright climbed up to 15,000 feet and then returned to base.

The next morning Wright was back in the air as Blue 1. Wing Commander Malan was again leading 92 and 74 Squadrons, this time at 28,000 feet over Dunkirk. In due course a formation of enemy aircraft was sighted beneath them. Wright identified them as Bf109s. 'I curved down to the right in a half roll, partially blacked out, and attacked'. Wright fixed his reflector sight on the rearmost starboard enemy machine. He fired several short bursts at close range.

> The formation had already seen me as they were diving down when I opened fire. My 109 took some evasive action by skidding and turning. One of my cannon tracers definitely hit him in front of the cockpit and a small stream of white-ish smoke started from him. He then straightened up a bit and his dive became steeper. I fired again but had to leave him as I could not hold my aircraft in the dive of over 450 mph and pulled out at 5,000 feet. He continued down steadily, going very fast.

Wright then saw another Bf109 just above cloud at 2,000 feet over Dunkirk. He closed to attack but only managed to fire a short burst before he lost it in cloud. Wright cruised around for awhile scanning the sky and then dropped down to sea level to head for home.

This was to be Wright's final victory with 92 Squadron. At this juncture he was absolutely exhausted from the fighting. He had been with the Squadron from the beginning; he had fought over Dunkirk, throughout the Battle of Britain, and been involved in numerous offensive sweeps across the Channel. If ever a fighter pilot deserved a rest from the action, it was Allan. But although he felt worn out, it was not the done thing to say so, but Wright was beginning to feel that his exhaustion was affecting his judgement in the air. In the end Allan consulted his medical officer and the very next day he was posted. It was 15 July 1941, the same day that he was awarded a Bar to his DFC. Wright's new posting took him to No. 52 Operational Training Unit at Crosby-on-Eden, where he was Officer Commanding B Flight. In September he was sent to HQ 9 Group, assigned to air tactics, and the following month he moved to HQ Fighter Command.

Early the next year Sailor Malan formed the first Pilot Attack Gunnery School at Sutton Bridge. Malan chose Allan as his Chief Instructor. On 19 June 1942 Allan married Barbara. Not long after, Allan, with his wealth of experience, was chosen along with three others to go to the USA to teach tactical and gunnery skills to the pilots being prepared for operations in the European theatre. The following year, Wright expressed his desire to get back on operations. Now a squadron leader, Wright was posted to join 29 Squadron as A Flight commander.

The Squadron was a night-fighter unit equipped with Bristol Beaufighters. Its role was to shoot down low altitude reconnaissance, and mine laying aircraft, which at night was proving a difficult task.

On 3 April 1943, Squadron Leader Allan Wright, DFC and Bar, and his Navigator, Flight Lieutenant G. S. Bliss, took off for a night patrol in Beaufighter 8274. Not long into the patrol they were ordered to investigate a 'bogey' with caution. Wright chased the unidentified aircraft for five minutes as it jinked violently. At 3,000 feet Wright tried to get into a position to positively identify the bogey but he throttled back a bit too far which caused his exhausts to flash white. The bogey opened fire with green tracer before taking violent evasive action. Wright pursued it by following the glow from its exhausts, still trying to identify the aircraft. The bogey continued to fire at his Beaufighter, so it was then deemed as hostile. At approximately 2101 hours, off Forenoss, Wright engaged the aircraft which he discovered was a Junkers Ju88. He fired a short burst from 1,000 feet, aiming between the 88's exhausts. A small flash was seen and he also scored strikes on the port side of its fuselage. Wright fired a second burst, this time using deflection, at the starboard exhaust but he missed the target. After a difficult chase, the enemy succeeded in escaping into the night. Wright took his aircraft back up to 3,000 feet and continued to patrol. At 2121 hours Wright attacked another Ju88 approximately fourteen miles north-west of Schouwen. Wright closed in to 2,000 feet and let off a short burst from the Beaufighter's guns. There was a flash and the enemy aircraft slowed down while returning inaccurate fire. Wright fired another two bursts, which caused an explosion. Wright and Bliss observed fire around the 88's fuselage. The enemy machine then curved away to port and plunged into the sea. Wright and Bliss returned to West Malling at 2153 hours. This night time aerial victory was to be Wright's last of the war.

Allan's experience was once again put to good use when he was asked to lecture bomber crews on how to lessen their chances of being shot down by enemy night fighters.

Wright was then posted to become Officer Commanding the Air Fighting Development Unit at Wittering. This new role involved Allan and his pilots flying new RAF and American fighters against captured enemy aircraft and developing appropriate tactics for use against the Luftwaffe. For this work, Wright was awarded the AFC on 1 September 1944.

On 12 February 1967, Allan Wright retired from the RAF as a Group Captain. In retirement he designed and built his own family home in Devon, where he still lives with Barbara, enjoying the peace of the countryside that he helped to secure in 1940.

CHAPTER 5

Pat Lardner-Burke

On Tuesday 2 December 1941, the *London Gazette* announced that, 'The KING has been graciously pleased to approve the following awards in recognition of gallantry displayed in flying operations against the enemy…' The sixth award mentioned was the Distinguished Flying Cross for a Pilot Officer by the name of Henry Patrick Lardner-Burke (87449), RAFVR, of 126 Squadron. The citation reads as follows:

> In November, 1941, this officer was the pilot of one of four aircraft which engaged a force of eighteen hostile aircraft over Malta and destroyed three and seriously damaged two of the enemy's aircraft. During the combat Pilot Officer Lardner-Burke, who destroyed one of the enemy's aircraft, was wounded in the chest and his aircraft was badly damaged. Despite this, he skilfully evaded his opponents and made a safe landing on the aerodrome; he then collapsed. Throughout the engagement, this officer displayed leadership and courage of a high order. He has destroyed five enemy aircraft over Malta.

Pat Lardner-Burke was born into a wealthy family on 27 June 1916 in Harrismith, Orange Free State, South Africa. He was the oldest child of three and when he became of age he was educated at a strict boarding school, where he excelled in athletics and horse riding. Before attending university, Pat trained as a quantity surveyor but his desire to fly would carry him to England at the declaration of war.

Unbeknown to his family, Pat paid for his passage to England himself and made it to London by 9 October to join the RAF Volunteer Reserve. His family would not discover his whereabouts until six months had passed. In June 1940, Pat began his training at No. 4 Elementary Flying Training School, Brough. He then went to No. 57 Operational Training Unit at Hawarden to continue his training.

While the Battle of Britain raged in the south of England, Pat continued to train as a fighter pilot. On 14 November, he flew a Mk I Spitfire (N9899) for

This photo was possibly sent from Pat with a letter to Betty on 20 March 1941 saying it was the 'Battle Grin' after a big flap over France with 19 Squadron. (*Martin Lardner-Burke*)

Lardner-Burke with Kupee the dog, 222 Squadron, 1943. (*Martin Lardner-Burke*)

the very first time at No. 57 OTU, Hawarden. Naturally he was delighted by the experience and recorded 'ATTA BOY!' in his flying log book. Pat spent the following weeks practising formation flying, aerobatics, battle climbs and mock-dog fighting.

A mishap occurred on 19 December when he crashed on landing. Pat wrote in his log book 'Undercart collapsed'.

With sixteen hours flying Spitfires under his belt, Pat was posted to Duxford to join 19 Squadron in early January 1941. His time with the Squadron would be fairly brief, but long enough to gain valuable experience from the likes of Battle of Britain veteran, Brian Lane, who, as Larder-Burke's CO, rated him as 'above the average'. It was at Duxford that Pat struck up a lasting friendship with another pilot named Denis Cowley. Through Denis, he also met Betty Mylcraine Freer, the girl he would end up marrying.

In an early letter to Betty, Pat wrote of his time at Duxford:

At the present I am sitting in front of a roaring fire in the Bull Hotel, Cambridge, waiting for Denis who has gone to the station to fetch Hazel, who will be staying here for a day or so. I was Duty Pilot the day before yesterday and had a bit of a jag that night. Yesterday they sent me up to do one hour's aerobatics and, so help me, I could feel whisky trickling down my nose into my oxygen mask. Awful, awful!

On 11 January 1941, Pat wrote to Betty once again, telling her about the hours he had spent flying Spitfires which he described as 'wonderful machines'. The day before, Pat had a troublesome flight when he got completely lost due to the country being covered in snow. His Spitfire ran out of fuel and he decided to force-land at Henlow, where his aircraft was then refuelled. Pat took off once again into the cold air but experienced engine trouble. He eventually made it back to base where he later wrote of the experience to Betty. 'I hate the idea of you being scared by the raids…We are a night fighting squadron as well so will be trying to look after you folks.'

Pat's spirits began to be dampened by the cold. On 19th, he wrote: 'The weather here is bloody awful. Snow everywhere and flying is so damn cold it's like sitting in a fridge.' The following week he saw little flying due to the poor conditions.

In February the Squadron spent a spell in a location that Pat referred to in a letter as 'out at G.I.' It was an unhappy time spent in tin huts, which was freezing cold, without water and light 'or any other bare essentials so common in modern civilisation'.

On 14 February Pat penned an action packed letter to his girlfriend:

Have been quite busy recently. A couple of days ago we went over France and met a lot of fairly accurate flak but no fighters came up. Then we did a low level attack on gun emplacements on the coast. Gave it hell. I was so bloody excited I nearly dived into a bloody road after gunning some bastards who were manning an AA battery. On the way back we chased a Ju88 but he got away as our gas was running out. Great Stuff!

Pat continued to describe his recent experiences as a fighter pilot:

We did a sweep over the North Sea and have been up twice at night but could not intercept the Hun, so I did some slow rolls on the moon as a target. Don't tell anybody these news items. We are off on a French jag tomorrow so hold thumbs.

During the remainder of February Pat continued to fly with the Squadron over France and Belgium. He seemed slightly frustrated by the lack of aerial activity, for he had seen enemy fighters during these offensive raids but they had yet to engage.

At the end of the month Pat wrote to Betty:

I am grounded for two days as they suspect bronchial pneumonia. I carried on flying but on the way back from the last show my ear drums packed up. I was nearly screaming with pain, everything went grey and I thought I had had it. Am missing a good show today, bloody nuisance. Hope the old drums are not perforated, too inflamed to tell at the moment.

Pat's attitude was typical of a fighter pilot who bemoaned having to stay behind while his colleagues went off on a show. The South African clearly loved being involved in the action, which would undoubtedly contribute to his success in the air. He was also a man that did not mince his words. 'Tell your friend,' he wrote to Betty, 'that searchlights are still bloody useless and always will be and are just turned on at night to dazzle fighter pilots'.

Pat was also an aviator that enjoyed everything flying an aeroplane had to offer. In early April he took off in a Magister and 'went around at zero feet beating everything up, cars, trains, pedestrians and cyclists'. Pat continued: 'I will have a sheet of complaints pouring in from the whole district. Nice going Burke!'

At 2300 hours on 9 April, Pat found himself alone, chasing an enemy aircraft at 15,000 feet. Pat recalled:

I saw him at the same time as two Hurricane boys and they were nearer so we gave him the works. He went down in flames and burst with a hell of an explosion. No one baled out. I figured "That's one for Rob" [a friend of Pat's who was KIA in March 1941]. The bloody swines. I go up two or three times a night and am bloody tired in the morning. Will need a rest.

On 21 April Pat continued to correspond with Betty.

> Sorry I have not written before but we have been up to the bloody eyes, flying
> every night and day. I was over London the night of the big blitz. Christ what
> a sight. It was amazing. My engine conked in and I bloody nearly baled but it
> coughed a bit and I juggled the bugger until it started. Got home and could not
> land as a bloody Hun was following me around the circuit and they would not
> give me the floodlight. I was pissing myself and eventually when the old crate
> gave a spasmodic cough I ignored the red light and came in and made an arrival
> (not a landing) in complete darkness. Got a hell of a pat on the back for it.

The following month Betty received a letter from Pat which exclaimed 'The
worst bloody thing possible has happened. I am going out to some unknown
destination next week ... Try not to forget me.'

On 15 May, Pat wrote again,

> I was overjoyed to get your letter today. Just in time. We push off from here
> tonight on the 'big push'. If I had seen you that Wednesday I would have got
> married quickly. Good scheme I thought. The first time I get home again we
> will. What do you say? Must scramble now.

In May 1941, Pat moved to Sherdown in Yorkshire before learning details of
his next posting. He continued to write of his days to Betty:

> I have been inoculated against typhoid and my arm is stiff and sore as hell.
> Got pissed last night with the boys. Damn fine crowd. I am billeted with a
> very pure and simple family. I clawed my way in and fell over a flower stand
> and they came out so I breathed 'goodnight folks' and they just got pale
> and held hands and gulped. I hovered gracefully and tripped up the stairs
> hiccoughing like hell. She came in this morning which was very nice. Poor
> buggers, if they only knew. We leave the night after tomorrow and sail the
> next day – we think. Hope the beer on the ship is good.

On 30 May 1941, Pat found himself onboard HMS *Gibraltar*. With not much
else to do but drink and sleep to pass the time, Pat took advantage of the
journey by putting pen to paper:

> We have had an uneventful voyage so far. Much drinking. Some types rather
> sea sick when it was a bit rough. The fun starts after we leave here. No beer
> in this joint and liquor a hell of a price. No black out. As all our letters are
> censored I can't say a hell of a lot. I don't know when I will be able to write
> again. It's going to be a bit sticky this job.

Pat now belonged to 46 Squadron, which was equipped with Hawker Hurricanes. The Squadron's destination was Malta, where it would form the nucleus of 126 Squadron. In his log book, Pat recorded: 'Transferred to HMS *Ark Royal* and took off on June 6 and flew to Malta; 400 miles; 4 hours.'

Pat's initial impressions of the island were not favourable. 'What a hole!' he wrote to Betty.

Raids the whole damn time. No rest at night. The Mess is a heap of rubble. Imagine a small island not as big as London with Italy about 60 miles away. They come in waves all the time. I did the first operational patrol in the squadron and saw some machines a hell of a way off going back to Italy. There is nothing doing here at all. No Europeans on the Island. Just crammed full of troops. Hot as hell and no ice in the drinks. Beer is bloody – so you see what a great time we are having. I long to be back again. We stay here for six months so I may be with you for Christmas…A chappie who is coming home by air is taking this letter for me.

Despite the dismal living conditions, the defence of Malta was of the upmost importance for Britain and her allies, for the tiny island sat at a strategic point between North Africa and Italy. It was absolutely vital for the RAF to keep the Mediterranean open for shipping vessels to pass freely with supplies and critically, oil.

While stationed at Malta, Pat Lardner-Burke would see considerable action with his Squadron in an effort to fend off the Italian Regia Aeronautica as it attempted to bomb the tiny island into submission.

Pat didn't mind the heat so much because it reminded him of his home in South Africa, but he did long for the nightlife back in England. In July he spent a week in hospital due to a blood poisoned leg but he soon recovered in the Squadron's rest camp.

While based at Ta Kali in Malta, Pat learned that his good friend Denis Cowley had been shot down and taken as a PoW. 'I am damn glad he is OK,' Pat wrote. 'Poor old type. Imagine spending the rest of the war in Hunland. Awful!' (Later Cowley managed to escape from captivity and made it back to England).

On 30 July, Pat once again propositioned Betty:

Only amusement here is swimming and drinking and am brown as hell again. Just like the old days in South Africa. You won't know me when I get back. Have never been so fit. It is hot as hell here, but that suits me. I think we should get married when I get back. What do you think? This is a formal proposal…What ho!

The next month was full of swimming, drinking and flying. 'This bloody island is driving us all mad.' Pat wrote, but just over a week later, things really began to turn serious.

During the morning of 19 August 1941, Lardner-Burke was airborne as Yellow 1, flying with the Squadron near Cap Passero. At around 1110 hours enemy aircraft were sighted flying at 23,000 feet and the 'Tally ho' call was given. Lardner-Burke followed Red 1, who turned left towards Cap Passero and flew about 5 miles inland. The two Hurricane pilots caught sight of a formation of six Italian Macchi 200 fighters flying at the same altitude as they were. Lardner-Burke also noted six more Macchi 200 fighters flying about 2,000 feet above. Red 1 turned towards the lower formation which split up into two sections of three and Lardner-Burke went after a Macchi flying in the rear of the second formation. He opened proceedings with a short burst that appeared to hit the enemy pilot. The Macchi turned over and spun towards the land. Lardner-Burke then climbed for height and turned his aircraft towards another Italian fighter, which he engaged from astern. The Macchi pilot pulled his aircraft's nose up and Lardner-Burke opened fire. His ammunition appeared to enter the Italian's cockpit before the enemy fighter spun downwards emitting white smoke.

Four days later Pat wrote of his exploits:

> I am getting bloody tired of this Island, but I suppose things could be much worse. Had a spot of fun a few days ago. The Flight Commander and myself attacked twelve Eye Ties and shot down three. I got two and had a chunk blown out of my tail and one aileron shot about. Right on their own ground over Sicily.

It appears Pat was very eager to tell Betty of this action because he wrote a second letter which would arrive sooner than the last one because a colleague was flying home with it. Again he wrote about engaging twelve enemy aircraft:

> I shot down two and he (Flight Commander) got one in the ensuing dog fight. The remainder fled and as I had half my tail blown off and a large chunk of wing and aileron gone I struggled home. Thank God none of them followed as things might have become somewhat boisterous. As it was highly pleasing, I got hoggers with the hogs in the mess. We had a champers party and all ended up in a shocking condition. All very funny. I am at readiness now in shorts and vest. No scramble as yet but anything can happen. Lots of fun and games. I am looking forward to getting home to some good old English beer.

Pat Lardner-Burke
in November 1943.
(*Martin Lardner-Burke*)

Pat concluded the letter: 'SCRAMBLE!'

Six days after his first 'real' action, Pilot Officer Lardner-Burke would claim another Macchi 200 as destroyed when flying in combat with the Squadron near Sicily. On this occasion Lardner-Burke was flying as Black 2 in a weaving role below the Squadron. Suddenly he heard 'Tally ho' over the R/T and positioned himself to attack the enemy at around 1715 hours. No. 222 Squadron's Red 1 dived and Lardner-Burke followed suit. One of the Italian fighter's broke off from the main formation so Lardner-Burke gave chase. The Macchi turned away and Lardner-Burke let off a quick deflection shot which missed. Lardner-Burke pulled back on the control column and climbed before making another pass at the evading fighter. This time his effort caused the Italian's port wheel to drop. The Macchi then went into a steep dive towards the coast of Sicily and Lardner-Burke followed it down at close range and concluded his attack with a long burst. The enemy aircraft's tail plane broke up and it dived straight into the sea from 1,000 feet. In his combat report Pat noted that the Macchi pilot appeared to be trying to abandon his aircraft before it went down. But the pilot did not escape the Hurricane's attack.

On the morning 4 September 1941 nine Hurricanes of 126 Squadron met approximately sixteen Macchi 200 fighters flying at 22,000 feet to the east of Malta.

Again, Lardner-Burke was weaving as Black 2 with the Squadron until he broke off with Black 1 to engage the enemy. An extract from his combat report describes his part of the action:

I went up [and] away from the formation. Black 1 was already attacking an E.A [Enemy Aircraft] with another on his tail. I engaged the latter and saw his wing disintegrate.

During this action Lardner-Burke was flying a cannon equipped Hurricane IIC, which had proved most effective in shooting the enemy out of the sky. The enemy aircraft was seen to turn over and its pilot baled out. As well as adding to the Squadron's tally, Pat had also rescued Black 1 from potentially being shot down.

Indeed the man from Orange Free State was proving to be a formidable adversary in the air. Pat was also a man that did not shy away from plain-speaking, which meant that Betty, was not spared from reading about the dangers that he faced.

In a letter dated 27 September 1941, Pat recalled:

I have bagged three more since I last wrote. Had quite a party one day while doing a patrol with another type. We got mixed up with a shower of the dreaded enemy and got to work with good results until my cannons all jammed and I had to streak for home with half the Italian air force after me but with the aid of a few heinous tricks shook them off and arrived back a bit shot up and a badly shaken type. You very nearly became a widow. Awful bloody show! I hate this blasted bloody hole more and more. Never again. I have been trying to get to Russia, anything can happen.

The following month, Pat found little else to lift his spirits:

The more I see of this blasted place the more I dislike it and want to get home. Have had a couple of binges with the boys in Valetta. The Union Club is the spot. It's for Officers only and you get decent drinks there. The beer is of course like dishwater. I feel sick after one mouthful.

On 12 October Pat wrote of some good news:

I am a Flying Officer as from 28th of this month. More money. I got another Eytie down a couple of days ago. The score mounts. I got so close to him that chunks of metal that were falling off his machine were hitting me. I saw the pilot later in the hospital. They are not very impressive.

On 8 November, Pat became an 'ace', when the Squadron was involved in one of the biggest dogfights it had been in for some time. Eighteen Macchi 200s and the new Macchi 202 fighters were intercepted on an escort mission for bombers bound for Malta. Lardner-Burke was flying Hurricane 'BD789' when he engaged and shot down a Macchi 202 near Dingli, but he was in turn fired upon from behind and wounded when a 12.7-mm bullet from an Italian fighter penetrated his seat armour and passed through his chest. Somehow, with a punctured lung, Lardner-Burke managed to land his Hurricane on Malta. Flight Lieutenant Tom Neil of 249 Squadron was off duty at the time, but he walked down to dispersal to watch a number of Hurricanes come in to land. Lardner-Burke's approach in particular caught his attention:

I noticed the battle damage and began to run. The propeller was still turning as I pulled down the retractable step and climbed onto the wing-walk, the slipstream clutching at my face and hair. The pilot still had his face mask attached but I recognised him immediately as Pat Lardner-Burke. I heard myself shouting, "Are you all right?" – then knew immediately that he wasn't. Pat's head was bowed and his shoulders slumped. He undid his mask, clumsily. "They've got me in the back." He was obviously in shock and pain. I sought to comfort him. "All right. Don't worry. Just hang on and we'll get you out." I shouted to those beneath. "Get the ambulance and a stretcher!" After which I began to consider how best to extricate him…Aware of the need to act quickly, I tried climbing onto the rim of the cockpit myself but found nowhere to put my feet. Then I thought about sitting on top of the open hood but saw immediately that I would not be able to reach down sufficiently to heave him up bodily. A pox on the man who designed this aircraft, I thought wildly, we would have to get a crane and winch him out. But there was no crane, or none that wouldn't take hours to find and fetch. I said urgently, "Pat, can you stand? Or climb out yourself? Otherwise we can't get at you." He said wearily, "I'll try," and painfully pulling himself to his feet whilst I grasped his shoulders, he croaked an entreaty which would remain with me always: "Don't shake me, Ginger…" Somehow we all reached the ground, to be faced with two airmen with a collapsible canvas stretcher.[1.]

Painfully, Pat was laid onto the stretcher and then lifted in to an ambulance which took him to hospital. As the ambulance drove off in the direction of Imtafa, Neil climbed back onto the Hurricane to inspect the damage. He found several bullets that had hit the side of the aircraft behind the cockpit. He was shocked to find that one had punched a hole in the armour-plate and penetrated the back of the seat, gone right through Pat, and carried on right through the dashboard and through the armour-plate in front. Several other pilots joined him, shaken by the sight of such powerful ammunition.

Pat sent a letter to his parents on 12 November 1941 from Ta Kali, Malta. He wrote the following:

Dear Pop & Mum,

I got your cable OK. I hope this gets to you fairly soon as I am sending it via Egypt. I am afraid I have not got any cheerful news. You may have got an Air Ministry cable by now. I don't know what the procedure is. I was shot down on Saturday and sustained a bad wound in the back. I am in hospital now. The shell that hit me was a .5 ammo piercing exploding job. It went in behind my left armpit and, after leaving most of itself inside; it came out about ¼ an inch from the left nipple. I tried to bale out as the machine was breaking up and my airspeed indicator was smashed, but could not open the sliding hood so I decided to try and land. I had a hell of a time as I lost a lot of blood and it was coming out of my mouth into the oxygen mask and choking me. I got down more by the grace of God than by good flying.

I was whipped off to hospital where they operated and yanked out the bits. Apparently I was very lucky as the lung is not badly injured. I should be flying again in a month or so. I feel OK at the moment and may get up for a bit in a day or so…There is nothing to worry about. I will be as good as new in a few weeks. I am very fortunate, the sisters are marvellous. Do anything for me…The medic has just come to say I can sit in a wheelchair for a bit. There is no more news now. I am about to have my dressing done – a hideous procedure.

My score here is mounting. I have had no letters from you for months. As I may not get another to you by Christmas, I hope you have a jolly time, etc, and a Happy New Year. Have a beer or two for me, and think of us drinking this Maltese hell brew. One of the captains of the convoy sent me a case of McKewans Scotch Ale. It was the most welcome gift I have ever received. The boys smelt it however so we all settled down and killed it off. The CO of the hospital told me next morning that he thought I had had rather too many visitors!

Love to all,

Patrick.

Unbeknown to his parents, Pat wasn't quite as okay as he had made out, for after he was removed from the cockpit of his aircraft, he was left for dead in

Lardner-Burke
in Aden, 1948.
(*Martin Lardner-
Burke*)

the hospital corridor until a nurse noticed that he was in fact still breathing. Later in the month Pat learned that he had been awarded the DFC for his leadership and courage in action. In January 1942, when he had sufficiently recovered from his injury, Pat returned to England.

On 7 March Betty received word from Pat, who was still recuperating:

> I am coming home via the Cape so will be back about the middle of March. Not fit enough to fly having had a hell of a session in hospital. Have lost tons of weight. I am going back to 19 Squadron as a Flight Lieutenant which is a good show.

Two months later, when Pat's health had improved, it appears from his letters that he was assigned as an instructor at No. 56 Operational Training Unit, at Sutton Bridge. But like all true fighter pilots, it was an unwelcomed posting when a war was still on.

On 7 May, he wrote to Betty:

> I got here OK to find that 56 OTU had left a month ago. Nice going. The next thing which gave me cause for joy was to see old Pat in the mess with Johnny Warfield who was our Station Commander in Malta so we settled down. 56 OTU is in Dundee so this does not please me and I get to figuring

Pat's RAF uniform.
(*Martin Lardner-Burke*)

ways and means of staying put. Guess who walks in next. You can't? Sailor Malan DSO & Bar, DFC & Bar. I had a long chat with this guy and told him where I had been etc, so he cancelled my posting and I am staying here in Fighter Wing on Spits. So don't write to OTU. The station is miles from anywhere but there is a nice local to which we repaired last night. It is very pleasant here and I think Sailor will fix it as he is as keen as hell to get me with him. He is going to see the G in C personally if these OTU sods raise any trouble, which they will, as I know the CO and Flight Commanders had my name down and a request for me to be sent to them.

Fortunately for Pat, his fellow countryman's intervention saw him join Malan's Gunnery Instruction Training Wing as an instructor, rather than joining 56 OTU in Dundee. Glad of the news, Pat wrote to Betty: 'I am keen and responsible type once more. I was getting a bit worried about my mental attitude but having got on the job again all is well. Bags of confidence.'

On 3 June 1941, Pat wrote to Betty:

I am glad you enjoyed the beat up. Sailor tore me off a strip! All the Spits are grounded for inspection so I am going to have a go at the Masters when I get browned off. Took a pilot on the course up yesterday who has shot nothing and thinks he is pretty hot.

The next day Pat wrote another letter:

Am sunbathing again. A trifle hot for aviating. Spent last evening in the mess and got to bed fairly early. Got a record score shooting at the drogue in the afternoon, which shook one or two people. The net result is that I am now considered a hottie on quarter attacks so have to give more instruction in the Masters. Bugger! Blast! That may be OK but I don't like it!

A few days later Pat vented his feelings by writing:

My mess bill rocked me. £12! The CO had a word and I got annoyed as usual and ended up by demanding to be sent to a Squadron where I could get away from all this bull. Have been pretty busy since. Only one op but no luck. Just had a squirt but saw no results. Was too busy looking around. We lost two types who had their fingers well in. Had a rare time coming back with a very duff engine. Could not get the throttle back and landed at about 140 mph with the engine switched off. When it stopped I got out and wrung out the old shirt and went in search of a new pair of pants.

On 19 June, Pat wrote to Betty, telling her that Sailor Malan had covered his Mess bill, which he referred to as 'bloody decent'. He also opened up about his state of mind: 'Have been doing a hell of a lot of flying and played lots of squash. Feel fine physically but complete mental wreck.'

At the end of July, another experience added to Pat's nerves:

Had a shaky do yesterday. Some bloody airman out of office from Manby wanted a trip in the Masters and got petrified with fright and put his knee on the stick. Damn near nosed us in. I had no control on the stick at all and had to try and land on the trimming tabs. It worked by the love of God and a very alert Wimpy pilot who saw I was in trouble and went around again. I was so relieved at walking away from it I did not bollock him but no more flips for those sods.

On 14 August Pat wrote again: 'Nothing of note happening here recently. Got a bit pissed with Sailor and some of the Yank chaps last night in Long Sutton. Ten of us in one jeep. What a riot. Feeling a trifle dazed this morning.'

Pat and Betty's letter correspondence continued to be consistent during the next few months and then on 9 December 1942, they were married at Rushen Parish Church in the Isle of Man.

Pat's flying helmet, goggles and oxygen mask. (*Martin Lardner-Burke*)

Three days after the wedding, Squadron Leader Brian Lane, DFC, was lost in action. He was last seen chasing two Fw190s over the North Sea. He never returned and was listed MIA. Hearing the news sometime later, Pat remarked: 'Poor old Lane has been shot down and bought it. His wife has taken it very badly. Bloody shame! I suppose I more or less hero worshipped him being my first CO.'

In March 1943, Pat received a new posting to No. 222 (Natal) Squadron as a Fight Commander. On 24 March, Pat wrote to Betty from Ayr:

This squadron is the Natal crowd. Henry and I are the only two with any ops! I took the flight up yesterday and they coped quite well so all should be OK. We leave here on Friday evening for Southend. Right into the front line. I am flying quite a lot and doing some night shows. Not much Hun activity – we will get all that in the estuary.

On 2 May, Pat caught a train and arrived at Hornchurch in Essex by 1300 hours. 'The weather cleared so we did the job,' Pat wrote. 'I had an awful feeling this morning that something was going to go wrong, but all was well.'

On 19 August 1943, a Spitfire IXb, that was built at Vickers in Castle Bromwich and air tested by famous chief test pilot Alex Henshaw, was delivered to 222 Squadron. This particular Spitfire, serial number MH434, sporting the code letters 'ZD-B', would become Flight Lieutenant Lardner-Burke's regular mount in the forthcoming operations.

The following Tuesday (24 August), Betty wrote to her mother:

> On Sunday afternoon I went down to Hornchurch, Sundays being the day on which females are allowed on the premises. Pat expected to have the afternoon off but when I arrived he was away on an unexpected sweep so the Adjutant met me with the Squadron car. Pat arrived back at four and we had tea, and then sat on the lawn. At 6 they went off on another sweep. I managed to get down to the aerodrome and watched them all take off. It was a marvellous sight, twenty-six Spitfires taking off at once. They were away for 1½ hours and then we watched them come back – one of the boys, Hesslyn, in Pat's squadron shot down one. Actually Pat was just going to shoot down the same one when, just as he was about to fire, he saw Hesslyn coming down on top of him and had to break away quickly to avoid a collision. Still it was another one for the squadron. We went up and talked to them as they got out of their machines – all looking very dirty and very tired as it was the third sweep they'd done that day.

Spitfire MH434 with Pat Lardner-Burke's 222 Squadron markings. (*Ben Montgomery*)

On the evening of 27 August the Hornchurch Wing was responsible for providing high fighter escort cover to 60 USAAF B-17 Flying Fortress bombers that were ordered to attack a target 4 miles north of St Omer Marshalling Yards. The Wing, led by Wing Commander William Crawford-Compton, DFC and Bar, was comprised of thirteen Spitfires of 222 Squadron and thirteen Spitfires of 129 Squadron. The Wing took off at 1833 hours, climbed from base and crossed over Dungeness at 16,000 feet. When the Wing reached Berck at 22,000 feet it rendezvoused with the leading box of bombers at 1904 hours and positioned itself to port of the Fortresses. The formation reached a point north-west of St Pol, turned left and flew north to St Omer and then on to Mardyck. Having escorted the first box of bombers some 15 miles out to sea, the Wing turned back for St Omer to pick up the second box of B-17s. Once again the Hornchurch Wing guided the Fortresses as far as they should go and then returned to escort the third box of bombers. But somewhere between St Omer and Mardyck at 1939 hours the Wing saw nine Focke-Wulf 190s dive at the third box of Fortresses in small and loose formations and then climb back up towards the bellies of the B-17s. No. 129 Squadron's Red Section and 222 Squadron's Yellow Section remained above as cover whilst Wing Commander Crawford-Compton led the rest of the Wing down to 15,000 feet to attack the German fighters.

Flying as Red 3 in Spitfire MH434, Lardner-Burke witnessed a Fw190 attack Wing Commanders Crawford-Compton and Davidson. Lardner-Burke shook the 190 off their tails by getting behind the enemy fighter and firing a two second burst from 350-300 yards range. His bullets struck the starboard wing and tail of the 190 which then turned sharply to starboard and dived away. The attack was seen by both Wing Commanders and the 190 was claimed as damaged.

Lardner-Burke then latched on to another Fw190, closed to within 300 yards range and thumbed the gun button for four seconds from dead astern. The enemy fighter dived and Spitfire MH434 followed it down in hot pursuit. Another burst, this time lasting two seconds from astern caused the 190 to dive vertically into the ground near Audrioq. This second action was witnessed by Red 4, Yellow 2 and Yellow 3 and for this reason Lardner-Burke was credited with 1 enemy aircraft destroyed.

Red 4 was Flying Officer Otto Smik, a Czech pilot who intercepted a Fw190 that had intended to attack Lardner-Burke out of the sun. Seemingly aware of Smik's presence, the 190 pilot put his aircraft's nose down and dived, but Smik followed it down and opened fire at 400 yards using his cannons. The burst hit the starboard side of the 190's fuselage and white smoke poured out into the air. The 190 pulled out of the dive, rolled on its back and the pilot baled out of the stricken aircraft.

Another 222 Squadron victory was scored by a New Zealander, Flying Officer Raymond Hesselyn, DFM and Bar. As Blue 3, he attacked a 190 as it broke away after it had attacked the bombers. A four-second burst from his guns caused the enemy fighter to dive. Hesselyn followed it down and fired another four-second burst from 300 yards astern and observed cannon strikes and large red flashes on the 190's fuselage. He continued to close in and ended the engagement with a lengthy six-second burst which most likely killed the pilot for the enemy aircraft went into a gentle dive and finally crashed 10-15 miles north-east of Guines. The engagement took place from 8,000 feet and down to 6,000 feet before the Fw190 was destroyed.

The general report written by Hornchurch's Sector Intelligence Officer on form 'F' includes some additional information regarding this sortie:

W/C Compton and Blue 4, 222 Squadron also fired but make no claim.

Blue Section 129 Squadron chased a F.W.190 but were unable to get within range.

One F.W.190 was seen going down vertically and smoking after being hit by the guns of a Fortress.

A Fortress was seen to crash in flames 10 miles N.E. of Fruges, but the crew is believed to be safe 8/9 parachutes were seen floating down.

After the engagement, our aircraft withdrew in small formations and one landed at Gravesend, the remainder landing at Base by 2017 hours.

Bombing was not observed but much smoke was seen coming from a wood north of St Omer.

Considerable heavy flak between St Omer and Mardyck accurate at bombers.

Four days later, Betty wrote another letter to her mother:

Did you hear the South African News Letter this evening? Have just been talking to Pat on the phone – apparently he figured in it rather largely. I didn't hear it, my wireless now being in the Temple and Pat was flying at the time,[2] but when he got back to the Mess he was greeted by jeers and shouts. It mentioned the Natal Squadron (Pat's) as being the top scorer of the sector, Pat being the only South African in it and a Flight Commander, that he shot down a Hun on Friday and damaged another. He said they were too busy with the rest of the Huns to have time to see what happened to that one. Two of the other boys shot down one each on the same sweep, so it was quite a good do. They ran into hundreds of Fw190s while escorting Fortresses on that show. Saturday was bad weather and Pat came up to town in the evening, we had supper in the flat and then went and met all the boys in Shepherds. Quite a celebration. He suddenly decided to stay the night but had to get up early next morning.

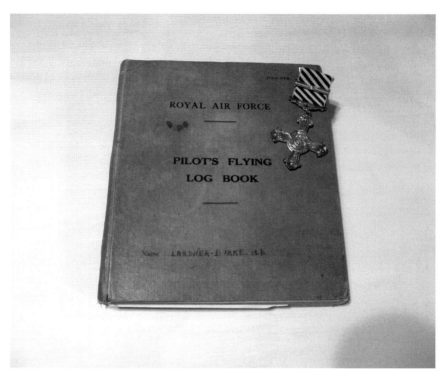

Pat's Log Book and DFC. (*Martin Lardner-Burke*)

Pat's Flying Boots. (*Martin Lardner-Burke*)

On the morning of 5 September 1943, Wing Commander Crawford-Compton led the Hornchurch Wing from its base to North Foreland, where the Spitfires detailed to act as high escort, rendezvoused with seventy-two B-26 Marauders that were instructed to attack the Marshalling Yards at Ghent/Meirelbeke.

The Wing met up with the bombers at 0800 hours and climbed towards Knocke, flew along the coast and crossed in at Nieuwesluis at 21,000 feet. A warning reached the Wing of enemy aircraft approaching from the north-east of its position, so the Spitfires began to orbit over Sas van Ghent and later east of Ghent. When bombs were seen to burst on the Marshalling Yards at 0829 hours the Wing turned to starboard from the target area. Approximately ten minutes later the Wing was bounced by about twenty Focke-Wulf 190s attacking out of the sun. Four sections of the Wing engaged the 190s and various dogfights followed.

With Yellow Section, Lardner-Burke climbed to port to head off half of the 190 fighters, one of which turned in front of his Spitfire and the South African opened fire. With a three-second burst from 400 yards astern, Lardner-Burke scored hits on the 190's engine and cockpit. The rest of Yellow Section watched the 190 turn over pouring smoke and then go down in flames in an uncontrollable spin.

Another 190 fell to the guns of Wing Commander Crawford-Compton's aircraft when later over Dunkirk he sighted three 190s and led his section down towards them at 7,000 feet. He opened fire at one of the fighters from dead astern and followed up with another burst as the enemy turned to port. The 190 spun and crashed into the sea east of Dunkirk.

Wing Commander Crawford-Compton then warned his wingman, Flying Officer H. L. Stuart of an enemy fighter on his tail and instructed him to break. Stuart broke to starboard; the 190 followed but overshot his Spitfire and then turned to port. Stuart's aircraft had already sustained damage to its port flap, his port cannon was shot away and there were strikes on both the Spitfire's wings, the engine and propeller. Nevertheless Stuart managed to get astern of the 190 and fire a one-second burst from 400 yards. He then followed it up with another quick burst from 300 yards range and finished with a two-second burst at 200 yards. Stuart saw strikes on the 190's fuselage and starboard wing before it went into an uncontrollable spin. The 190 was last seen by Stuart at 2,000 feet going down vertically. Both Stuart and Crawford-Compton were of the opinion that the 190 could not recover and the enemy aircraft was claimed as a probably destroyed.

Stuart's damaged Spitfire was streaming glycol but he managed to safely land it at Manston.

During this engagement, Squadron Leader E. Cassidy, DFC, and Flying Officer Daniel Thiriez of Red Section were bounced by four Fw190s, but the enemy fighters overshot them. Two of the 190s turned to port and Cassidy and Thiriez went after them guns blazing. One of the 190's was struck by their ammunition and it went down vertically streaming white smoke. Both Cassidy and Thiriez were convinced that the pilot had lost control of his aircraft or was killed. This Fw190 was claimed as a shared probably destroyed.

The tense battles had proved favourable for the pilots of 222 Squadron, who landed back at base at 0935 hours. But Sergeant Carmichael of 129 Squadron failed to return. He was last seen diving with a Fw190 on his tail.

On 8 September 1943 Pat was airborne yet again in Spitfire MH434. The Hornchurch Wing, comprising of twenty-five Spitfires were flying as high cover to a formation of bombers that were detailed to attack targets in the Boulogne area between 1740 and 1817 hours. On this occasion the Wing was led by Squadron Leader H. Gonay, Croix de Guerre (Belgian) of 129 Squadron because Wing Commander Crawford-Compton was unable to take off at the appointed time due to engine trouble. He did however take off in another aircraft and joined the Wing over the target area shortly after it arrived.

The Wing crossed the French coast at 22,000 feet at 1740 hours and then three patrols were carried out between Hesdin and Audricq. No. 222 Squadron patrolled at 24,000 feet and 129 Squadron flying 1,000 feet above.

At the end of the third patrol, twelve Messerschmitt Bf109Fs were sighted by 222 Squadron, which were then at 25,000 feet. The 109s climbed except for two of the fighters which dived to port. The General Report written by Hornchurch's Intelligence Officer describes Lardner-Burke's involvement as such:

F/Lt. H. P. Lardner-Burke D.F.C., and F/O O. Smik (Blue 1 and 2) dived down on the leading e/a [enemy aircraft] which was diving steeply to the S.E. while Blue 3 and 4 followed, covering their attack. F/Lt. Burke opened fire from about 10 degrees closing to dead astern at 350/300 yards range. He fired two bursts of 3 seconds and one of 2 seconds. Black smoke was seen to pour from the e/a which appeared to be in difficulties. F/Lt. Burke broke to port to enable F/O Smik to fire a 14-second burst from 300 yards dead astern, closing to 250 yards. He expended all his ammunition and broke off the combat at 7,000 feet. The e/a continued to dive at about 500 m.p.h. (Both Blue 1 and 2 were diving at 470/480 m.p.h.). The starboard wing tip of the e/a fell off and it dived straight in the ground 10-15 miles S.S.E. of Boulogne. The crash was also witnessed by P/O Wyllie (Blue 3). This Me.109F is claimed as destroyed.

129 Squadron did not see any of the enemy fighters. There was intense heavy flak over the target area and five large fires were observed as a result of the bombing.

Escort missions continued for the Wing and on 27 September, whilst escorting seventy-two Marauders that were detailed to bomb Conches

Betty and Pat Lardner-Burke in 1966. (*Martin Lardner-Burke*)

Pat, 2nd from right, at Sutton Bridge, 1942. (*Martin Lardner-Burke*)

aerodrome, 129 Squadron claimed two Fw190s destroyed, one Fw190 damaged and two Messerschmitt 109s damaged. A single claim was made by 222 Squadron after Flying Officer Smik shot down a Messerschmitt 109F. As Red 1, Lardner-Burke confirmed Smik's claim.

While turning to port Smik saw the enemy fighter attacking a Spitfire from 200 yards line astern. Smik tightened his turn to help the Spitfire pilot, who having been warned of the fighter on his tail broke away leaving Smik behind the enemy aircraft. From a 180-yard range, Smik opened fire with a long burst from his cannons and machine guns which raked the 109's engine and cockpit. The starboard underside of the cockpit exploded and the starboard undercarriage leg dropped. The 109's engine then stopped and finally after a port spin, pouring black and white smoke, the enemy aircraft crashed 20 miles south of Rouen.

After the meleé most of the Spitfires re-formed above the bombers and came out at St Valery-en-Caux at 1750 hours. Slight heavy flak was encountered and one Marauder received a direct hit and went down in flames. None of the crew was seen to bale out.

On 3 October, seventy-two Marauders took to the air to bomb Beauvais/Tille aerodrome. The Hornchurch Wing climbed from base and crossed east Hastings at 15,000 feet to rendezvous with the bombers about 30 miles north of Dieppe at 1703 hours. The Marauders carried out their objective as accurate bombing was observed to strike the dispersals and airfield at Beauvais. Four minutes after leaving the target area the Wing was bounced by forty 109s and 190s that dived straight towards the Marauders from out of the sun. Wing Commander Crawford-Compton ordered 129 Squadron to remain above as cover while 222 Squadron went down after the enemy fighters.

Flight Lieutenant Hesselyn was seen to attack the rearmost aircraft, a Messerschmitt Bf109, which after being set on fire crashed in a wood as Blue Section pulled out at 1,000 feet. The Spitfires then climbed rapidly but were bounced by two Fw190s at 15,000 feet. One of the enemy fighters was seen to fire a short burst at Hesselyn's aircraft which soon caught fire and, after turning on its back, went down in flames, poured black smoke into the air. Flight Lieutenant Lardner-Burke saw the action from his own cockpit and reported seeing a parachute below. He was convinced that Hesselyn had baled out when turning the Spitfire on its back...and he was right. Hesselyn was able to successfully abandon his aircraft suffering burns and wounds to both legs. He was soon captured and became a prisoner of war.

At the end of the engagement the majority of the Wing re-formed and came out behind the last box of bombers before returning to base. That day, Betty wrote to her mother about Pat's Investiture at Buckingham Palace:

> We did not get away after all; the Squadron Leader went off sick so Pat had to be about. We have been very lucky as it has been awful weather all

week and no flying – Pat had to go back to camp for a few hours every day to sign his name to things, etc, being the acting Squadron Leader of the Squadron. Yesterday it was clearing up and he was fairly late getting back in the evening. Today has been very nice so he had to go off early and will probably be late getting back but he's getting two days off tomorrow and Tuesday and I am due back on Wednesday. It wasn't a nice day at all last Tuesday (28 September 1943) for Buckingham Palace. It was teaming with rain until nine, and I had visions of arriving dripping wet but it cleared up, thank goodness, though very wet underfoot and dull. I wore the fur cape in the end and was very glad of it and the rest of the wedding regalia. We arrived at ten and had to queue up – as somebody said it was like going to the pictures! The doors opened at 1015 and we slowly moved in. Didn't get very far inside the Palace, the Investiture was in the first room and we came to, in fact it was more like a hall. I thought I had a very good seat, right at the end of the row with a perfect view of the dais. But when all the men filed in I couldn't see at all except without peering between but I had a good view of everyone before they got their medals! There were masses of OBEs, lots of civilians, several military matrons and one nurse. I could just see the King's head and Pat's when he got his medal, they had a few words – asked Pat if he'd been in Malta. It's a very nice medal, silver, with the date on the back. Emerson Gelling from Douglas was also at the Investiture. I think he's in the Merchant Navy. I saw his wife and sister at the back of the queue when we were waiting to go in but I didn't feel like losing my place to go back and make myself acquainted and I didn't see them again. The King came in just after eleven and we got out just after 1230. We rushed straight out and no efforts were made to photograph us! Not being famous enough. Peter Scott was there and very much in the limelight. There were several Beefeaters in full regalia, which livened up the proceedings and we had music.

On Wednesday 20 October, Betty wrote the following to her mother:

The weather has been pretty foul and Pat has been up every evening so we've spent the night at the Temple. This evening I was on duty so he did not come up. On Saturday evening I went out to Hornchurch for the dance. There were masses of people there, including the AOC, Group Captains, etc, and well known people such as Al Deere, Don Kingaby – fighter pilots. It was a very good dance, Pat had an extra bed put in his room and I slept there. Sunday morning was very wet so there was no flying and I stayed around until the last minute. The Hun aeroplane, which was shot down during the raid on Sunday night, crashed, complete with full load of bombs, on the Hornchurch dummy aerodrome – very lucky. Pat said the explosion was terrific, shook the whole Mess, windows flung open and curtains blown in

Pat Lardner-Burke at Sutton Bridge, 1942. (*Martin Lardner-Burke*)

– bits of aeroplane all over the place. Monday and Tuesday nights Pat came in and we shut ourselves up in the flat – too wet to go out – and concocted some sort of supper. Pat produced six oranges last week which he got from an American ship – some milk chocolate which tastes of nothing after being used to the strong chocolate we get now. Pat is about to leave Hornchurch any moment now. He should really have left for a rest a month ago having done 150 sweeps and I don't know how many flying hours. Today he had to go and see the AOC of 11 Group (the top notch group of fighter command) and see group captains, etc, about getting a new job at Fighter Command at HQ. This is at Stanmore so if everything turns out alright, he'll be there for the winter. All very nice – it's a bit further away than Hornchurch, takes 50 minutes in the tube – but no complaints. Also it means he'll be made an acting Squadron Leader. We are having a nurses dance here on Friday night but if Pat is leaving on Saturday he'll probably be having a farewell party in the mess that night, also celebrating his promotion.

Pat's new posting to HQ, Fighter Command meant that he would now be serving with Group Captain Bobby Oxspring, DFC and two Bars. Oxspring wrote the following of his new appointment:

Spitfire MH434 in flight at Duxford. (*Ady Shaw*)

Pat Lardner-Burke with his good friend Dennis Cowley, 19 Squadron, 1941. (*Martin Lardner-Burke*)

222 Squadron at Hornchurch, 1943. Pat is with 'Kupee' the dog. (*Martin Lardner-Burke*)

Before my leave expired, an order arrived cancelling my return to Sicily but instead to report to Fighter Command at Stanmore. A vacant slot needed filling in the Tactics and Training branch of the illustrious headquarters, and I joined a formidable squad of fellow tour-expired veterans whose cavalier approach to their work sent spasms of horror through the dedicated Staff College graduates. The tactics and training publications directed at the day fighter squadrons were entrusted to three of us sharing an office.

Jackie Urwin-Mann, a pre-war vintage Canadian who had sweated through the Battle of Britain and the Western Desert, occupied one chair. The third desk was the domain of Pat Lardner-Burke, a rugged South African who, with Hornchurch sweeps and Malta behind him, displayed a refreshingly irreverent attitude to all senior officers with whom he disagreed. Facetious comments filled the minute sheets of numerous files which we solemnly circulated between ourselves, and on rare occasions to other departments. Delaying as long as possible any publication from Fighter Command on our particular subjects, our natures rebelled at the preposterous notion of issuing a training directive to the likes of Johnnie Johnson, or a tactics manual to Sailor Malan.[3]

In April 1944 Pat took command of 1 Squadron, which he successfully led until December that same year.

During this time he and Oxspring would meet again when the latter was assigned as Wing Leader of the Detling Wing. The meeting was almost disastrous, when, one morning the Wing lined up on Manston's large runway to take off for Detling, and something went wrong with Oxspring's aircraft, as he recalled:

> I had almost gained flying speed when my engine cut dead. Holding rudder against the torque I couldn't prevent a violent swing across the path of Pat Lardner-Burke formatting on my wing. Pat hauled back on his stick and his aircraft literally jumped over the top of me. I can still visualise every single rivet on his under fuselage as he careered over my canopy. Bouncing down off his kangaroo leap, he demanded: "What the hell goes on, Bobby?" The Wing roared away as I trundled off the runway with a fuel starvation problem; I didn't need to remove my helmet, my hair shot up so straight it just pushed it off. Pat's lightning reactions avoided a messy pile up. Years afterwards we still chilled over the memory. Such dramas tend to play hell with the nervous system. As Pat remarked, "Man, we bloody near became a couple of chattering wrecks."[4]

Pat's final sortie of the war took place on Christmas day. He saw his first Me 262 screaming through the air but no contact was made. A few days later Pat was promoted to Wing Commander Flying and moved to RAF Coltishall. In February 1945, Pat was awarded a Bar to the DFC. His citation reads as follows:

> This officer continues to display a high degree of courage and resolution in his attacks on the enemy. Recently, he has led the squadron on many missions in the Ruhr area and throughout has displayed great skill and tenacity. Squadron Leader Lardner-Burke has destroyed seven enemy aircraft in air fighting. He has also most effectively attacked enemy targets on the ground.

By the end of the year Pat had attended a course at No. 1 OATS, Cranwell, and taken command of Horsham St Faith airfield. Then for three months he served as Wing Commander Flying at Church Fenton.

After fulfilling a number of varying appointments in the service for a number of years, Pat applied to remain in the RAF. For awhile he was retained on the RAF reserve list but, perhaps due to his medical record, he was not granted a Permanent Commission. Considering all Pat had given to the air force during the war, it seemed a cold way to end his commendable career.

The South African fighter ace eventually settled on the Isle of Man with his wife, Betty, where for several years he ran a public house.

After a period of ill-health, Wing Commander Pat Lardner-Burke, DFC and Bar died of renal failure on 4 February 1970. He was only fifty-three years old; two of his four children were still in school.

Pat with 222 Squadron Spitfire EN473. (*Martin Lardner-Burke*)

Pat on the right, Ray Harrington left, and Phil Tripe centre (222 'Natal' Squadron, 1943). (*Martin Lardner-Burke*)

Pat, top middle, with Blackpool airshow display pilots in 1947. (*Martin Lardner-Burke*)

In April 1983 Spitfire MH434 was sold at auction to its most illustrious owner, Ray Hanna and became one of The Old Flying Machine Company's founding aircraft.

Today this incredible Spitfire, which Lardner-Burke christened 'Mylcraine' (Betty's middle name) in August 1943, can be found at the Imperial War Museum Duxford, in Cambridgeshire.

MH434 is arguably the most famous and iconic airworthy Spitfire still flying today. It has starred in several movies including *A Bridge Too Far*, *The Battle of Britain*, *Dark Blue World*, *The Longest Day*, as well as the Television series *Piece of Cake* and *Heroes of the Skies*.

At present MH434 is painted in 222 Squadron markings bearing the code letters 'ZD-B'. The name 'Mylcraine' and Lardner-Burke's personal scoreboard have been painted onto the port side of the cockpit to replicate the South African's markings in 1943.

Pilots who have flown MH434 in modern times have described the aircraft as an absolute delight to fly, beautifully responsive and extremely manoeuvrable.

In late September 2012, Paul Bonhomme flew MH434 on a special journey to Malta to commemorate the 70th anniversary of the island being awarded

MH434. (*Chris Brookes*)

the George Cross. As well as flying at The Malta International Airshow, Bonhomme carried out a wonderful display over the Grand Harbour. To have an aircraft so well connected to Pat, flying in that once ferocious arena over Malta was truly a special occasion. In fact I can't possibly think of a greater tribute to Pat Lardner-Burke than to see and to hear his remarkable Spitfire still soaring through the skies in all its majesty.

CHAPTER 6

Finn Eriksrud

On a late Autumn evening in 1940, two young men struggled forward on the east side of the Iddefjord. On the other side of this long fjord was Sweden. That's where they wanted to go. Both of them had been thinking of escaping German capture for some time already, and their first semester at the University of Oslo had not been spent studying, but rather making plans for their escape to freedom. They had both heard of young men, just like themselves, escaping Norway to continue the fight against Nazi Germany. One of the boys, who had now been walking for two hours in the pitch black by the long lake, was Finn Eriksrud. The other was his friend from the University, Gunnar.

They both knew that the quickest way to Great Britain was across the North Sea, but neither of them had any contacts on the Norwegian west coast, and they had quickly let go of such plans. They had settled on a plan which seemed as easy as it was simple. Gunnar had heard rumours that, if they managed to get themselves to Stockholm, they would be transported to London on the first available flight. Naive perhaps, but they decided that the rumour was good enough. In reality, this was surely not the case, but maybe it was for the best that they did not know. They would take the train to the border town of Halden, Norway, and then make their way down the east side of the fjord looking for anything that might help them across to the other side. It sounded easier than it really was. There was no moonlight, and it had been raining the entire time. They were wet, tired and getting desperate.

With another half-hour passed, they finally located an old rowing boat. As honest young men from the University, they decided to leave 50 NOK under a rock as payment for the sudden disappearance of a poor man's rowing boat. They made their way across the fjord and found a little cabin to satisfy their need of sleep. By daylight, they made their way to the Swedish town of Strømstad, and were quickly apprehended by eager Swedish policemen. The Swedish police, probably handling plenty of these Norwegian escapers, asked if the two of them had done anything wrong back home, since they had come all the way to Sweden. Yet again naive, the two Norwegians denied having done anything wrong. They simply stated that they did not like the Germans and would like to go to the Norwegian embassy in Stockholm. The Swedish police had no reason to keep the two boys, and sent them back home. They were told that next time they came to Sweden, they should at least have a good story to tell. So, they returned to Norway, feeling foolish and disappointed with their efforts.

Finn Eriksrud remained enrolled at the University until Christmas of 1940. Then he decided to have another go. In the meantime, he had got in touch with another friend, and they were now three in the group. Gunnar had changed his mind about the best way to escape Norway, and said that it was much easier to simply take the train to a small Norwegian border town, walk across the border, and get on the train again at the other side. Finn did not agree with Gunnar's daring plan, and teamed up with his other friend, Børge. They decided to go on skis over the border in a more secluded place than close to railway tracks. As it turned out, Gunnar arrived safely in Stockholm three days before Finn and Børge did.

As for Finns second attempt at escape, he knew what to tell the Swedish police once they got hold of them. This time he told the police a great story about being involved with illegal papers. This was accepted, and Finn Eriksrud was approved for travel to the Norwegian embassy in Stockholm. In the embassy, they told the Norwegian officials their story, but had to be honest concerning military background; they had none. Their easy flight to London was officially denied. It was a disappointment. Finn had to settle in Stockolm for the time being, waiting his turn to get the necessary funds and papers for further travel. A second massive hurdle was money. They had none, and a journey on this scale, going around the planet to eventually end up in London, was an expensive one. However, if Finn could get the money himself, the embassy would act more quickly and could also help them with the necessary visas.

Finn had no money and no rich family in America. Luckily, they got hold of someone walking across the border the next day, and he would bring the message back to Finn's parents to send money. All he had to do was wait. Within fourteen days, the money arrived. He now needed the necessary visas for entering Canada. Not Great Britain yet. Finn wanted to be a pilot, and Norway's training camp for pilots was located in Canada.

In the beginning of March 1941, Eriksrud finally got his visa for entering Canada. As for getting to Canada, he had to start by taking an epic route to Moscow, Odessa, Basra and Bombay. His money reached only that far. In Bombay, he had to rely on the hospitality of English ships bound for Canada or Britain. His long journey began a whole year after the German invasion of Norway. Finn wondered if the war would actually be over before he arrived and could do his part. Finn Eriksrud's first ever flight was from Bromma in Sweden, to Moscow in Russia. He enjoyed it, and his plan to become a pilot was settled once and for all. With his friend Gunnar, he joined up with a larger group of Norwegians in Moscow, all going to Odessa.

After two days on a train, they arrived safely in Odessa. There had been little conversation on the train, as none of the Russians seemed to understand either English, French or German. Their official papers stated that they were ordinary tourists, and they managed to attend a few operas and do some casual sightseeing in Odessa. The next day, they would take a boat to Istanbul. From a rough train ride from Moscow, they now enjoyed a very nice boat trip. It was a shock to them to realize that the boat would stop at Varna in Bulgaria as this city was occupied by German forces. Just in case, they stayed below deck as they were told that Germans would photograph them and send pictures back to Norway. In retrospect, Eriksrud assumed it was all rumours but, at the time, it was a deadly serious business. After a day or so in Istanbul, the journey continued onwards to Baghdad, Iraq. During Easter of 1941, they arrived in Baghdad, and were met by representatives from several hotels in the city. When Finn and his group of Norwegians did not understand what these people were saying, they started to argue with each other. Apparently, it was something to do with which hotel was the best, and who could entertain the Norwegians the best. Finn spent a whole week in Baghdad, and thought of the city as hot, dirty and hostile. Finn and Gunnar walked around the city alone and, on one occasion, the Iraqis started to throw rocks at them. They mistook the two Norwegians for being British. Fourteen days after Finn and Gunnar had left Baghdad, there was rioting among the Arab population. Luckily, they managed to get on a boat bound for Bombay, and they were both pleased that they did not have to stay in Baghdad for a minute longer.

In Bombay, they approached the Norwegian Consulate for transportation to Canada. At that moment, there were no boats bound for Canada, and the Norwegians had to wait. When Finn had left Sweden, they had been four Norwegians. By the time they arrived in Bombay, there were over 150 men who wanted to report for duty. It took another fourteen days before they finally got lucky and boarded a British transport ship. Still struggling with the intense heat, Gunnar and Finn stayed with their faces well planted into the air vent in their quarters for fresh and cooler air. They spent their time on the boat reading for the most part. After several short stops along the way, their final destination would be Montreal, Canada. On board the ship were several other Norwegian Air Force officers, and Finn, as keen as ever to become a pilot, kept asking them questions about what it was like to be a pilot. They told him that one of the exercises he had to do to become a pilot was to stand on one leg, both hands stretched out and his tongue sticking out. They told him that the longer he could stand like this, the better his chances were of being accepted. It was all a joke, but Finn took it seriously and practiced until he could stand in such a position for over five minutes.

A happy, young Finn Eriksrud in his Norwegian naval uniform. (*FMU*)

Finally, on 27 June 1941, they arrived in Montreal. The next day, Finn and Gunnar took a train up to Toronto and 'Little Norway', the Norwegian training base for air force personnel. It had been an epic trip across large parts of the globe. At the station in Toronto, he knew he was in the right place as he quickly saw a soldier walking with a pretty Canadian girl. The soldier had 'Norway' embroided on his shoulder. Five and a half months after he escaped from Norway, he had reached his first goal.

By the time Finn arrived at Little Norway, most of the camp was already constructed. It was surrounded by barbed wire, and the camp's own police force kept a strict look-out. If anyone was caught outside the fence, they would be fined ten, fifteen or twenty dollars, all depending on the degree of disobedience. Most people thought hard about making a run for it and living it up in Toronto for a night or two. North, towards the Maple Leaf stadium, the camp had a large wooden fence. It was impossible to climb it so that part of the camp had no guards. A few of the boys had noticed this, and sawed a hole in the fence. They even put in a door. For a long time, this route was used by the Norwegians, but it was eventually discovered.

One night, the guards knew they would catch many of them, and gathered as a large force. When one Norwegian after the other showed his face through the hole, he was caught and put under the arrest. The camp police also did checks around Toronto, especially in restaurants. If they found anyone drunk or making trouble, they were promptly detained. At the beginning of the Norwegians' stay in Toronto, they were a welcome addition to the population but, commonly, where Norwegians set foot in other countries, there was bound to be much drinking and trouble. So, over time the Canadians became a bit less welcoming, but it never got a point where Canadian girls were advised to stay away from dances and restaurants where Norwegian Air Force cadets attended in large groups. On the contrary, many Norwegians married Canadian girls and were welcomed into Canadian families.

Finn Eriksrud was to report to Ole Reistad, commander of the camp, when he arrived. He showed up early in the morning, but he was not the only one coming in early to report for duty. Six others were already lined up in front of Reistad's office that morning. They had all arrived in Toronto the day before. One via New York, another by the same route as Finn and another all the way around the world via San Francisco. One was a Norwegian-American from Portland, Oregon, and his Norwegian was more than a bit rusty. Finn went through an interview with Reistad and was accepted. He was fully vaccinated and given his uniform. Eriksrud wanted to be a pilot, and he went through several tests. Reistad had, again and again, explained that, for every pilot, they needed ten ground crewmen. These were sobering statistics, and Finn's heart sank a little each time Reistad talked about this. Luckily for him, Finn was one of the few who was accepted for pilot training. By August, he had got into the thick of things, and tried to focus on his studies. The weather outside was sunny and warm, and sometimes it was hard to stay inside studying meteorology. Eriksrud also bought his own car, as his expenses for travelling from Stockholm were reimbursed by the Norwegian government.

Finn Eriksrud's next stop was Elmsdale, north of Toronto. It was time for all his theory to be put into practical use. He would now start flying. When Finn arrived, it turned out that they all had to sleep in tents as there were only a few buildings at the site. The very next day, Eriksrud would start his flying training. He would train on Fairchild Cornells. He made slow but good progress. His landings went from being extremely dangerous to at least being likely to walk away from in one piece. His instructor seemed more and more pleased with his flying and before long, he could land the Fairchild by himself.

However, he always found comfort in the fact there was a skilled pilot behind him. One day, after his third landing, the instructor left his seat and let Finn do it alone. At first, Finn felt shocked and terrified, but, sooner or later, he had to land one of these aircraft himself, and it turned out to be sooner rather than later. His instructor seemed to have faith in him, perhaps more than Finn had in himself. He got a funny sensation in his stomach, exactly like he had back home when he went ski jumping in large hills for the first time. He started to sweat and his hands started to shake. It was too late to turn back now. Several of the other students had already flown their first solo, and all had gone well for them. He had no more time to think about things as he was cleared to take off. Finn tried to forget all his worrying, which wasn't so difficult as he had enough to concentrate on with holding the aeroplane on the right course going down the runway. All went well, he did everything he was taught and his confidence soared. Finn flew around the sky and felt as free as bird.

But when the time came to land again, the former feeling came back. Finn felt it was easy to get the Fairchild flying. It was the landings he was scared of. He circled the airfield a few times and saw his instructor looking up at him. He prepared to attempt his landing. His speed seemed to be alright, and Finn thought he would make it with no further problems. It was easier said than done, though, as his height was too great, and he practically fell out of the sky and onto the grass runway. The undercarriage held, thankfully for Eriksrud, and he could taxi back to his instructor. He was pleased enough by Finn's efforts, but no more flying would take place that day. He would be back in the air flying the next day, though, and would now learn to spin, roll and loop.

Navigation flying was also coming up, something which could be dangerous over the vast forests of Canada. Finn was told that, if he got lost, he must not become nervous or scared and start to fly in circles. Furthermore, he was instructed to keep on flying until he reached something he recognised. It seemed very simple. Not so when Finn tried his first navigational flying sortie. He got lost. Darkness started to fall, and Finn knew the situation was dangerous. He could not recognise anything below him. He contemplated jumping out but decided to stay with the plane until the last possible moment. When he was about to give up, he finally spotted a light below him. A car. If he could follow the road, he would, for sure, find civilisation. By looking at the lights and the buildings below, Finn recognised the town as Huntsville, just a short distance from Elmsdale. By the time he arrived over Elmsdale, it was dark, and Finn had never tried to land at night before. His landing was rough, but the undercarriage held once again. The landing was not important. Eriksrud was just happy to get away from his first navigational flying sortie with his life intact. His instructor was not very pleased though, and Finn had to offer apology after apology followed by detailed explanations of why he had got lost. And why did he get lost? He had performed several aerobatics which threw him off course. The result was one week confined to camp. However he learned his lesson. By December 1941, the same day that Japan attacked Pearl Harbor, Finn Eriksrud packed up his bags and left Elmsdale.

Up until this point, the training had all been with a Norwegian instructor. Now, the Norwegians would be split up into two groups. One destined for fighters, the other for bombers. Finn went to bombers, and was sent to Medicine Hat, far out in Western Canada. The base had mostly Canadian ground crew and soldiers, but the pilots were British. Finn experienced, more than once, a bit of friction between the Canadians and the British. On one occasion, a fight developed in town. There were several Norwegians stationed at Medicine Hat, and they were a bit hesitant about who to side with in this little struggle. They decided, perhaps for tactical reasons, to side with the Canadians. Because of this, Finn and his fellow Norwegians could always leave the camp when they wanted, while the Canadians treated the British much more strictly and always reported it if someone came late back to the camp. Other oddities also occurred. Every Saturday, there was an inspection arranged. Shoes, clothes, buttons – everything had to look its absolute best. The Norwegians did not have the same equipment as the Englishmen, and the English sergeant who did the inspection had no knowledge of the Norwegian rules and what they demanded. Finn, on the other hand, had no idea how to satisfy the English rules, so it all ended with the Norwegians taking life easy while their English colleagues had to work like slaves to get their equipment up to par.

At Medicine Hat, Finn Eriksrud trained on Airspeed Oxfords. A strange thing happened to his confidence when flying Oxfords; he suddenly became scared of flying. When Finn was told to go up and fly, he did what he was told, but the will was no longer there. He felt as if it was the Oxford that flew him, not the other way around. He was not sure what he was afraid of, but he had never experienced this fear before. He didn't want to tell his friends, and kept going in this way for over a week. However, his instructor noticed Finns condition. The English instructor did not react angrily. He decided to give Finn his confidence back, and spent several hours getting him back into shape while flying. Suddenly, Finn's confidence came back.

After Medicine Hat, Finn moved to another course before finally leaving for a well-deserved holiday. With his friend, Harald Odman, a Norwegian-American, he went to New York for some proper sightseeing. Having 'Norway' on their shoulders contributed greatly to the locals' welcoming reception. Everyone wanted to buy them drinks. If Finn tried to tell them he wanted to pay for himself, or that he'd had enough to drink, the Americans simply ignored him and kept buying him drinks. By the time they got out onto the streets again, from whatever restaurant or bar they had visited, their spirits were considerably lifted. By the time they left New York, they actually felt rather relieved that they would no longer be bought so many drinks.

Finally, in January 1943, Finn Eriksrud was on his way to the United Kingdom on the Queen Elizabeth. His friend Harald had by this time gotten bored and frustrated with the waiting. He had applied for a transfer to fighters and got accepted. Finn stayed with his group of bomber pilots and, after four days at sea, they were escorted by British fighters up the Firth of Clyde. By that evening, everyone was transported to London by train. For Finn, it seemed that Harald had got the better deal, as he was quickly sent to a fighter squadron somewhere around London. Finn Eriksrud, on the other hand, was given the task of writing birthday and greeting cards to the Norwegian personnel in their Air Force. But his frustration would soon end as he was sent to an Operational Training Unit (OTU) near Bristol.

It was different flying aircraft in Britain, and more training had to be done. From the OTU, Finn was sent to Leuchars to fly Mosquitos with the Norwegian 333 squadron. The squadron's A-Flight was flying Catalinas out of Woodhaven, and now, a brand new B-Flight would be formed at Leuchars. When Finn arrived, the Mosquitos had not arrived, and two English Beaufighter squadrons operated from the base. Fourteen days later, the Mosquitos arrived, and the Norwegians could start training on these fantastic machines. Finn thought the cockpit was a bit cramped, and he was lucky to get a navigator who was not too large in size. His name was Erling Johansen.

In June, the Mosquito flight would start their operations. Finn had by this time been training as a pilot for a whole two years. Their first sortie was met with excitement and joy. No. 333 Squadron Mosquitoes would undertake recce sorties over the Norwegian coast, reporting back about U-boats, German shipping and other interesting things they might set their eyes on.

No. 333 Squadron scored their first kill in the middle of June 1943 when Knut Skavhaugen and his navigator Jan Heide spotted a Dornier Do 24T-1 flying boat, and promptly shot it down in the Haugesund harbour on 13 June with several onlookers on the ground. It was reported that the flying boat had at least ten Germans on board, and that they were most likely all dead. Back at Leuchars, Finn joined in the celebrations. Skavhaugen decided to re-enact his kill using his own body. He got up on a chair and tried to demonstrate to his audience how he shot the flying boat down. To show everyone how the German went into the sea, he dived down from the chair – head first. He got up again, a grin all over his face, and looked at his watch. He told everyone how the Germans now had been dead for six hours, thirty minutes and fifteen seconds. He repeated the performance several times, re-calculating the time. The incident left its scars.

For Finn's first real mission on 2 July 1943, they would reach the Norwegian coast by daylight, and he was, therefore, woken up in the middle of the night. Eggs and bacon for breakfast was a welcome treat and after eating their breakfast, Finn and Erling reported to the operations room. The ops room had a large map covering Scotland, the North sea and Norway. A red line was stretched out from Leuchars over to Norway. Also on the map were yellow markers – British submarines. Two black markers were pinned near Sognefjord, and these were German U-boats. For Finn's first mission,

A 333 Squadron Mosquito taxiing out. Notice the Beaufighter in the left corner used for practice flying. (*Magnus Eide*)

he would patrol from Bergen to Ålesund. They could decide if they wanted to fly north to south or south to north. Finn went for the northerly route, making landfall around Bergen. It was considered safer than entering Ålesund as the Germans had Focke Wulf Fw190s in the area. For the recce, he would be flying Mosquito with the code mark E on its fuselage and the serial number DZ7520.

It was still dark outside when Finn and Erling walked down to their Mosquito in the hangar. The ground crew had been working on it all night, and it was ready for the sortie. Finn realized that Ole Reistad had been right when he said they needed ten men for every pilot, and he felt humbled to be given the chance to fly. By the time they were airborne, it had started to become light, and they could see the silhouettes of the Scottish mountains behind them. With the magnificent speed of the Mosquito, they prepared to make their first sight of Norway after a long time away. Neither of them had set their foot in the western part of Norway before, but they felt confident they could do the job well. And then it showed up on the horizon; Norway. Lost in the sensation of joy in seeing their homeland again, they forgot to check where they were. Under them a little boat appeared, and the Mosquito roared over it. The man in the boat waved like crazy, and Eriksrud decided to do an extra turn around the mad Norwegian for national pride.

Suddenly, red and green lights appeared all around them – flak. For a moment, they had forgotten all about the war, being too excited about seeing Norway. There was certainly a war on, and Finn changed height and course to avoid the flak. When they passed Sognefjord, they looked for the German U-boats, but they had already disappeared. North of Florø they spotted a German convoy, and Erling photographed it. The Germans fired hells at them but luckily, they missed. They wanted to end up on the eastern side of Ålesund to avoid the German fighters, and they had the feeling that they were already there, waiting for them. Coming in on the east side of Ålesund, all was quiet from the German fighters. Finishing their patrol, they turn around and set course for home.

Then the Focke Wulfs appeared. Four of them, about 2,000 feet behind. Finn increased speed and headed for Leuchars as fast as he could. There was no point getting into a dogfight with four Fw190s. There were no clouds to hide in as it was all sunny. They had to rely on their speed. The thought that the German fighters did not like to go further than 100 kilometres from the coastline was comforting. After another few minutes of fear, they finally saw the Germans turn back to their base. They could now head home with no one chasing them. There was a sense of relief from both men in the cockpit. After they landed back at Leuchars, the ground crew started their work, and Finn reported back about their sortie.

Finn Eriksrud was always of the opinion that it was better to be a pilot than a soldier. His squadron had beds, a roof over their heads at night and every modern convenience. He was also happy that he did not have to watch friends suffer close up, as they do on a battle field. However, there were always situations when Finn wished he was somewhere else, like the time they had been out flying for two hours on a naval sortie. He noticed that they had been flying on the wrong course. They flew on 360 degrees instead of 180 and were well on their way to Svalbard. The only thing he could do was to maintain course until Erling had calculated a new course back home. On this occasion, the Shetland Isles. The time when they should have seen Shetland came and went, but they saw nothing. They feared they were flying straight into the open Atlantic ocean. However, half an hour later, they saw land. They got safely down, and realised they had reached the northern tip of Scotland. The reason for this was the wind. It had changed considerably since take off, and Erling had used the wind since then to the best of his abilities. Back in the ops room, there was great concern when they saw that Finn and Erland were flying north instead of south.

In late June or early July 1943, two Mosquitoes were sent up to Sumburgh Head, and Finn Eriksrud was one of them. Finn enjoyed his time up there,

Filling up a Mosquito at Leuchars, 1943. (*FMU*)

especially since they were so close to the Norwegian coast. They could reach Bergen in a short time. Their time off from flying, however, was quite dull as there was nothing much to do up there. At Sumburgh, there was also a squadron of Beaufighters, and cooperation with them improved as time progressed. However, Finn's joy of flying to Norway started to slowly drain away. If he knew in the afternoon that he would fly a sortie the next day, he often lay awake the entire night planning it, especially when it came to the 190s. It was essential to surprise them, so that they weren't waiting for them when they arrived at the coast. For Finn, it was perhaps another incident that made him less enthusiastic.

Before they left for Sumburgh, a Norwegian Mosquito had gone down just off the runway during landing. None of them understood why it had happened, as the pilot was considered to be very skilled. This was Mosquito E/DZ752 flown by Midshipman Tryggve Bjørn Schieldsø and the squadrons radio officer Trygve Øverli. Originally, it was Schieldsøe and Petty Officer Gunnar Helgedagsrud that would do the training sortie, but Øverli took Helgedagsruds place to test radio equipment. Interestingly, after Helgedagsrud had avoided death in such tragic manner, he stayed with the squadron and eventually became one of the longest lasting members of the flight during the War. Perhaps understandably, none of the Norwegians wanted to fly again that day. They had seen it happen to British pilots before but, this time, it had was a little closer to home, and their morale took a beating.

On 9 July, their second mission this month, Finn Eriksrud and Erling Johansen took off for a recce from Sumburgh on what they now simply called 'the Norge coast' using the Norwegian name of Norway. They sighted and attacked what they thought was a Junkers 88 (it was in reality a Focke Wulf 58). Finn approached from behind, and the German fired a red cartridge followed by another, five seconds later. The Norwegians were slightly confused, but opened fire with their cannons. Finn observed hits all along the fuselage, and the port engine caught fire. Erling saw the Focke Wulf 58 go down in flames, and crash into the sea. Finn Eriksrud's impression of the incident was that the enemy had not recognised them as an enemy. There was no return fire from the enemy. The patrol was flown in bad weather.

Going into summer and the early autumn of 1943, the flight kept losing pilots and crew over the Norwegian coastline. The flight had already lost their leader, Lieutenant Håkon Offerdal in a mid-air crash very close to Leuchars. He had crashed with an Airspeed Oxford during landing. Anton Christopher Hagerup and his navigator Just Wilde Meinche Finne were lost in late June. Other losses were Alf Sundt-Jacobsen and Christian Bernhard Aagard, they were lost during a night flying exercise. The two Norwegians had been told to wait north for clearance to land north of Leuchars, and had crashed into the sea.

For Finn and Erling, the most devastating blow came when their closest friends, Hans Olai Holdø and Jan Erling Heide, did not come back from a sortie on 28 August 1943. The crew had taken off after noon and were expected back around six. Finn and his navigator were about to go to the cinema for the evening, but suddenly decided they would wait for their friends. By 1830, they started to get worried, as still nothing was heard from the crew. In the ops room, they were worried about the delay and, as each minute passed, they gradually understood that their friends had made their last sortie to Norway. From time to time, they had discussed what one crew would do if the other was missing. Jan was of the opinion that a major party was needed, and insisted that if he did not make it, Finn and Erling had to go out on the town and drink.

They tried to do what Jan had told them to do, but it did not go very well, so they gave up and went home. The loss of their two friends was too big a

A Norwegian Mosquito at Leuchars. (*Per Einar Jansen*)

blow. Finn had calculated the odds of survival, and had settled on a one in seven chance. He had the feeling that Jan believed he would not make it, but Finn himself was never in doubt that he would be the one in seven to actually survive. By late August 1943, the flight had lost five Mosquitoes.

One day, there was a lot of commotion in the ops room. Finn was told to be ready to go up in five minutes. The German cruiser Lützow was observed heading south in the early morning, and now a scout was needed to find the massive ship. The job was given to Finn and Erling. They understood how dangerous such a mission could be. The cruiser was escorted by naval vessels and plenty of fighters were ready to come to its rescue. However, they also understood how important it was to find it, and report back to at once so that an attack could be launched. Finn was to fly his Mosquito from Kristiansund to Bremanger. They headed out, and the tension increased as they approached the Norwegian coast. However, nothing was to be seen, no fighters came to meet them, and everything ended uneventfully. After they landed, they were told that the cruiser had been spotted outside Haugesund, so their anxiety had been for nothing.

With autumn now well under way, 333 Squadron had taken a hard beating. Only Finn and Erling were now left of the original crews. They had very few Mosquitoes at their disposal, and those they had lacked spare parts. For the Flight, there was nothing for it but start all over again with new Mosquitoes, and

Finn's friend Jan climbs
into the Mosquito
for his final trip to
Norway. (*FMU*)

new crews. However, the Flight's losses had been so extensive that they could
not obtain either pilots or Mosquitoes in good time. It took until November
1943 until the Flight was again operational. For Finn, 22 November would be
a day to remember. He took his Mosquito with serial number HP860 marked
R on a recce in the Stavanger-Lista area. Around 1000 hours, they sighted a
Junkers 88 (D7+BH) at 2,000 feet and 130 degrees. The weather was cloudy,
and the Germans kept flying in and out of the clouds. Finn tracked the Junkers
down and opened fire from dead astern. Pieces flew off the fuselage, and one
of the engines caught fire. When Finn flew past the Junkers, Erling took up his
camera and snapped a photo of the doomed German. The Junkers then glided
down towards the sea and disappeared in the dark waters. Finn Eriksrud had
scored his second German victory.

Going into winter of 1943, the weather worsened and less flying took
place. One afternoon, on 18 December, the weather was decent enough for
a recce, and Finn prepared for a trip that would take them from Stavanger
to Bergen in Mosquito HP861 coded N. When they were a few miles off the
Norwegian coast, the weather suddenly worsened considerably, and they

Above: Finn Eriksrud
and Erling Johansen
shoot down a Junkers
88, 1943. Johansen
photographs it just
before it hits the water.
(*Ulf Larsstuvold*)

Right: Mosquitoes lined
up at Leuchars in 1943.
(*Magnus Eide*)

found themselves in a storm. They were supposed to see land any minute, and if they did not, they would turn back. Just in time, the weather cleared up and they turned north. The weather worsened again and by the time they reached the point where they were supposed to turn for home, they decided to fly south again as the weather could have helped to hide important things they needed to report back on. So instead of turning out to sea, they headed down the coastline again. They felt they were safe, since the weather was so bad that they doubted any Germans would be up to greet them. When they had crossed the area where the weather had been bad on their first pass, they decided to set course for Leuchars. Only a minute later, Erling spotted something flying across their own course. A Focke Wulf 85 Weihe (KR+CW). Lady Luck seemed to be shining on the two boys. A FW85 would not pose a major threat, and Finn went in for the kill. He decided to attack from the side as the speed of the Mosquito was so much quicker. Finn fired his first burst, and pieces flew off the Weihes tail. Another burst, and the engine caught fire. The attack was going very well, but the Norwegians celebrated a bit too early. They passed under the Weihe, and flew straight through the fire and the smoke streaming from it. It blinded Finn, and all he could do was to keep flying straight and get out of it.

The FW85 was doomed. Finn was sure about that. Before the German crashed into the sea, he had managed to fire a few shots at the Mosquito, and had hit their starboard engine. Fuel was running over the edge of the wing, and Finn had no choice but to cut the engine and feather the prop. With the FW85 gone into the sea, they only had themselves to think about. Their other engine was also acting up, but they decided to try and make it to Leuchars on one engine. It was a difficult decision, as Finn did not know how bad their running engine had been hit. Suddenly the liquid cooling temperature went through the roof, and the answer was clear: they had to turn back to the coast of Norway. They quickly found out that if they did, they would not even manage to get over land and would have to land the Mosquito on water. Erling and Finn strapped in as best as they could, and opened the hatch which was located above them in the cockpit. The Mosquito came in like a flying boat. A massive wall of water hit the wings from both sides, and, with great speed, it continued going forward before the heavy engines pulled it up to a full stop. Their straps held and they were unharmed. Finn got out and inflated his Mae West. Their rubber dinghy was also in the water. Local Norwegians had seen what was going on, and two young boys came out to greet them in a boat. The two Norwegians from Leuchars got onboard with them, and saw their Mosquito quickly disappear into the depths while they rowed away. The last original 333 Squadron Mosquito crew had met their fate.

Finally, they arrived at the shoreline. Both Finn and Erling were completely wet and very cold, and had to get out of their clothes. While they did this, several German soldiers appeared and told them they were now prisoners of war. Finn could not do anything but accept this sober fact. The Germans gave them a small room for the night, under supervision. Finn kept thinking about the people back at Leuchars, now wondering why they had not come back. Finn had also invited a lovely girl from Dundee to the Christmas party that they would arrange at the station, and he hoped someone would be so kind as to tell the girl that he was missing and could not attend. For Finn, it was a valid reason to not show up.

The next morning, Finn did not understand where he was. It took him a few seconds to realize what was going on. A German guard entered and told him to follow. From now on, Finn and Erling were not allowed to be in the same room together. The next morning, a boat would arrive to pick them up and take them to Bergen. The boat arrived, and Finn was given a meal and a few cigarettes. One of the German sailors told him that he had volunteered for the German invasion of Britain that would come within months. Soon, he would be in London smoking Chesterfield cigarettes. Finn could do nothing but stare in disbelief at the German. From Bergen, they were transported over the mountains and to Oslo. When Finn passed Geilo, he could not help but to look and smile. He had spent so many holidays there as a child, and now he came back in such an unfortunate state. Having arrived in Oslo, they were taken to the airfield of Fornebu for interrogation. The Luftwaffe officer who performed the interrogation wondered why the RAF had bombed Hamburg into such a poor state. Finn said that it was just like what the Germans did to Norwegian towns in 1940, only on a smaller scale since the Norwegian towns were smaller. The German declared that the bombing of Norwegian towns was legitimate as they were military targets. Finn did not bother to discuss it any further. At that, the German became more aggressive and threatened Finn with the Gestapo and what would happen if he left him with them. Among other things, Finn saw a file that contained detailed information about the Mosquito. The documents were signed by a colonel in the RAF. They could have been fake, but Finn did not think so.

Finn spent Christmas Eve of 1943 in captivity at Fornebu, waiting to be transferred to Germany. He remembered he had bet a bottle of whisky with a fellow pilot that he would be back in Oslo and celebrate Christmas at home by 1943. He had done his part so to speak, and considered he had won the bet. The circumstance was, perhaps, not as planned but, even so, he was back home.

On 3 January 1944, Finn was woken at two in the morning. He would now be taken to Germany. He was placed in a bus with three Germans, and was driven down the harbour and a waiting ship. It was full of German troops on their way home to Germany. The journey took three days. The boat went to Denmark, and he was then transported into Germany on a train. In Germany,

Finn got plenty of hateful looks as civilians took him for one of the pilots who had bombed their cities. He managed to cover himself up with a backpack so that they could not look directly at his uniform.

Finn arrived in Frankfurt the day after. He was given his own small cell. In one of the cells next to him, he understood that there was an American. On the third day of capture, Finn overheard the prison guards talking to the American. The prisoner was also of Jewish heritage, and Finn heard Germans warn the American that he should be careful as he was a Jew. If he did not sign his name on certain forms, the Gestapo would take over. The American refused, and, in the end, he got so mad at his captors that he started to cry. One last chance was given, and if the American didn't sign, the Gestapo would come. The prisoner still refused. Finn waited with tension for what how this situation would end. However, no Gestapo came, and the American left the prison with fifty other Americans.

Finn was relieved. Their threats about the Gestapo seemed to be just talk. The day after the American had left, Finn was visited by the same German. He told him it was interesting to meet a Norwegian, as he insisted they belonged to the same race. Finn thought it was quite funny that the German was not such a good representative of the Aryan race – small and chubby with thick glasses. At first, he had a very friendly tone, but as Finn too refused to sign the forms he brought with him, the German worked up a rage. He wanted to know where Finn had been flying from, which squadron, what aircraft and other military questions. Finn refused, and the German got increasingly angry. Finn thought it could not be good for the man's blood pressure to keep doing this sort of routine every day. The German left none the wiser and gave up.

After fourteen days in Frankfurt, Finn was taken out of his cell and transported further. He got his watch back, but it was completely dead due to all the sea water. He also met his navigator Erling again. He had become terribly thin and had a lot of facial hair. Finn guessed that he didn't look much better himself. Together again, they were transported to Sagan. Stalag Luft drei Belaria. Soon after arriving, they were greeted by a British colonel, the most senior officer in the camp. Finn and Erling had to prove that they were indeed who they were said they were. It happened from time to time that the Germans put their own people into the camp to spy on the prisoners. After this, they were greeted by other prisoners and given a cup of tea before the questions started. When would the invasion of Europe come? When would the war be over? In reality, the prisoners knew more about these questions than Finn did. The only thing Finn could give them was local news. When the invasion was finally reported as having started, the prisoners reacted with comments like, 'It's about bloody time!'

As time passed and 1944 came to an end, Finn could at times hear artillery fire in the distance. One evening, two hundred British pilots came into the

A graceful Norwegian Mosquito at Leuchars in 1943. (*FMU*)

camp. They had marched 200 kilometres in temperatures of -20 degrees Celsius temperatures, without either sleep or nutrition. They were in terrible shape, and Finn understood that they too, could be suddenly told to do such a march. The prisoners started to prepare as best as they could. It did not take many days before the Russians had established bridgehead over the river Oder, and the prisoners hoped that the Russians would arrive quicker than the Germans could react. Nothing happened over the next days, and the prisoners started to breathe a bit more easily. Maybe the Germans had given up attempting to move 10,000 prisoners. However, one night at the end of January 1945, the message came. They would start to march. The British colonel protested wildly and said that moving so many prisoners in such harsh temperatures was madness. The Germans did not listen. The only thing he managed to secure was another thirty minutes to get ready. Finn and the rest of the prisoners got ready as best as they could before they were to march out. They each got a packet from the Red Cross at the gate. The smart ones had brought their cigarettes with them, trading them in for bread. The very best exchange that Finn heard of during that time was that an American traded twenty cigarettes and a box of cheese for a horse and a sledge.

The prisoners walked 80 kilometres in one week in the bitter cold. The morale was high even in these tough conditions, as they believed the Russians would eventually catch up with them. Finally arriving in the town of Spremberg, they were all taken on board a train to Luckenvalde, about 50 kilometres south of Berlin. In Luckenvalde, the Germans had a camp with about 15,000 to 20,000 prisoners of all nationalities. They arrived there late in the afternoon. When Finn woke up the next morning, he was shocked to hear that there were 1,500 Norwegian officers close by, among them General Otto Ruge. The General made arrangements with the German for having the newly arrived Norwegians brought over to their part of the camp, including Finn. The time in Luckenvalde was unpleasant, and there was very little to eat. The only glimmer of light was the news they got daily. The war was going in the right direction.

As spring arrived, things were looking up for Finn. It was of interest to know who would arrive first: the Americans, the British or the Russians. Finn heard artillery fire in the distance, so the front was not far away. It came from the south-east, so they expected it to be the Russians. One morning, they had the regular count of the prisoners. Afterwards, the German commandant simply left with a group of German guards, leaving some guards behind to keep an eye on the prisoners. When these poor men were not relieved as normal, they understood they had been left behind, and became both confused and frustrated. One guard sold his gun to a prisoner for ten cigarettes, and then he disappeared. Quickly thereafter, all the guards disappeared, and the prisoners were left to take care of themselves. The leaders of the prisoners were now General Ruge, a British colonel and an American colonel. The prisoners hung up white sheets all over the camp. Twenty-four hours later, the Russians arrived. It was 21 April 1945. Finn Eriksrud was free man once again.

Finn Eriksrud died in 2004 in Oslo.

CHAPTER 7

Arne Austeen

Arne Austeen was born 1 July 1911 in Vestfold, Norway. His parents were Johan Gustaf and Ragnhild Austeen. In all, the Austeen family had six children. Hans, Ellen, Maia, Kirsten, Ragnhild and Arne. Johan, Arne's dad, was well known amongst the local population of Vestfold as the headmaster of a famous agricultural college at Fosnes. He was later elected for government positions in two periods, and was also the administrator of another well known farming college at Ås, just south of Oslo.

As a young man, Arne started his university education at Norges Tekniske Høgskole (NTH, Norwegian Institute of Technology) in Trondheim. His friends from his time there remember Arne as a solid character with a bright and open mind.

It was later said that Arne always reacted harshly to injustice. He spoke his mind with no thought for his own advantage, nor for what people would think of him. Everything came from his heart, and nowhere else. He was also seen as a kind and happy person who created a lot of fun around himself. When he was still at university, he went with his friends on long summer night-trips to a cabin used exclusively by the students of NTH. After the war, his friends from the university still remembered these trips vividly. Arne was also a master on skis, and his friends spoke particularly about his 'crazy ski trips'. What they meant by this is not known, but it may have included ski jumping, downhill slalom and many other daring skiing adventures.

Perhaps the most interesting character trait that his friends talked about was that he was a real Norwegian patriot. He loved Norway and everything Norwegian. This, and his honest heart, would later earn him an important place in Norwegian military history. Arne Austeen was well educated, an individualist, and a bit of a daredevil. He was perhaps an ideal fit for a fighter pilot.

Arne graduated from NTH as an engineer. Already with a burning passion for aviation, in 1932, he applied to and was accepted at Hærens Flyskole (Army Flying School) at Kjeller, the birthplace of Norwegian aviation just outside Oslo, and earned his wings there. He seemed sure of what he wanted

Left: Arne Austeen, newly graduated from Norway's military air force. (*FMU*)

Below: Arne Austeen at work at Øveraasen in Gjøvik. (*Sverre Anthonisen*)

to do with his military service. After graduating and finishing his year of military service, he got a job at the Øveraasen Motorfabrikk engine factory and mechanical workshop in the little town of Gjøvik, Norway.

The factory is still there, equipping airports, road authorities and railways with gigantic snow removal machinery. Gjøvik is located on the shores of the biggest lake in Norway, Mjøsa – today, a two-hour drive north from Oslo. In Gjøvik, Arne met a girl named Ruth Asla. They started dating and after some time, they got engaged to be married. Ruth came from Hamar, a town on the other side of the lake. She was a trained hairdresser and opened her own hair salon in Gjøvik in the 1930s. From 1934 to 1935 Arne participated in Winter military exercises and in 1936, he completed the 'Speiderkurset' scouting course for Norwegian Army pilots.

When not working at Øveraasen, Arne spent time at Gjøvik's local flying club and became a flight instructor of civilians who were keen to get an introduction to flying. Rolf Hvalby wrote in one of the flying clubs anniversary publications:

It was vital that we found an instructor so that we could start learning. Again, we were lucky. We had one in our ranks. Arne Austeen had moved to Gjøvik in 1938 as an engineer at Øveraasens Motorfabrikk. He was trained as a military pilot, and was more than willing to take on the job of being an instructor. First, he had to attend a short exercise at Steinsfjorden by Hønefoss (1939). With his aviation background, he had no trouble getting approved as an instructor. During Easter of 1940, Arne decided that some of us were ready to fly solo. We were dragged up to 150 meters [in a glider], then released to fly straight on. You needed to reach 30 meters to pass the A-test. All of the students got through this with no trouble. In Gjøvik in those days, opportunities for flying were few and far between, and still exotic for most people. During the Winters, the club used the frozen lake as a runway for their glider.

The flying club, too, is still there, with their own small runway up in the hills of Reinsvoll.

Arne spent most, if not all, of his free time involved in aviation or with Ruth. His friends from Gjøvik flying club talked of Arne as a fair person with a lot of courage and a strong will to fight for a Norwegian and Allied victory over Germany. People who knew Arne at different stages of his life spoke of him using much the same language and vocabulary – as a strong, solid and patriotic character.

When Germany invaded Norway, Arne had been a member of Norway's defence force, guarding its neutrality, as had many other pilots from Kjeller before the War. He was registered as a combatant at Elverum, Norway, only

Airborne in the glider over lake Mjosa in Norway, winter of 1940. (*Erland Hvalby*)

Arne in the glider, getting himself ready for a flight. (*Erland Hvalby*)

Arne Austeen here in white overalls instructs a new pilot ready to take his glider up over lake Mjosa, winter of 1940. (*Erland Hvalby*)

a day after the invasion. On the day of the invasion, Arne was out on lake Mjøsa, anticipating a day of flying. He did not know there was a war on. Hvalby continued:

Frode Jahr and yours truly had three B-tests again, and it was decided that we would take these tests before we went to work on the 9 April. We left around seven in the morning and, on our way down to the pier, we met journalist Helge Waale. He told us that Germany had attacked Norway, and that fighting was already taking place in the Oslofjord. We went down to the pier anyway. Arne Austeen came just after us, but he had not heard anything about the war. Arne, a lieutenant in the Army Air Force, had to leave for Kjeller for mobilization as soon as possible. He decided that we would still finish the tests we had started. It was over quickly, and both of us qualified before we left for work that mornin. Before Arne went back home to change into his uniform and leave for the War, he told us that we had to move LN-GAN [their glider] to a safe place.

Arne with two of his sisters. (*Sverre Anthonisen*)

As a patriot and as a trained serviceman, Arne was needed for the struggle ahead. He did not hesitate to do his part for Norway in the fight against Nazi-Germany. He took part in the fighting in Norway until the Norwegian capitulation in June 1940.

In the winter of 1941, Arne escaped occupied Norway. He could no longer stand back and watch the injustice that Germany inflicted upon Norway and across Europe. He felt strongly that he could do more for Norway's cause from outside the country. Later on, the collaborating Norwegian government would cancel Arne's Norwegian citizenship as punishment for his escape.

Arne escaped to Sweden, like many other Norwegians who had the same plan in mind: to fight for freedom. He travelled to Stockholm and to the Norwegian embassy where he got the necessary help for further travel through Finland and Russia. As someone with a military background and valuable flying experience, he was given priority. From Moscow, he took the Trans-Siberian railway, and reached Vladivostok, where he wandered around in the harbour area looking for a chance to board a boat bound for the USA. It was not uncommon for young Norwegian men to be either in Vladivostok or Japan at that time, looking for a way across the Pacific, sometimes staying for months to find the right boat with someone willing to bring them over the vast Pacific Ocean.

Amazingly, Arne met an old friend from when he lived at the agricultural college at Fosnes with his mother and father. The skipper of a Norwegian Wilhelmsen boat, Hans Akselsen, was a former neighbour of the college and was greatly surprised to recognise Arne. Akselsen understood what Arne was trying to do, and invited him to come onboard. Arne then worked his way over to the USA, performing small tasks on the boat so that could contribute during the voyage. After he arrived in the USA, Arne travelled up to Canada and to Toronto where the 'Little Norway' Air Force training camp was located. It had been a long and hard journey, but he made it.

In August 1941, Austeen left Toronto for Halifax and further travel to the

United Kingdom for active duty as a fighter pilot. During his time at Little Norway, Arne was close friends with fellow pilots Olav Ullestad and Eiliv Strømme, both acquaintances since their time at Kjeller. The friends were known to many as 'The Three Musketeers', due to their somewhat wild behaviour. They also had a taste for practical jokes, and were often found cooking something or other. Fellow pilots later said that it was the oldest of them that did the planning, which the other two executed with great willingness.

Arne was the oldest of the three, and was probably the mastermind behind these practical jokes, in much the same way his friends from NTH spoke of him. During the goodbye party at the Royal York Hotel in Toronto, the Musketeers saw fit to have some good, old-fashioned fun. According to Kristian Nyerrød, who became a pilot with 331 Squadron, the Musketeers emptied a champagne cooler over the head of a Norwegian Lieutenant, who had spoken proudly of his adventures on 9 April 1940 when he shot down a German bomber. This unlucky fellow was more than likely Rolf Torbjørn Tradin, later killed in action with 611 Squadron. The Musketeers were good fun, but not everyone enjoyed their antics.

Before the night of departure from Halifax, the boys had a night out on town. Tarald Weisteen travelled together with Arne Austeen and several other Norwegian pilots. In 2004, he wrote the following about their journey in his book, *Nattjager* (Nightfighter):

In the harbour, a 22,000-ton passenger ship waited for us. It was so old it was rumoured that it would be scrapped as soon as it arrived in the UK. We boarded the ship but stayed in the harbour for several days. The real date for departure to England was strictly top secret. There was an excessive number of soldiers onboard, and there were queues everywhere. Canadians were in the majority. Then, one day, we left Halifax. The day we boarded, I had noticed that the captain was heavily intoxicated. When we finally left, he seemed, thankfully, to be sober. The commander of the convoy was onboard our ship. All in all, there were 64 ships in the convoy now heading out into the Atlantic, with the danger of the German submarines. The convoy that had left before us had suffered horrible casualties. Almost half of the ships had been sunk. We, on the other hand, were lucky. As far as I can recall, we lost none of the boats even though the alarm went off three times during the sixteen-day journey. The convoy also changed its course three or four times. On two occasions, depth charges were released from escorting ships. Our ship had depth charges as well, and sometimes we increased speed and zig-zagged in front of the other ships. Overall, we had a quiet journey. The sea was also quite calm in August. We sailed into the port of Liverpool during the first days of September. A Norwegian from our Air Force greeted us, and led us to the railway station where we took a train down to London. It is possible we spent the first night at the County Hotel. After that, we stayed at the Gloucester Hotel.[1]

On the same ship as Austeen were also pilots Bjørn Næss and Kristian Nyerrød. Bjørn Næss, from Elverum Norway, joined a Halifax squadron and was attacked by a Messerschmitt Bf110 nightfighter over the north sea in 1943. The Halifax was never seen again. Kristian Nyerrød had a long and highly successful career, flying Spitfires with 331 Squadron and Mustangs. He survived the war. Another practical joke was played out by the Three Musketeers on their voyage to the UK; Austeen, as an officer, was placed in charge of the group of travelling Norwegians.

Lower-ranked Kristian Nyerrød was ordered bring their backpacks up from storage for an official inspection. To reach them, he needed to move a considerable amount of equipment around. While hard at work, Nyerrød got frustrated at this obviously futile task and remarked that he knew it was all done just for pointless fun. The frustrated comment was noticed by one of the Musketeers, and Nyerrød would later pay for it. When he had finally completed his task, and had brought the backpacks up to the deck for inspection, he was told to put everything back the way it was. Onlookers had plenty of fun, but Nyerrød was not very amused.

According to Tarald Weisteen, Austeen was the most steady of the Three Musketeers, and was someone to be trusted. Unfortunately, only one of three would survive the war. Olav Ullestad, besides his somewhat wild and drunken behaviour, was a charming and handsome young man, around whom girls flocked. He ended his war service with 80 Squadron flying Hawker Tempests, as one of very few Norwegians to fly the glorious Hawker product. He also had a spell with Alex Henshaw as a test pilot. He was simply called 'Ullis' among friends, and had been a boxer before the war, hence his skill at fist fighting. Olav Ullestad would be shot down on 1 March 1945 and captured by the Germans. He said his arm got stuck when he was about to bail out and joked that it became 'as long as his mess bill'.

In London, things didn't move as quickly as Austeen and his friends would have liked. They stayed in the English capital with nothing much to do for a frustratingly long time before finally being sent to an Operational Training Unit (OTU). After the long wait, Arne was sent, on the 7 October 1941, to Aston Down to train on Hurricanes. Tarald Weisteen was with Arne and wrote;

> It took a month before I was sent further through the system, to Number 52 Operational Training Unit. I arrived there on the 7 October. I would finally complete the last couple of tests on the British training course before I was

sent to an active squadron. The first thing we pupils were ordered to do was to sit firmly on the ground with ear phones and listen to British air traffic conversations. It was important for us to learn key expressions so we could receive instructions and reply, listening to what was going on around us while we flew. It wasn't until 12 October that I took a Miles Master up. Two days later, I got to fly a Hawker Hurricane for the first time.[2]

Tarald Weisteen finished his training in November of 1942, and was sent to 331 Squadron at Skeabrea. In a group picture from Aston Down, Tarald Weisteen is actually sitting next to Arne Austeen. Arne finished his training at the same time. At Aston Down, the group of young Norwegians flew old and worn-out Hurricanes. One day, a Hurricane came in with fabric flapping in the wind. On another occasion, a Norwegian landed a Hurricane with thick, black smoke pouring out of the engine. Frightened by the dangerous amount of smoke, the Norwegian jumped out as soon as it was safely down on terra firma. But he was a bit too quick to exit as the Hurricane had not yet come to a complete stop. He fell off the wing and got a concussion.

Finally, the training was over. The Norwegians decided to invite Aston Down's station commander to a farewell party, together with all of their British instructors. They all gathered in a local pub in the evening. The oldest of the Norwegians, Hertzberg, was in charge of the party. The Norwegians served their British friends Aquavit and beer alongside their meal. Hertzberg made well-performed speeches, and arranged for games to take place after the dinner was over. The drinking had its effect on most of them by then, and they decided to take the party over to the officers' mess. More alcohol was served, more games were organised. However, some of the games took on a violent aspect, and some of the mess furniture did not survive the night. Some of the participants did not make it unscathed either. One young Norwegian pilot fell against a hot oven and got blisters all over his hands. A strong, tall Norwegian was a little too rough with an English officer and the poor Brit broke a collar bone. Another Norwegian sprained his ankle. It was also time for Austeen and Ullestad to get their revenge on Nyerrød for his comments during the journey over to Britain. A drunken Ullis had not forgotten his old boxing skill, and hit Nyerrød with a solid upper-cut. Nyerrød crashed into the wall and saw stars in his eyes. He got away with no real injuries, but Ullestad was not ready to set aside his fighting abilities so soon. Another Norwegian, Søren Liby, had to stop him from causing serious damage to poor Nyerrød.

The next morning, a queue developed outside the doctor's office. Station Commander Grandy took full responsibility for the wild party, and the Norwegians heard no more about it. They arrived in London late the same afternoon. For dinner, they went to the smartest hotel they could find, and ordered anything that looked remotely good. In Canada, food had been mediocre, and now it was time to make up for lost time food-wise. Austeen and company looked like they had just come from some exotic battlefield. Many of them had bandages, Nyerrød had a big bruise on his forehead and several were limping around. When they asked to pay for their fancy meal, they were told that it had already been taken care of. Someone obviously thought that they had just arrived back in London after surviving a terrible battle somewhere.

From Aston Down, Arne was sent to 124 Squadron at Biggin Hill, and spent Christmas there. With him was Olav Ullestad. Both of them were then sent back to the Norwegians early in 1942 when 332 Squadron was being formed at Catterick. They both stayed with 332 for a short time, leaving almost as soon as the Squadron was officially formed on 19 March 1942. They had arrived on the 5 February but left again on 30 March to join 64 Squadron. Austeen did manage to fit in a few official sorties with 332 Squadron and the 23 March was an eventful day. Austeen was scrambled with Arve Aas. Unknown intruders had been observed 12 miles east of Scarborough. Aas and Austeen broke off from their normal routine flying and commenced a hunt for the unidentified aircraft. Ground control spread them out to cover a greater area, but neither of them found anything out of the ordinary, and they both landed back at Catterick disappointed. Also on 23 March, Nils Ringdal had a hairy moment when his engine cut during a mock dogfight. From the Operational Record Book:

> Sergeant Ringdal had a rather exciting experience today. At 1500 hours on his way back from a practice flight, his engine cut out and failed to pick up again. As he lowered his under-carriage, the aircraft lost speed, and he made a heavy landing on the aerodrome. Aircraft category AC but the pilot was uninjured.

As well as the Austeen and Aas scramble, there was another scramble in the evening but, yet again, the pilots of 332 Squadron had to land back at base with nothing to report.

For Arne, it was time to move on to 64 Squadron as a Captain, and he took Ullis with him. The Squadron had several Norwegians in their ranks from 1942 to 1943. In June of 1942, they were joined by the third of the Three Musketeers, Eiliv Strømme. The Musketeers were finally reunited in the same squadron. Ullestad and Arne stayed together until August when Ullis was transferred to 331 Squadron at North Weald. Interestingly, Tarald Weisteen later saw a Spitfire named 'Ullis' while he was at 85 Squadron flying Mosquitos. A Spitfire squadron stationed at West Malling later received some of 331 Squadron's old Spitfires, the ones that Ullestad had flown.

Not long after his arrival at 64 Squadron, Arne Austeen found himself in

Arne Austeen with 64 Squadron in 1942. Arne is third from the left, front row. (*Sverre Anthonisen*)

combat with German Focke Wulf Fw190s. On 30 July 1942, he was flying as number two to Squadron Leader Wilfrid Duncan-Smith (later Wing Commander in charge of 331 and 332 Squadrons at North Weald). Strømme and Ullestad also participated in the sortie. On their way back to England, Austeen spotted a dogfight about 4,000 feet below them. He made Duncan-Smith aware and they both dived down towards the fight. Smith picked out a 190, which was on his way back to France, and fired on him. Arne followed Smith while keeping an look-out behind for enemy fighters. After Smith was done firing, Austeen observed thick, white smoke gushing out of the engine of the 190. Arne manoeuvred himself into firing position behind the damaged enemy and fired a two-second burst. The white smoke changed colour to black with flames starting to pour out of it. As Austeen pulled away from the 190, he saw the German lose control of his plane before it span downwards. Smith and Austeen claimed the 190 as a shared. Smith on the other hand, claimed another 190, as did pilots Steward and Donnet. Both of the other two Norwegians fired short bursts, but were unable to claim anything owing to lack of camera guns.

No. 64 Squadron took part in the ill-fated Dieppe Raid in August of 1942. Austeen's day started at 0615 when the Squadron was called to readiness to cover other squadrons back in England for refuelling. A few hours later, Arne and 64 Squadron escorted twenty-four Flying Fortresses with 401, 402 and 611 Squadrons to bomb Abbeville Aerodrome. The mission was a success and most of the bombs hit their target. Everyone returned safely at 1100 hours. One hour later, Arne took off for another sortie, now covering shipping withdrawals. The Squadron found action and attacked several Dornier 217s. Messerschmitt 109s were also in the area and Tommy Thomas shot one down. Don Kingaby claimed a Do217, but could not get it confirmed. Stømme also flew with the Squadron. They landed at Hawkinge on their way back. Austeen had a quick lunch in dispersal, and took off again close to 1500 hours to protect more returning shipping. This time they ran into more Dorniers coming from the Le Touquet area. Tommy Thomas claimed a Fw190 shot down, which was confirmed. Donnet, Austeen, Rogers and Barnard all fired bursts at the Dorniers but none of them saw any results.

Duncan-Smith and Austeen then attacked another Dornier bomber. According to Duncan-Smith, the pilot of the Dornier must have been a former fighter pilot, as the German handled the bomber amazingly well. While Duncan-Smith fired at the bomber, with Austeen sticking tightly to his tail, the German gunners suddenly got in a lucky shot at Duncan-Smith. The engine of his Spitfire caught fire and he had to bail out. When he pulled back the hood to get out of the plane, his face was instantly hit by a stream of oil from his engine. Luckily, Duncan-Smith managed to bail out and he landed safely in the channel. Austeen saw him land in the sea and reported his position. Fortunately, it didn't take more than thirty minutes before a Royal Navy vessel, on its way back to England, spotted the Englishman in the Channel and picked him up. Duncan-Smith hardly had time to get wet compared with some. He wrote, in his book, *Spitfire Into Battle*:

My number two, Arne Austeen, flew past rocking his wings. On reaching the sea, I released my parachute too high off the water, and went into it head first. As a result, my legs got caught in the shroud lines and I had quite a job freeing myself with the aid of a knife attached to my Mae West. In all the mix up, somehow my rubber dingy attached to the parachute seat, came adrift and I lost it. Bobbing about on the swell like a cork, I searched frantically but it was nowhere to be seen. After only a few minutes, the chill of the English Channel seeped through my uniform to my bones. If I was not picked up soon I was going to be in trouble. Dimly, I could see the coastline in the distance. "It must be France", I thought. Except for the swish of the wind and the occasional sound of a breaking wave, I couldn't hear anything definite.

After about half an hour's suspense, I heard the deep-throated throb of engines. I was chattering now with cold, my thoughts tumbling through my head one upon the other. The noise I heard connected somehow in my brain with an ocean liner. What was an ocean liner doing here? I still could not see anything but the distant shoreline and the water. Overhead, the clouds had closed in, scudding darkly across my line of vision.

The throbbing note of engines got louder – I swung round in the direction of the noise and saw the low silhouette of a motor launch approaching. I waved and shouted. Cutting a wide arc with the high stern wave kicking up foam, it circled in my direction. For a horrid moment, I thought it might have been a German boat, particularly so close to France. Actually, I found out later I was about four miles off the Somme Estuary.[3]

The rescue boat gave Duncan-Smith plenty of whisky, and told him his Dornier had crashed into the sea about two miles away. No. 64 Squadron did not escape the day without losses. Sergeant McCauig was lost, and they were later told he was buried at sea. Another 64 Squadron pilot, Stewart, was leading Blue section as Don Kingaby had to return early owing to engine trouble. Michael Donnet heard Stewart call out on the radio saying, 'Be careful! You're firing at me!' That was the last they heard of Stewart, and he did not return. However, the Hornchurch total score was 10 destroyed, 1 probable and 14 damaged; perhaps a bit optimistic. Duncan-Smith was promoted the next day, now taking over the Norwegians at North Weald as a Wing Commander.

On the 29 August, Arne Austeen rendezvoused with twelve Flying Fortresses in the fine but slightly cloudy sky. Their goal was Courtrai. Following the Americans as escort, the bombs seemed to hit the target, and they set course for home. Then the Focke Wulf Fw190s came in. Arne Austeen and his wingman, Rogers, were suddenly jumped by ten enemy fighters. A nightmarish situation was upon the two pilots, trying to evade five times the number of fighters to their own. Apparently separated from the rest of the Squadron, Austeen and Rogers fought for survival to the best of their ability. Back at Hornchurch, the ground crew looked on as Austeen came back alone. His Spitfire had bullet holes in its undercarriage. Rogers landed at Manston, barely getting back over the Channel. He had a bullet in his arm, and his Spitfire was a complete write-off. A shaky Arne Austeen was released off camp in the evening and Duncan-Smith was a popular appearance in the bar that night.

On the first day of September 1942, Arne and Strømme went on patrol over Canterbury. The sortie was uneventful, but was an example of how close the Three Musketeers were able to remain for large parts of the war. They spent much time together in the air, and on the ground. On the 5 September, the Squadron escorted thirty-six Flying Fortresses to the marshalling yards at Rouen. Over the French coast, they were jumped by a group of Fw190s, and the Squadron lost two pilots. One was picked up in the Channel the next day, still alive. Duncan-Smith and Austeen flew together a lot in 64 Squadron. Duncan-Smith was later spoken of as one of the best Spitfire pilots of the war. No doubt, Arne Austeen learned a lot from this famous Battle of Britain veteran.

A less hair-raising incident happened on the 8 September when the Squadron was out experimenting with how long drop tanks lasted. They found out they had enough fuel to last an extra 35 minutes. When they landed, Arne burst his left tire. It was noted, with some frustration, that it was the fourth tire burst in a week. Austeen was not injured. The next day, Eiliv Strømme and his wingman, Michael Donnet, were vectored onto two Fw190s over Benck Sur Mer. They chased the two Germans for 10 minutes before they lost them in the haze. They found another pair of 190s in the area, and Strømme went in for the attack, loosing Donnet in the process. When Strømme was about to fire, suddenly six more 190s appeared, all shooting at him simultaneously. Luckily for Strømme, Donnet reappeared and managed to confuse the Germans enough to buy the two Spitfire pilots some precious time. They ran for their lives barely managing to keep the Germans at a safe distance. They landed back at base, very happy to be alive.

A few days later, Austeen and Strømme said their goodbyes to their friend as Ullestad was transferred back to the Norwegians of 331 Squadron at North Weald. The Three Musketeers were parted once again, and this time for good. Eiliv Strømme would loose his life on 11 October. The weather was lovely, and the squadron went on a 'Rodeo' – a sweep over enemy territory. A considerable number of Spitfires had to return due to problems jettisoning their tanks. With only four Spitfires from the Squadron left, four Fw190s went in for the attack. Strømme was bounced and hit. He was last seen lifeless in the cockpit of his Spitfire V.

Olav Ullestad, Strømmes closest friend together with Austeen, flew on the same mission but with 331 Squadron. It was a devastating blow to Ullis when he heard that his close friend had died on the same sortie that he himself had taken part in. Pilot Officer Dowler also went missing, which meant that 64 Squadron had lost another two men. There would never again be a practical joke carried out by the Three Musketeers.

Three days later, Wing Commander Duncan-Smith re-appeared, and this time he had brought two Norwegians from 331 and 332 Squadrons with him: Wilhelm Mohr and Rolf Arne Berg. No. 64 Squadron still had several Norwegian pilots in their ranks, and Duncan-Smith kept them all well entertained until midnight, partying in the officers' mess.

On the last day of October, Austeen and Pilot Officer Patterson patrolled Dungeness when a big formation of German bombers came over to bomb Folkestone. The ground controller gave them several vectors, but never told them which area was actually being attacked. Austeen and Patterson were frustrated about not getting the formation, but not for long. Suddenly, they came across two 190s, which came out of a cloud and tried to bounce them. In the corner of his eye, Austeen saw Patterson escape into a cloud with tracers flying everywhere, and Arne came to the conclusion that his wingman had most likely 'bought' it. Arne shook off the attackers and came in to land at Manston. Much to his surprise, Patterson came in unhurt, and they both stayed at the airfield over night. The Squadron had stayed at Fairlop in October, and moved back to Hornchurch the next month.

November and December 1942 brought bad weather, sometimes with strong wind. No. 64 Squadron spent their time at Hornchurch, but also stayed at Redneck airfield in Cornwall for several days, including the Christmas period. On 24 December, Christmas Eve parties were in full swing by the afternoon. For Norwegians, Christmas Eve is the most important and special day of Christmas, and not the 25th as with the British. A beautifully quiet Christmas Day followed, and the Squadron kept a section at readiness. All pilots attended a lunch in the airmen's mess and, afterwards, most of the Squadron pilots went for walks on the cliffs or on the beach. Flying Officer Houlton even went for a swim. Christmas dinner was held for the officers, followed by a dance. The next days were quiet and calm except for a scramble to lead in a Mitchell which was shepherding a flock of Airacobras who were lost over Exeter.

Arne's time with 64 Squadron was coming to an end. He had been with them for almost a year. On the last day of 1942, he was posted to North Weald as instructor on tactics. He was also promoted to Major. His posting would mean he would be very close to the two Norwegian squadrons operating from the airfield. He would stay there as an instructor for eight months before going back to active duty.

Next stop for Arne was the legendary 611 Squadron as a Flight Commander. Arne arrived at the now very familiar Hornchurch on 9 August 1943. He was not the first Norwegian to fly with the squadron, as Rolf Torbjørn Tradin had been with them up until his death in May 1943. Tradin had attacked a 190 but did not manage to pull up in time. Both the 190 and Tradin went into the sea. Austeen and Tradin had of course, crossed paths before, certainly in Canada before departing for Britain. Jon Tvedte, another Norwegian pilot and a friend of Tradin, later wrote a book about the Spitfire in a novel-like style, telling a story about a Norwegian pilot named Rolf Steen who flew with 611 Squadron. Jon Tvedte too, flew with 611 in 1943, and was a first hand witness to life at the squadron. Obviously, Tvedte wrote the story in dedication to and remembrance of his good friend Tradin. An extract from the book is worth quoting, given how similar Austeen's experience was.

"0730, sir. Your tea, sir,"

The batman touched Rolf slightly to wake him up. He walked around and made chit-chat to get the boys to wake up, and not close their eyes again.

"You're Norwegian, sir. Glad you got out of the country? Would you like your buttons polished, sir?"

"No! Take it easy. Don't use your cloth on them. They are Norwegian oxidised buttons."

The batman was more than pleased.

"Okay sir. Saves me plenty of work."

He walked away with Rolf's shoes to give them some attention.

The atmosphere in dispersal was intense. A message had come from the control room about several 'tip and run' attacks on the coastal towns down south. The enemy fighters had come over the Channel just above sea level, swept over the towns and released their load before disappearing again. There were no point in the attacks other than to create panic. One flight was put on standby. The pilots were strapped into their cockpits, ready to go up. Rolf could see them in profile through the crystal clear hoods. Most of them sat there with a magazine or a newspaper and seemed to be quite relaxed.

Suddenly, a roar came through the speakers;

"611 A-flight scramble!"

At the same moment, the siren went off at full strength. The ground crew ran to the starting batteries. Six propellers started to turn slowly. The engines fired up, one by one. Starting batteries were disconnected. The Spitfires rolled a few meters forward to get a clear line down the aerodrome. The noise of the engines increased in volume. Off they went. Seconds later, the six aircraft were just dots, high up, turning south.[4]

Arne Austeen's first mission with 611 took place on 14 August 1943 when the Squadron was escorting thirty-three Beaufighters to the coast of Holland for an attack on a German convoy. The convoy was not found and Austeen landed at Coltishall at 1315 hours.

On 16 August, 611 Squadron were escorting thirty-six Marauders to Bernay in France. Wing Commander 'Laddie' Lucas was in charge of 611 Squadron on this sortie. The bombers hit their targets on the ground and several fuel-depots started to burn. Just as the Marauders were turning towards England, 15 Focke Wulf Fw190s showed up and attacked the bomber force. No. 611 Squadron reacted instantly. Lucas shot down a 190 while Arne got behind one of the other 190s, and fired both his cannons and his machine guns. Hits were observed, but no one saw the German plunge into the ground. Disappointingly, Arne had to settle for a 'damaged'. The entire squadron landed at Hornchurch with no losses.

Austeen continued to fly with 611 Squadron during the late summer of

1943. Arne was usually the leader of white section and flew as 'White 1'. He also led the Squadron on several occasions.

The 18 September was a day full of action for Arne and 611. Their mission consisted of escorting twenty-four Beaufighters to Holland. The Beaufighters would attack several German minesweepers not far off the coastal town of Texel. The torpedoes launched did great damage to two of the minesweepers and they managed to sink a third. Arne, as 'Black One' for the day, was in charge of A-section. They spotted a Messerschmitt Bf109 in the area and chased him down. Arne got into firing position and fired short bursts at the German. Unfortunately, Arne was unable to see what happened to the enemy. Luckily, it was later reported by a Beaufighter pilot that a German went into the sea outside of Texel. The observations by the Beaufighter pilot matched those of Arne's.

I was leading Black section at 800 feet when we followed the Beaufighters down towards the minesweepers outside the coast. When we passed target number one, I saw to Me.109E come down towards us from a southerly direction. I turned hard right to cover the attacking Beaufighters. Then I saw two new Me.109E dive towards the Beaufighters from a northerly direction. I dived after them and they aborted their attack. I then followed the closest of them who turned left and dives eastwards. I managed to close to 500 yards and then fired a two and a three-second burst at 400 yards, but observed no results. The enemy had clipped wings and I think this was a Me.109E. A Beaufighter pilot, Fg. Off. Ellsworth of 254 Squadron, reported later that he saw a section of Spitfires close in on the 109's who attacked the Beaufighters. Seconds later one of the flicked over on its back and dived straight into the sea from 300 feet.

I claim this Me.109 as destroyed.

Arne took over the command of the Norwegian 331 Squadron in late September. He was now Squadron Leader. Since the ill-fated Dieppe raid in August of 1942, the German presence in the air had been less frequent, and met the Germans in dogfights less often. The Germans had suffered great losses they had not been fully able to replace, and several of their squadrons had also been sent to the Eastern Front.

Arne received Spitfire Mk IX MH828 as his personal aircraft. MH828 survived the entire War and was sold as scrap in the summer of 1950. Just a few days after his arrival, Arne led 331 on a mission for the first time. The Squadron was sent down to Halesworth to escort B-26 Marauders to France. Enemy planes were spotted and attempted to attack from an advantageous angle, but the attack was not a success due to too many Spitfires being in the area. In fact, the other Spitfires were more of a hindrance than a help to 331

Squadron in repelling the attack. After one and a half hours in the air, 331 Squadron landed at North Weald at 1230 hours. Svein Heglund claimed a 109 destroyed, and Arne reported that he did see a German aircraft being shot down at the same height and place as Heglund reported.

October 1943 would be one of the last months of the war where the Norwegians met heavy German resistance in the air. After a rather dull start to October, 331 got into the thick of it with German fighters between the 20th and 30th of that month.

Arne led the squadron on the 20th over St Quentin at 32,000 feet. There were reports of enemies to the south. Two boxes of enemy aircraft were then spotted by 331. Most of the Germans broke away to starboard when they saw the Spitfires, while a few of them turned to port. Arne picked out the last German in line of the group who turned to port, and fired at 500 yards. He saw no results, and got in closer before he fired again. He saw several hits on one of the wings and around the cockpit area. Several big pieces fell off the plane before it flicked over and spun downwards. The pilot of the enemy plane was observed jumping out by Lt. Fearnley of 331. Arne claimed the plane as destroyed.

Just two days later, he was back in action with 331. Arne was leading Blue Section on this occasion, and they were at 26,000 feet when they spotted twenty-five German planes below them, heading west. Austeen gave the order to dive down on the Germans. He picked out the closest aircraft, but changed his mind when he saw that Red Section was heading for the same targets. Arne attacked the middle of the formation instead. He fired cannons and machine guns at 300 yards, and didn't stop until he was at 100 yards. Suddenly the enemy plane exploded and its undercarriage dropped down. To avoid a collision, Arne pulled hard to starboard. The enemy fell downwards in a ball of fire.

Just after pulling out of the near-collision, Arne saw eight 190s straight ahead, descending slightly. He gave chase and followed the Germans down when four of them broke off to the left and the rest to the right. Arne picked out one of them and fired. He shot from a great distance, but struck the 190 anyway, and saw several hits just behind the cockpit area. Going in closer, he opened fire again and, this time, the engine started to burn before the enemy simply fell out of the sky. In just a few days, Arne Austeen had shot down three enemy fighters.

Two days later, on 24 October, Austeen was in action once again. Together with 332 Squadron they passed four Bf109s at great speed. Arne threw his Spitfire after the 109s but, due to their high speed, he couldn't catch up. He broke off the attack. On his way back to rejoin 331 he was suddenly on a head-on course with two 109s. After barely avoiding a collision, he managed to sneak up on one of them. He fired at 400 yards and kept firing until closing to 100 yards. The 109 received several hits and started to spin. It went down into the sea with flames streaming from its engine Arne and his number two, Sergeant Nilssen, again tried to get back to the rest of the Squadron but, again, they ran into enemy fighters. This time, several 190s dived on them. Arne attacked two of them. He saw several hits but was not able to see the result of his attack. After landing at base, he claimed two damaged and one destroyed. In only five days, Arne had shot down four enemy planes.

After these dogfights, there would be quieter times for Arne Austeen. November gave the Squadron a lot of bad weather with strong winds and less operational flying.

December brought much of the same for Austeen and 331 Squadron. The start of the month was troubled with bad weather and a lot of fog. During the middle of December, the weather improved, and Austeen took his boys up for formation flying practice and other training.

On Christmas Eve of 1943, 331 Squadron escorted bombers to the continent. They spotted the friendly bombers just south of Hastings and escorted them over France. They saw no Luftwaffe aircraft, and they were all back safely just before 1330.

The year 1944 started on a sad note. On 4 January, one of 331 Squadron's most experienced pilots, Bjørn Bjørnstad, collided with newcomer Stenstad in mid-air. Bjørnstad managed to bail out of his Spitfire while Stenstad was killed instantly. The rest of the Squadron, with Austeen leading, continued their mission towards the Somme-Abbeville area with no further problems.

On the 4 March, Austeen flew two missions with 331. Both missions were uneventful. The first took place between 0855 and 1025 hours. All returned safely. These would turn out to be some of the last tasks that Austeen would perform with 331 over enemy territory. The next day, 5 March, the Squadron flew down to RAF Southend for low-level attack practise with a small bomb attached to each Spitfire. Because of bad weather, the practise was reduced to three days and, on 13 March the Squadron returned to North Weald. Over the next few days, they were on exercise with the Canadian Army. Practise with the Canadians end on 20 March 1944.

Three days later, and Arne finished his operational tour with 331. The Squadron was taken over by Major Leif Lundsten from Eastern Toten in Norway. Amazingly, 331 Squadron was under the command of men from the same small local area of Norway for almost an entire year during the war.

Next stop for Arne was the Central Gunnery School in Yorkshire, as Chief Instructor. According to a later Squadron Leader of 331, Ragnar Isachsen, only the best of the best were selected for instructor duties at this particular school. You not only needed to be an excellent fighter pilot but you also needed a technical background, which Arne had.

Isachsen got to know Arne well at the Central Gunnery School, and he characterised Arne as a clear-thinking and fair-minded man. In the evenings

d overrekkelsen av
e Distinguished Flying Cross
18.mars 1944

Arne recieving his DFC at North Weald in 1944. (*Sverre Anthonisen*)

and on Sundays, Isachsen and Arne went on bike rides around idyllic English villages on the east coast. They spent many hours with the locals. Isachsen tells in a letter to Arne's sister, Ragnhild, that Arne had the greatest respect and admiration from his friends in the squadrons, including English friends, and also among his superiors. After this little 'holiday', Arne was ordered to Transport Command for delivery of aircraft from America to Great Britain.

Arne was back on active duty in February 1945. He took command of 126 Squadron, stationed at Bentwaters in Suffolk. The Squadron was flying Mustang Mk III fighters (as the P-51 B/C was known in the RAF), escorting bombers all the way to Germany and back. Arne participated in the famous Shell House raid in Copenhagen on 2 March 1945 – he flew escort for the Mosquitos. Careful planning was needed before the raid could take place, including large models of the city and the Gestapo building. The pilots had to study the surroundings down to the tiniest details. Intelligence said that the entire Gestapo staff in Denmark was located in the building. The raid was requested by the Danish Resistance. The Mosquitos took off in three waves of six at exactly 0900 hours, perfectly timed with when the Gestapo staff would

From the same day in 1944. From left to right: Kaj Birksted, Arne Austeen, Werner Christie, and Nils Jørstad. (*Sverre Anthonisen*)

be arriving at the headquarters. The journey to Copenhagen took two hours. The Mosquitos stayed low. In fact, they were so low that Wing Commander Kleboe struck a building and crashed into one of the city's boulevards.

Several of the other Mosquitos mistook his crash and the subsequent fire for the target, and attacked it instead of the building. Arne's Mustang squadron played a dual role in this attack. They not only escorted the Mosquitos outbound and on their return journey, but they also had the task of attacking flak positions in the area. However, the attack was such a surprise to the Germans that the flak batteries did not react before the Mosquitos turned for home. Four Mosquito bombers were lost, along with two Mustangs. Arne Austeen survived the raid, but fellow Norwegian Herman Becker, a navigator in one of the Mosquitos, lost his life in the attack. Herman Becker was young

Arne Austeen's Mustang III at Bentwaters in 1945. (*Erland Hvalby*)

man with Jewish background from the Stavanger area. His family had, by
then, perished in the concentration camps.

For a few more months, Austeen continued to escort bombers
to Germany. Now, it was just a matter of time before the Germans
surrendered, although a great number of missions still took place. The
Luftwaffe was almost completely beaten, and the danger of being shot down
came almost entirely from the ground.

On the 4 May 1945, only four days before the war would officially be over,
Arne flew a Mustang III, registration number KH578, on a mission to the
northern part of Germany. On this mission, Austeen and his Squadron would
accompany Beaufighters in attacking German U-boats in the Flensburgerfjord.
As Squadron Leader, Arne dived first towards the U-boats. This would make
the task easier for the rest of 126 Squadron, as most of the flak would be
directed towards Arne and not them. U-155 was under command of
Oberleutnant Friedrich Altmeier, and his anti-aircraft guns blazed at Arne
during his dived. U-155 hit Arne's Mustang.

The Mustang went down towards the sea with Arne still inside. With
little altitude left, there was not enough time for him to get out. No chute
was reported and Arne crashed into the sea. The Mustang went down at
coordinates 54'55N 10'07E. No trace has ever been found of either the plane
or of Arne Austeen – a tragic fate after surviving a whole four years as a fighter

pilot. German official records include a letter written in 1977 that describes the attack.

Dear Mr. Künzel,

Thank you very much for your letter from 5 July 1977. I read about the incidents you describe with great interest. Of course, it is unfortunate that your [photographs/pictures/images/film/celluloid/cinefilm] did not develop very well, but this may help for us to meet again "on board", as you suggested. Like you told me, you have sat at the same table as Großadmiral Dönitz. How did that happen? How is he getting along? Did you speak with him as well?

After our time in the dockyard, we were ordered to depart towards Kiel… In Kiel, we took on supplies…After the leader of the flotilla bade farewell, we cleared the port and headed for Flensburg. We stayed there for a few days and then received an order to sail for Norway.

In the bay of Gelting, some other boats were lying in wait. As far as I know, our group was assembled there, consisting of the boats *Altmeier*, *Niemeier* and ourselves. We sailed in with *Altmeier* leading, followed by *Niemeier* and then us. As far as I can remember, in the afternoon, we sighted aircraft. This could have been in the Kleine Belt area (Lillebælt), or maybe between the island of Alsen and the shore. It was a beautiful day and the sun was shining.

After the air raid alarms went off, all stations were manned quickly on board all boats. When the first aircraft turned in towards us, we knew the attack was coming. The aircraft targeted the boat in the middle and approached our group at low level. In the meantime, at least two more aircraft went into a low-level attack. The first aircraft strafed the boat *Altmeier* and all of us returned fire. The bullets splashed into the water and over the hull of the boat. To this day, I cannot understand how none of the crew were injured.

After the *Altmeier*'s tower, the aircraft overflew the boat and crashed into the water. All this happened within seconds and after the plane crash, the other aircraft turned away and climbed. They circled our position for a while at altitude and then they disappeared. To my knowledge, no bombs were dropped.

After nightfall *Altmeier*, *Niemeier* and I met for a short briefing. During our voyage, the order arrived: "Complete Stop. Take no further action. Await orders." At that time, we were offshore near Fredericia, and we destroyed some secret documents and the torpedo deflection aiming computer, and we destroyed the torpedoes by firing them at the shoreline where they detonated. This period is a dark shadow in my memory – we were dealing with so many things at the time. We had to take down the flag and we finally got the order to enter port at Fredericia. Everything else you will certainly remember yourself.

Dönitz certainly had a plan to reassemble the remaining U-Bootwaffe, (which surely sounds like a bit of a fantasy) to continue the U-Boat war from there, or (which seems more likely to me, although not very likely in the situation) to have a better diplomatic starting point for negotiations with the Allies. To my knowledge, setting course for Argentina has never been mentioned."

Those fairytales about Nazis and treasure seem to me to be wishful thinking, and the scuba divers to U-534 will be disappointed in this regard, as well. After the surrender, they came asking questions about Nazi officers on our boat, too. That was the belief of the Allies; but I myself never met such people on any of the U-Boats...

[Translated from German by Maik Lutterklas]

4 May 1945. The squadron operations record book tells a short and tragic story:

> The squadron led by Major Austeen set out to escort Beaufighters attacking shipping amongst the Danish Islands in which the Germans were desperately trying to escape to Norway. Whilst the Squadron was still away from base, having landed on the continent after the show, the news came through that Germany has given in Denmark, Holland and the remainder of NW Germany, so that this will probably be the last operation over the European continent by this Squadron. Occupied Norway and Czechoslovakia are the only big outposts of German resistance left.

> 5 May 1945. The squadron returned to base after landing at Luneburg where they spent the night after the operation on the day of the 4th. They brought back the melancholy news that our Squadron Commander, Major Austeen, had been shot down into the sea by a submarine while he was strafing it off the Flensburger fjord in the Little Belt. He had only been with the Squadron for a couple of months, but had already proved himself to be a very efficient commanding officer. Our aircraft damaged four submarines before losing the commanding officer, and the Beaufighters sank one submarine, damaged one D/D, three submarines and one M/V of approx 5,000 tons.

No. 64 Squadron, ironically Arne's former squadron, flew with 126 on the mission and wrote the following of Austeen's tragic death:

> The squadron provided escort for Beaufighters attacking enemy shipping off the coast of Denmark. These vessels were trying to escape from Kiel

and other ports. Our Mustangs, owing to lack of petrol decided to leave the Beaufighters, after the latter had successfully attacked submarines and shipping, and headed south of Lübeck. On the way three submarines were seen on the surface which were attacked with m.g, and strikes were seen on all three huns before they submerged. The Wing reformed, headed south again. On reaching Kiel Bay we saw four more subs, escorted by flak ship. No. 64 Squadron and 126 Squadron attacked again, seeing strikes again. The C. O. of 126 Squadron, Major Austeen was seen to suffer a direct hit from a U-boat and he went straight into the sea, on fire. After re-forming again, the Wing carried on to Lübeck where they rendezvoused with Gold section led by F/Lt Kelly who had continued in company with the Beaufighters. The weather deteriorated so the Wing landed at Luneberg. Here it was that we met old boys of the Squadron F/Lt Gaze (ex CO in 1942), F. O. Bernard (Bob) and F. O. Boots. During the evening in the bar, the good news came through that the Huns had surrendered to Monty. Free drinks on the house, consisting of Hock, Whiskey and Gin. The boys got shockingly blotto. The C. O. took a jeep on a looting expedition to Lungeberg, and returned with some booty. The party went on well into the morning, most of the boys sleeping perforce, in the hospital with many ex. PoWs.

The South-African, A. R. Hall DFC, former Squadron Leader with a Dutch Spitfire squadron, wrote a letter to Arne's mother after the loss of her son. A. R. Hall arrived on the 7th to take over command of the Squadron, and it fell to him to write to Austeen's mother about her son's passing. Hall had met Austeen for the first time in 1942. During the intervening years, Austeen and Hall became good friends. Hall, as with many others, only had good things to say about Austeen. According to Hall, no one that met Arne had anything bad to say about him. Hall was also of the opinion that the attack on the U-boats was likely to have been 126's last mission of the War, which did indeed turn out to be the case.

Dear Mrs Austeen,

I wish I was writing this letter under more happy circumstances. It's my duty to write to you concerning tragic events that have taken place, something I truly wish I did not have to do. It is with great pain that I have to inform you that your son, Major Austeen, has not returned from operations of war. I know this will be a devastating blow to you. Please allow me to give you my deepest condolences, and from everyone in the Squadron your son commanded.

Your son was very well liked, and was highly regarded in the Squadron, something I hope will give you some comfort. For me, the loss of Arne is very personal, as he was a dear friend of mine. I met him in 1942, and our friendship grew strong in the intervening years. I liked and admired him greatly. All those he met, liked him immediately. I have yet to meet anyone who had anything negative to say about Arne.

Arne excelled during the war, and was, because of his skills and courage, awarded Norwegian war medals as well as the British Distinguished Flying Cross (D. F. C.) He also participated in the war against Germany with great energy, and was always to be found in the heat of the battle.

It was so tragic that Arne was shot down during an attack against German submarines not far off the Danish coast on the 4 May 1945, in what was most likely the Squadron's last offensive operation during the War.

We all miss him deeply, and remember him with pride and dignity. You may with pride say, "He was a man."

Yours faithfully,
A. R. Hall.

The loss of Arne took a great toll on his fiancée, Ruth. After the war, she was always very hesitant to ask about what happened to her dear fiancée, but her daughter Elisabeth understood that she had been engaged to someone who died during the war. It stayed this way between mother and daughter for many years.

The day before Elisabeth was to get married, that would change. She received a bracelet from her mother as a wedding gift. Ruth told her that this bracelet had meant a lot to her, and now it was hers. Ruth had received it from Arne. Elisabeth's mother then told her daughter the entire story of her relationship with Arne Austeen. According to Elisabeth, it was quite obvious that it had been a deep and special love between Arne and Ruth. Arne was a loss that Ruth never truly recovered from, and she never forgot him. The couple had also started preparing for their wedding, that would take place when the war ended. Four more days, and the wedding would have taken place as planned.

In the town of Gjøvik, Arne Austeen is commemorated on a monument in a park close to the train and bus station. He is listed as the last of locals to lose their life during the war. He was also given his own street in Gjøvik, named *Austeens Veg* (Austeen's Road). It can be located just north of the high school, and across from Gjøvik Hospital. For most people, Arne Austeen is a forgotten hero.

Up until 2011, it was thought that Arne stayed with his Mustang when it hit the water, and never did get out of the cockpit. During recent years though, there has been some debate about this. A Norwegian journalist and a German researcher found a grave in Hamburg with only a date: 4 May 1945. They were almost entirely convinced they had located the grave of Arne Austeen, one of

Norway's most decorated fighter pilots of the Second World War. Researching the few men killed in action that day, it looked like they were onto something. Perhaps Arne was found floating in the sea, and then buried in Germany in an unnamed grave.

In 2012, the author was contacted again by another local source around the area of Flensburg. He insisted that this was not the case, and that Arne was still in his Mustang. Perhaps we will never know the truth, but the fact stands; the Allies lost one of their very best men that day, 4 May 1945.

CHAPTER 8

Kaj Birksted

Kaj Birksted was born in 1915 in Copenhagen. He was number three in a line of eight children. In his first years, the family moved to the United States of America, and Kaj grew up in Boston, MA instead of Denmark. Because of this move, Kaj became fluent in English, which would come in very handy later in his life. Returning to Denmark in 1927 due to illness in the family, Kaj went through the Danish school system as most children did. He had begged his parents to let him stay in the US as he wanted to become a surgeon, but he came with the family back to Denmark.

In 1932, aged seventeen, he saved a girl from drowning. The girl went through the ice on Lake Furesøen, on the eastern Danish island of Zealand, and Kaj decided to risk his life to save her. The rescue was a success, and he was awarded a silver clock by the Department of Justice.

Kai started an apprenticeship in his grandfather's timber business, but he had already decided to do something else with his life rather than being a salesman. He wanted to become a pilot, and applied for pilot training with the Danish Naval Air Service in 1936. He was accepted, and graduated two years later. Denmark, like Norway, had cut back on their military budgets considerably coming into the 1930s, and Kaj did not have very modern equipment at his disposal. Nevertheless, he became a pilot and fulfilled his ambition.

Denmark's answer to the German invasion on the 9 April was even more helpless than Norway's. After the initial shock of being under attack had set in, the Norwegians managed to pull themselves together to fight their invaders. Denmark however, remained passive. Taking up arms against the Germany's massive military power was considered hopeless and would only end in a catastrophe. Kaj was on duty that day in Copenhagen, and could not do much more than to phone his superiors informing them about what was happening. Denmark's response to the invasion was a major embarrassment and frustration to Kaj. It was also humiliating to the Danish forces as the Germans took over their quarters and buildings with little trouble. Kaj could do nothing more than to remain calm outwardly, and watch as the Germans made themselves at home. Inside, he was furious.

He did not stay calm and quiet for long though. He got in touch with a colleague, Charles Sundby, and the two young men decided that enough was enough; they would escape from Denmark as soon as possible. The Norwegians had not surrendered yet, and Kaj saw Norway as the place to continue the fighting. Their plan was simple; escape to Malmø in Sweden over the Øresund strait.

Today, a large bridge connects Copenhagen and Malmø making travel between the two countries easy. Not so in 1940. On 16 April, Kaj and Charles got drunk with Danish and German soldiers in Copenhagen and decided that, after the party was over they would put their plans into action. They had to get hold of a proper boat to take them over the strait. It is only four kilometres across, but Kaj and Charles had only a small boat with a very small engine at their disposal. They had trouble getting the engine to start, and were both on alert for German troops, and their own military as well.

After a whole night of travel, they made it in one piece to Malmø and Sweden. In Malmø they had to be aware of the Swedish police and the possibility of being sent back to Denmark as illegal immigrants to Sweden. Thankfully, it did not happen and the two Danish boys set off for the Norwegian border, heading north-west. Without any money, it's remarkable that they made it so far.

On 26 April, they crossed into Norway. Norway's fight against Germany was desperate. Their military forces were already on the brink of surrendering to the enormous German war machinery and support from a British task force had not been successful. The Germans were, by and large, the dominant force in the air and the situation got worse by the hour. Birksted and Sundby made contact with Norwegian forces as far north as Namsos. The Norwegians sent them to a British destroyer. Since Kaj was fluent in English, and could easily make himself understood by the Norwegians, it seemed like a perfect match. The British forces in Norway were too small and came too late. Defeated, they left Norway on 3 June bound for Glasgow. Luckily for Kaj, the British looked at him as an asset, and let both him and Charles stay onboard rather than being left for the Germans to deal with.

Kaj's journey towards his ultimate goal, fighting with the RAF, went smoothly until his arrival in London. The British did not seem interested in his services and he was left bitterly disappointed. The high point of the Battle of Britain was several months away, and the Battle of France was in its early stages. The RAF did not feel that they needed more pilots, and foreigners were a long way down the list. Little did they know what was just around the corner, or perhaps they would have thought differently.

The Danish ambassador in London was even more hostile towards Kaj, viewing Kaj as a deserter who should be shot. Not feeling very welcomed by anyone, Kaj and Charles left London on a Danish boat and took up work as crewmen.

Kaj Birksted at the Danish Club in London. (*Esben Aakjær*)

At this point, Kaj must have felt like his dream of being a fighter pilot was in shreds. But a few days later, they heard news of Norway's new training base for pilots in Canada. Both boys made themselves known to the Norwegians using the boat's telegraph. They wanted to join, and were told they would be accepted. When the boat arrived in Cuba, they left their jobs behind and took a flight to Miami.

Eventually, they arrived in Toronto and the 'Little Norway' training camp in the autumn of 1940. Recruits to the camp kept flooding in from all parts of the world. Students, sailors, whalers, and former pilots, who were mostly Norwegians but also Danes and some Swedes. Even Norwegians who had risked crossing the Atlantic Ocean in fishing boats, directly from Norway to Canada, arrived to do their part in the war effort. Little Norway also had a direct connection to the Norwegian Royal family, now living in the area after escaping from Norway. This connection would be useful to Kaj through most of his later life.

Kaj was promoted to Lieutenant and was given a place among the first fighter unit to be formed, the initial batch of Norwegians destined for the brand new 331 Squadron. Among others in the unit were future legends such as Finn Thorsager, Leif Lundsten and top scorer Svein Heglund. On 12 May 1941, Kaj Birksted arrived at RAF Sutton Bridge, a year after he first came to Britain with hopes of flying in the RAF. At Sutton Bridge, Kaj first met the workhorse of the Battle of Britain, the Hawker Hurricane. At that time, the station was under the command of John Bisdee, widely known as 'The Bishop' and a very popular chap throughout the RAF. At Sutton Bridge Kaj, went through RAF training with his fellow Norwegians, among them Finn Thorsager, Werner Christie and Henning Leifseth.

After Sutton Bridge, Birksted was sent briefly to 43 Squadron at Tangmere. Kaj arrived at 331 Squadron on 27 July as the first pilot to report for duty at Catterick. The same day that he arrived, the Squadron received their first Hawker Hurricane. Three days later, he took to the skies as the first pilot to fly for 331 Squadron, flying their first aircraft. The Squadron came together at Catterick, but were shortly sent to Castletown in Scotland. On 13 September 1941, 331 Squadron was declared operational, and Kaj Birksted was the first pilot to be placed at 'Readiness'. From Castletown, 331 Squadron were sent up to Skeabrae to protect the naval base at Scapa Flow. The days were spent flying patrols and practising scrambles, but not much was seen of the Luftwaffe. However, while at Skeabrae, the Norwegians replaced their old Hurricanes with Spitfires, a signal that the RAF did not want them up north and away from the front line for very long. At Skeabrae, there was an incident where two pilots landed on the same runway from opposite directions. One of them was Kaj Birksted, the other Martin Gran. Both of them got away without crashing head on, and Kaj claimed he had landed with a tailwind on purpose.

A few weeks before Christmas of 1941, Kaj was ordered to take B-Flight up north as far as Sumburgh. During a particular take-off, Kai had a scary moment. He was a bit too quick in retracting the wheels, and the propeller blades of his Spitfire touched the ground, which sounded like machine gun fire to onlookers. Kaj didn't realise how close he had come to crashing, and spent the next 30 minutes according to his schedule. When he came back down, the propeller tips were bent outwards, and not inwards as would have been expected.

During this period, some pilots noticed that Kaj seemed to feel a bit depressed. His friend Charles Sundby had joined up with Canadian Forces instead, and Kaj was left as the only Dane with the Norwegians at the time. Added to this, he was also stuck in a deserted place like Sumburgh were the weather was tough and the days were bleak. Kaj was often seen walking around on his own, deep in thought. Finn Thorsager was notified of Kaj's appearance and took it upon himself to praise their flight leader during his New Year's Eve speech, and Birksted seemed to cheer up considerably.

Something which did not improve though, were the communications at Sumburgh. Several times during their time there, the Norwegians could have engaged the Luftwaffe if it hadn't been for the slow response of the controllers on the ground. Kaj might have shot down his first aircraft at Sumburgh if things had worked properly. While Birksted and another pilot orbited their base, a Junkers 88, presumably from Norway, passed the islands just 4 miles out from their position. Kaj noted down all of the issues in his report when he returned to Skeabrae with B-Flight.

Back at Skeabrae in January 1942, the Squadron and Kaj had to put up with bad conditions as the water pipes froze up. Kaj was frustrated, and wondered how pilots could be efficient under such conditions.

After more than half a year at Skeabrae, Kaj and 331 Squadron were finally sent south to North Weald in Essex. The Squadron arrived in May, and the officers took up residence at Hill Hall. It's said Kaj ended up in a 'heavenly bed'. This was a major change from the conditions he had to endure at Skeabrae. Between their first sorties, lead by twenty-two-year-old Wing Commander David Scott-Malden, life at North Weald included visits to local pubs such as the Kings Head and the Thatched House, as well as weekend trips down to London and the Wellington Club. There was a complete contrast between their lives on the ground and what they were doing in Spitfires over the channel and the continent. Kaj blended in well with the locals around the Epping area, and so did the Norwegians. Some locals even felt that the Norwegians, and the few Danes with them, were the easiest of all the Allies to handle, as their attitude and approach seemed very similar to the English.

However, upon their arrival in the North Weald, Epping-Ongar area, the Norwegians did not handle the big change from their days in the deserted Skeabrae area very well, and went a bit wild in the villages. This was especially the case in Epping, after having had considerable amounts to drink. Local girls were of interest as well, and things got a bit out of hand. Helge Mehre, Commanding Officer of 331 Squadron, decided that Epping was to be out of bounds for everyone for at least a week. The local press got hold of the news and wanted to know why the Norwegians were not allowed to visit the town. Kaj Birksted decided to get involved. He went to Helge Mehre and appealed for the ban to be dropped and let the Norwegians back into Epping. Mehre relented. After a while, the whole thing fizzled out as the Norwegian boys got used to both alcohol and girls.

Kajs flying career and indeed his young life could have ended just a month later, when 331 Squadron attacked two flak ships just outside Knocke. Kaj himself was surprised to survive to fly another day. With 331 Squadron leading 222 Squadron, Scott-Malden ordered 331 Squadron to break off and protect

Kaj Birksted and Wilhelm Mohr at a wet Catterick in the spring of 1942. (*Wilhelm Mohr*)

331 Squadron pilots in November 1942. Front left: Reidar Haave Olsen, Kristian Nyerrød, Fredrik Fearnley with mascot Varg, Kaj Birksted, Tarald Weisteen. Middle, standing: Helge Sognnæs, Leif Lundsten, Stein Sem, Knut Bache, Anton Chr. Hagerup, Rolf Arne Berg, Philip Yatman, Rolf Engelsen. Two at the very back: Johannes Greiner and Martin Gran. Haave Olsen, Fearnley, Sognnæs, Lundsten, Sem, Bache, Hagerup, and Berg would not survive the war. Hagerup was not part of 331 Squadron, and was visiting the squadron when this picture was taken. He perished in a Mosquito flying with 333 Squadron in 1943. (*Susanne Zima Feierskov*)

222 Squadron as they were being engaged by several Focke Wulf Fw190s. Birksted and 331 Squadron attacked four enemy fighters first, and Kaj seemed to be a good shot as he claimed to shoot one down, emitting white smoke and looking to be out of control. He had no time to dwell on it though, as he was attacked head-on by another 190 which scored hits on his wing. Kaj fired back, and saw several hits on the 190.

The attacker was last seen diving vertically below Kaj's Spitfire. He observed several splashes, and a Spitfire being shot down in flames. More 190s got tangled up in the fight, and the North Weald wing pulled out of the area. Suddenly, 331 were a long way ahead of Kaj, heading for home. As one of the last Spitfires out of the area, he was attacked by six Fw190s. Kaj tried to out-turn them, and also kept turning into their attacks. He performed every manoeuvre he could possibly think of to shake off the attacking Germans. He continued to throw his Spitfire around just above sea level, descending to no more than 200 feet. Some of the Germans did not care for Kaj's low-level manoeuvres, opting not to follow him. Others seemed to leave him alone after exhausting their ammunition. Kaj was on full boost and revs, stretching his Spitfire Mk V to the limit of its capabilities. Getting desperate, Kaj pulled up hard and then half-rolled back down to sea level several times. To Kaj's great surprise, this shook off the last of the attacking 190s, and he landed back at North Weald just after noon. It was a great achievement to have avoided being shot down by superior numbers of 190s and to return safely. A month later, Kaj was promoted to Captain and A Flight Leader in 331 Squadron. There was indeed a fine line between living and dying.

As new pilots joined the Squadron, the two experienced members who excelled most in welcoming and taking care of the new lads were Kaj Birksted and Rolf Arne Berg. According to author Cato Gunfeldt, both had exceptional leadership skills. They were highly respected but they were also informal and good at making personal connections with 'new faces'.[1] Kaj would even tip his hat to greet those of lower ranks when they saluted him. He was indeed a popular character among both ground crew and pilots. Kaj wasn't a pushover though, and several Norwegian pilots remember a certain episode after the Squadron had been down at Manston. They were flying back to North Weald in a loose line-astern formation with Kaj as number three. At one point Kaj lost his place in the formation, and one of the lieutenants in the Squadron, either Leif Lundsten or Rolf Arne Berg, decided to have a little fun with their popular Flight Leader. One of them went on the radio and appeared to impersonate David Scott-Malden's voice, saying that number three in the formation was not flying line astern. Then the second of the jokers came on the radio and followed by asking if number three could not perform formation flying. After landing, Kaj was not in a good mood. He reprimanded the boys for their poorly disciplined use of the radio. Neither of the jokers uttered a word. Kaj then pointed the finger at poor Knut Bache, who had to practise formation flying for a whole week with no operational flying.

Going into August 1942, Kaj participated in the Dieppe raid along with 331 Squadron and their sister squadron, 332 Squadron. No. 332 Squadron had arrived at North Weald in June, a month after 331 Squadron took up residence at the already historic airfield. During the first sortie on a particular day, Kaj claimed a 190 as damaged. On their second sortie, both squadrons tracked down several Dorniers and shot them down.† For the Norwegians, the sorties over Dieppe had arguably been a success, and David Scott-Malden later said, 'There is not better fighting group in southern England'.

In September, Kaj was again promoted. Now a Major, he became a Squadron Leader of 331 Squadron. On the 5 September, the day that he got his promotion, the Norwegian Royal Family came for a visit. King Haakon, originally being a Dane, obviously looked with pride on all of his pilots, but having a Dane as a Squadron leader must have been particularly special for him. Wilfrid Duncan Smith later wrote, in his book *Spitfire Into Battle*, that Squadron Leaders Birksted (331) and Mohr (332) ran very efficient units. To Duncan Smith, the Norwegian squadrons' close ties to their Royal Family, who were on first name terms with many pilots and ground crews, was a pleasant surprised to him. In September 1942, both squadrons were equipped with new Spitfire Mk IX.

A month later, Kaj was awarded the Distinguished Flying Cross (DFC) and the Norwegian *Krigskorset med Sverd* (War cross with Sword). He had participated in forty-five offensive sorties. He was noted for his selflessness, generosity and kindness to his fellow pilots. His organisational skills were regarded as excellent. In the October, he was credited with two enemy aircraft destroyed and two damaged.

Ever since the Squadron had been at Skeabrae, they had had a German shepherd named Varg as a mascot. It was bought by John Nordmo, who had drowned soon afterwards in the cold North Sea after wanting to go swimming. Since then, Varg had several owners that took care of him. After a while, it was said that anyone who looked after Varg would die, as several pilots who took care of him were lost on operations. Eventually, no one wanted to take care of Varg to avoid bad luck, and he was left as an orphan. Kaj thought this was too much and decided to adopt the dog. His ground crew wanted none of it, and told Kaj that if he went ahead with his adoption plan, they would shoot the dog. They were completely serious, and Kaj decided not to take Varg.

From October 1942 until March 1943, life was more quiet than it had been. The US 8th Army Air Force had arrived in large numbers, and Kaj led his squadron in escorting the American bombers during those months. The

---

† For more information, see the chapter on Leif Lundsten.

Above: Wilhelm Mohr, Helge Mehre and Kaj Birksted during King Haakon's visit, 5 September 1942. They all received the Norwegian War Cross with Sword. (*Susanne Zima Feierskov*)

Left: Kaj Birksted, decorated with the war cross with sword DFC, North Weald, late 1942. (*Susanne Zima Feierskov*)

Kaj Birksted lights
up a cigarette for
Leif Lundsten,
spring of 1943,
North Weald. Both
are given their
tributes in this
book. (*FMU*)

Norwegian Squadron still lost pilots, but now more during low-level attacks over the continent than to Luftwaffe fighters. It did not take long until 11 Group stopped these dangerous sorties altogether.

Kaj's duties as a Squadron Leader included sad things that were all part of the job. For example, during the the Christmas of 1942, pilots received Christmas presents sent from as far away as the USA and Canada. Some of the gifts were addressed to pilots who had been killed in action while the parcels were en-route to North Weald. One was a well-wrapped cake from Washington for Peter Lockwood Owren. Owren had been killed in action with Fw190s in November, so the pilots decided to share the cake between themselves. Birksted wrote to the sender later on, thanking her from the cake and explaining how it was disposed of, hoping that she would understand. Kaj would also be woken up in the middle of the night by screams from his fellow pilots who were having nightmares in other rooms. He never forgot those screams.

In March 1943, everything seemed to change. On the 7 March, Kaj was scrambled with Red Section together with Blue Section, and were directed towards the Clacton area at 30,000 feet. They were vectored nicely onto two Messerschmitt 109s which were above them. Kaj had not yet reached 30,000 feet, and was at 28,000 when he spotted the 109s above him. Tactically, he led his Section 'up sun' and turned into the two Germans. The two 109s spotted them at that moment, and the Germans half-rolled and dived towards France. Blue Section gave chase to one of the 109s, and Kaj led the chase on the other, diving almost vertically downwards after it. During the dive, he lost his number two, but kept going and gained on the intruder. Suddenly, the German pulled out of his dive, and started to climb again, perhaps thinking he was safe from Kaj and his Spitfire. Trying to gain height, the German suddenly stalled, and started to weave very gently. At 200 yards, Kaj opened fire and parts of the Messerschmitt 109 exploded. Kaj had no time to react, and flew straight into a giant fireball of oil and smoke which covered his windscreen. Birksted found the German again after his windscreen cleared enough for him to see. The 109 was still flying under control but with its engine on fire. Kaj fired another short burst which ripped the wing off the 109. The last Kaj saw was a splash in the sea, a parachute and a body nearby. The German had managed to bail out. His cine-gun was working, but oil from the 109's engine obscured a good video which was to be shown later.

Seven days later, 331 Squadron had hardly sat down in their chairs at dispersal when they were scrambled. Focke Wulf 190s were inbound over the British coastline, and Birksted led 331 Squadron out to meet them head on. Twenty minutes later, the Norwegians shot down six of the 190s with no losses on their side. It was Birksted's brilliant tactical thinking that led them into a position where such a score was possible. 'Norwegian bags six Huns before breakfast', wrote the newspapers, and 331 Squadron was becoming the crack squadron of 1943. Indeed, they became RAF's top fighter squadron that year, and they topped the score list by the end of the year, without doubt thanks largely to Birksted. Rolf Arne Berg and Arne Austeen (for more information, see the chapter on Arne Austeen) were 331's two other Squadron Leaders that year.

Kaj got into a fight once more, seven days later, this time with a Messerschmitt Bf110, arguably a relic from Battle of Britain days. The 110 was seen attacking B-17 Flying Fortresses around St Nicholas. Birksted dived down on the 110 and fired a three-second burst. He saw hits on the 110's tail but it kept flying. Knowing it was under attack by a Spitfire, the 110 pulled sharply up and to the right, which signed its death sentence. Kaj fired another three-second burst, and he hit the 110 around the cockpit area and engines. The port engine stopped and the starboard engine caught fire. It was a sure kill and Kaj pulled away, watching. For twenty seconds, the Messerschmitt 110 shuddered, and then it fell into a vertical dive, never to pull up. That was the last that Birksted and his number two saw of the 110. No parachutes were seen. After Kaj landed at North Weald, it appeared that the engine cowling and the spinner of his Spitfire had been hit by parts flying off the 110.

After sixty sorties with 331 Squadron, Kaj was finally sent on a brief rest period as an instructor. Leadership of the Squadron was taken over by Rolf Arne Berg. Kaj wouldn't be away for long, though. He was back in July, acting as a Wing Commander for the entire North Weald Wing. As previously noted, the Wing would, under Kajs leadership, have considerable success.

On 14 September 1943, Birksted led twenty-four Spitfires to Belgium as escort for 36 B-26 Marauders. On this occasion, Kaj flew with 332 Squadron, acting as bottom cover. The Marauders decided to cancel their operation due to bad weather, but the Dane led the Wing over to Belgium anyway. It turned out to be a good decision. Over Belgium, they spotted several Fw190s at 32,000 feet. Kaj led 332 Squadron upwards. They were at 30,000 feet, and the enemy was above the entire Wing. When they had gained enough height, Birksted went in for an attack, but the Germans dived away. Another group of Germans soon arrived on the scene, this time Messerschmitt Bf109s. Kaj took 332 Squadron with him and bounced the incoming Germans. Birksted picked out one of the 109s and fired at 200 yards. His aim was perfect as the tail of the 109 suddenly broke off. The doomed German went vertically downwards while Kaj pulled away, observing it until it disappeared. He then attacked a second 109, but the Germans decided that enough was enough, and broke off their attack, diving away. Altogether, Kaj had fired his guns for a mere 12 seconds. Just five days later, Kaj led the Wing on an attack on Merville airfield, and claimed another Focke Wulf 190 as destroyed.

His success as a Wing Commander was considerable and was plain for everyone to see. The numbers spoke for themselves, and Kaj kept on leading the Wing on missions with great results. On the 3 October, Kaj led 331 and 332 Squadrons on a sortie to France. They were quickly informed by the Beachy Head controller that the Wing had company from at least fifteen enemy fighters. The Wing first spotted them at the same height as themselves but climbing. Kaj and his North Weald Wing turned and gave chase. A second formation of Fw190s and Bf109s then appeared. Kaj ordered 332 Squadron to deal with them as 331 Squadron chased down the first formation and went in for an attack. A massive dogfight took place, and Kaj picked out one of the 109s, flying with his leader. He fired short bursts at it and saw hits. He could not follow it up as he had to break away due to another enemy aircraft coming in on a collision course. He then looked for his first 109, saw it diving and fired off a few bursts. It looked like the 109's engine had stopped but, yet again, Kai had to break off violently. Kaj shifted focus to the leader of the two, and dived after him instead. He fired a four-second burst at 500 yards and saw several hits on the fuselage. An explosion followed and the 109 dived vertically down. Once again, Kaj had to fly straight through the debris. His

Kaj Birksted during one of his rest periods. (*Tim Elkington*)

windscreen was covered with oil, and was still not clear by the time he landed back at North Weald. It was another superb mission led by Wing Commander Birksted – on return to North Weald, the Norwegians claimed seven German aircraft either destroyed or damaged for no losses of their own.

Another Birksted claim came on 22 October when he led both squadrons over France for a ramrod fighter sweep in the Abbeville area. A large group of enemy fighters appeared below them and 331 Squadron went flat out, turning in for an attack from behind. Quickly, Birkstead selected one of the Germans slightly to port. He fired a four-second burst and the 109s engine erupted with smoke. He overshot the 109 but managed to see that its engine had stopped completely, and the German bailed out of his stricken aircraft. He flew the entire sortie with his reserve tank still on, as he was unable to release it due to a malfunction.

Kaj's time as a Wing Commander, and the Wings considerably good numbers, did not pass unnoticed. In November, he was awarded the Distinguished Service Order (DSO) and was promoted to Lieutenant Colonel. Birksted had led the

Wing on seventy sorties, and he was nearing 180 operational sorties himself. The British loved the Danish tactical mastermind. He was psychologically well balanced, calm and easy going. He kept his Danish humour intact, perhaps not far removed from British humour with that special sense of understatement. Adding his fluent English to the mix, it is easy to understand how Kaj Birksted became a shining star among both the Norwegians and the British.

It was said during the war that Kaj Birksted only had one fault: he did not like girls complicating the lives of pilots. He was of the opinion that marriage while on active service made pilots prone to becoming soft, perhaps losing their edge. Norway's top scorer during the war, Svein Heglund, married while Birksted was his Wing Commander. In his book *Høk over Høk* he suggested that perhaps Birksted's view on married pilots was one of the reasons why he was not allowed to come back to the Squadron after his rest period, but instead went to 85 Squadron flying Mosquito night fighters. However Kaj did accept fighter pilots' marriages, including Tim Heiberg's marriage to a Canadian girl who he managed to bring over to Britain. But Kaj had his own ideas on girls and plans for marriage. As early as June 1942, he noticed a girl at a dance in the officers' mess at North Weald. She was Sonia Jacobsen, married to one of the Norwegian pilots, Lt. Karl Jacobsen. Kaj asked about the who she was, but was told she was married. He held back and simply said, 'I can wait'. Sonia's husband was killed in action only a short while later on 19 June 1942, but Kaj waited until December of 1944 before getting in touch with Sonia, perhaps due to his own opinion on fighter pilots, girls and marriage.

Kaj's final combat victory came during the early days of 1944. Over Cambrai as Red One, he engaged three Fw190s. The 190s were in a turn and did not see Birksted coming from behind, cutting inside them. Kaj fired at the number two of the group and hit the engine and cockpit several times. The 190 exploded into a great fireball and that was the end of it. It was his tenth and last combat kill.

During the war, Kaj went to the dentist about a tooth he had problems with. Instead of filling the tooth as the normal procedure, the dentist simply pulled the tooth out. When Kaj asked why, he was told that fillings for fighter pilots were a waste of time. The dentist did not have much hope of them surviving for very long.

The RAF liked Kaj Birksted and in March of 1944, he was transferred to 11 Group HQ at Uxbridge. Hjalmar Riiser-Larsen, the head of the Norwegian Air Force, wrote Birksted a personal letter, telling him that he still regarded him as one of their own, even if he now would be more under British command than Norwegian. The feeling was mutual. Birksted would now take part in organising and coordinating the upcoming invasion of Europe. He was the only foreigner at this level in the chain of command in the RAF. During the invasion itself, Uxbridge got a few short messages of how things were going

Leif Lundsten, Kaj Birksted and Helge Sognnæs outside the dispersal, North Weald, spring of 1942. (*Kristian Nyerrød*)

in the heat of battle, but it was not enough for Kaj Birksted. He decided to see for himself, and went to Northolt and borrowed a Spitfire.

He proceeded to fly over the beaches where fierce fighting was still ongoing. He then flew back and reported directly to HQ on the situation. One can only imagine what he saw. It's possible that Kaj Birksted was the first pilot to witness the landings, but Kaj never laid any claim to this. His character was not of the type to claim personal glory.

Birksted stayed on with 11 Group until March 1945. He was then brought back for operational flying as Wing Commander for two British Mustang squadrons at RAF Bentwaters. This Wing included Arne Austeen's 124 Squadron where he flew as Squadron Leader. If it was Birksted that especially requested Arne Austeen for the position is not known. Nonetheless, the two men once again teamed up for another partnership, one as a Wing Commander, the other as a Squadron Leader. Birksted flew his last sortie of the war on 3 May 1945. It brought him back home over Denmark as escort for Bristol Beaufighters attacking German shipping, which was still very active and aggressive – quite a homecoming for Birksted. During the last months of the War, Kaj wrote a final letter to Sonia in case he was killed.

Five days after VE Day, Biksted returned to Denmark in his personal Mustang. On 9 June 1945, he married Sonia Irgens, very much in accordance with his opinion of marriage and fighter pilots.

Kaj Birksted died in 1996. His urn was placed in peaceful Norwegian cemetery in Kragerø. Among others, the famous John 'Cats Eyes' Cunningham spoke at his funeral.

CHAPTER 9

Leif Lundsten

Leif was born in the municipality of Vestre Toten on 24 May 1918. His parents were Otto and Laura Lundsten. Otto was the stationmaster of Bilitt train station at Østre Toten, and the family lived in the station's main building. A couple of years later, Laura gave birth to Leifs brother, Bjarne. Otto's brother was stationmaster at the neighbouring station of Kraby. Today, neither of these stations are working as the entire railway line in Østre Toten has been dismantled.

During his youth, Leif kept himself busy with normal activities for Norwegian children during the 1920s and 1930s – football during the summer, skiing in the winter. According to his brother Bjarne, Leif won a medal in a ski jumping competition up in the mountains of Toten. These competitions were held every Easter. Near a small lake called Skjeppsjøen, there was also a hill that was widely used for ski jumping during the cold winters. Sadly, ski jumping was halted when the lake was designated as a source of drinking water. Leif also ski jumped at a hill called Bratlandsbakken at the nearby village of Kapp.

However, it was neither ski jumping nor football that kept Leif busy. He is still renowned in the area for his amazing model cars. Roald Lundsten, Leifs cousin, got a wonderful model of a truck from Leif as a gift in 1937. Leif built it all from scratch. He also built them for himself and raced them down the small hills around Bilitt. There's no doubt Leif had a talent for construction.

At school, Leif performed well and after elementary school he continued his education at a high school in the town of Gjøvik, in preparation for university studies. Somewhere between school, model cars and sports, Leif developed a burning desire for flying. Olav Gundersen, a classmate of Leif from Gjøvik, says that the two of them had different ideas on what they wanted to do with their lives. Leif wanted to be a pilot in the Norwegian Army Air Service, whereas Olav wanted to join the ground forces. With Leif's exceptional grades from school to commend him, he was accepted for the Army flying school at Kjeller in 1938.

In the same year, the entire Lundsten family moved from Billitt to a place called Rånåsfossen in the county of Akershus, where Otto became

Leif Lundsten as a
young boy, perhaps a
school picture from
Toten, Norway. (*Morten
Lundsten*)

stationmaster on another railway line. This also brought them very much closer to Kjeller, where Leif was now busy with his pilot's training.

During the late 1930s, a man called Leif Feiring was the commander of the Army flying school, with Captain Ottar Engvik as his second in command. Twenty pupils started the course in the summer of 1938, and this group of young men would turn out to include some famous and exceptional pilots: Rolf Arne Berg, Tarald Weisteen, Stein Sem, Werner Christie, Kristian Fredrik Schye, Peder Mollestad and of course, Leif Lundsten. In parallel with their pilot training, they also took part in long marches lead by Lt. Jean-Hansen. According to Tarald Weisteen, these marches were very unpopular until Jens S. Hertzberg took charge of them. Hertzberg took his fair share of the load on his back, just as the boys did, and he also carried the loads of others if they got tired. The marches actually became popular after the change of leadership.

On 20 February 1939, Lundsten and his friends left Kjeller for a winter exercise at Tisleia between the villages of Gol and Fagernes. They used Tisleia as their airfield, and they used the Tislefjorden lake for target practise. The pupils lived at the Oset Hotel. Navigational flights as far as Gardermoen

With an ever-lasting love for anything with wheels, wings or engines, Leif Lundsten is here on a motorcycle before the war. (*Morten Lundsten*)

(now Oslo Gardermoen Airport) was also among their tasks. After a month or so, they returned to Kjeller in their Fokker C.V-Ds & -Es and De Havilland DH.82 Tiger Moths.

The class of 1939 would also become the least expensive as no pupil wrecked a single aeroplane. Kristian Fredrik Schye was on his way to becoming the best of the group if it hadn't been for a very unsuccessful shooting exercise at Tisleia. Who did become the best is uncertain, but the author has received several confirmations that it was Leif Lundsten. Schye would get into a fierce dogfight with Bf110s over Oslo on the 9 April, and subsequently crash-landed his Gladiator, surviving the encounter.

After graduation, Leif left Kjeller for Gothenburg in Sweden to study at a technical school of excellence. It didn't take many months before he was called back in Norway for neutrality service with the military. The studies had to wait. Several of Leif's fellow students from Kjeller were called in to serve at Oslo Fornebu Airport, but Leif was ordered north together with Rolf

Leif in his Army Air Force uniform with his family before the war. (*Morten Lundsten*)

Arne Berg. According to Leifs brother, Bjarne, he was still up north when the Germans invaded Norway. Stationed at Bardufoss were also future Spitfire pilots Henning Leifseth and Morten Ree.

For the entire winter of 1939 to 1940, Leif was in northern Norway. The Hålogaland flight had six Fokkers at their disposal, and these were spread out on three separate airfields – Bardufoss, Banak and Seida. On the 8 April, the order was given to move all of the Fokkers to Bardufoss. Rolf Arne Berg had, up to this point, been at Seida, while Morten Ree and Henning Leifseth had been at Banak. Leif is also thought to have been at Bardufoss. They soon feared that Bardufoss would be bombed by the Germans, so they gathered all the Fokkers at Moen in the Målselv municipality of Troms county in northern Norway. From Moen, Lundsten flew recce missions, without actually knowing where the front lines were. Soon, they were given orders to move the flight to Rundhaug by lake Tanaelven. Rundhaug was not an airfield but just a farmer's field, which they used as best as they could. Most of their gear and equipment were still at Bardufoss, and Ree talks about how they flew there when they needed fuel or ammunition. From Rundhaug, they kept flying recce missions, photographing the German lines when they could find them. The men also invented something they called the Halling Throw. This included manoeuvring the Fokker to drop bombs by hand in a particularly effective way.

On 14 April 1940, the flight started a series of bombing attacks that lasted for three days. According to Ree, it was the most successful campaign they conducted up north. Leif Lundsten did not participate, but the other pilots did their very best to attack Junkers Ju52s on a frozen lake (also attacked by Swordfish biplanes from HMS *Furious*).

The men got plenty of action at Rundaug, and one of the most famous of incidents happened when Svein Eggen and his tail gunner, Håkon Kyllingmark, attacked a Heinkel 111. Eggen crash-landed, and Kyllingmark had to leave him, badly injured and stuck in the wreckage, to search for help. This was not the only crash at Rundhaug. Leif Lundsten was involved in the other.

Morten Ree told the author of a book that came out shortly after the war:

> Leif Lundsten had a terrible crash at Rundhaug. He put the Fokker down too far into the field and overshot, ending up on a fairly steep hill approaching the river. The Fokker went right up on its nose and was reduced to a pile of scrap in the subsequent crash. Both Lundsten and his scout, Mensen, were stuck in their cockpits, and the aircraft caught fire. Mensen eventually got out on his own, but we had to break Lundsten free using a saw. He was badly injured, and the Fokker was a write-off.[1]

At the beginning of May, some aircraft arrived from the south, but these were in such a poor shape most of them were written off on the spot. The flying school's popular leader on those long marches at Kjeller, Jean-Hansen, showed up at Rundhaug with a Fokker that had a piece of cut timber in place of one of the undercarriage wheels. The conditions at Rundhaug deteriorated significantly when the snow started to melt. Ole Reistad moved operations to Takvann, most likely with a still-injured Leif in the middle of it all.

On 18 May 1940, Morten Ree and fourteen other pilots escaped Norway with the Polish ships Czobry and Batory. According to Bjarne Lundsten, Leif escaped with King Haakon VII and the Norwegian government on board HMS *Devonshire* on the 7 June, together with fellow pilot Kristian Nyerrød. Cato Guhnfelt (of Spitfire Saga fame), however does not list Leif as part of the group on the *Devonshire*. It's more than likely that Leif left with Ree on the Batory instead. A third option, but less likely, is that he left Norway as early as 6 May.

Morten Ree remembered:

> We boarded at Evenskjær but on 15 May, the ship was attacked by German Heinkels in the Vestfjord. The ship took several direct hits, and the Czobry started to burn. A Norwegian and three-hundred English evacuees were killed in the attack. It was obvious to everyone that the ship had to be abandoned, but it was not very tempting to jump into the freezing waters. Luckily, two

British destroyers arrived and we jumped straight over to them. We didn't get very far on our first attempt at escape, but after a short spell in Harstad, we boarded Czobry's sister ship, Batory, on 18 May. The ship only had a few senior British officers on board besides us, fifteen Norwegian pilots. To avoid German ships, Batory went very far north on its way to England. We were all the way up to 80 degrees north to get out of the danger zone, and seven days passed before we arrived in Glasgow.

Kristian Nyerrød wrote of his experiences on board the *Devonshire*:

I was on deck until my country disappeared beyond the horizon. Then I went down to the mess. Dinner was already being served, and a plate of soup was put in front of me. I took a mouthful and it nearly took my breath away. This had to be what dynamite tastes like. The cook must have dropped his box of spice into the pot. Life on board was not so spiced up, though. Our beds were always cleared out for the day, so we had to be on our feet for the entire day. We took a stroll around the deck, but were told to disappear by a very angry Norwegian officer. Our only breaks were the meals.[2]

On the 23 May, Batory arrived in Scotland. Leif Lundsten and most of the Norwegian Air Force personnel were quickly sent to Dumfries. The stay would last for three weeks and, according to Nyerrrød, there was little to do in the small Scottish town. The cinema and local dances were frequently visited.

Originally, the plan had been to establish a training base in France for the Norwegian pilots, but with the fall of France, a new plan had to be figured out. Captain Bjarne Øen made plans to establish a training base in Toronto, Canada. And so, on Friday 21 July, the Norwegians left Dumfries for Canada. Many of the pilots were frustrated with the decision to leave, and Wilhelm Mohr (later Squadron Leader of 332 Squadron) felt it was like taking a bucket of water and leaving when the house was on fire. The Battle of Britain had just begun, but the Norwegians had to leave Britain. Captain Øen later defended his decision of leaving by saying he did not want the few Norwegians he had at his disposal at the time to disappear into RAF squadrons. It was an opinion that was never shared by the Norwegian pilots. They wanted to fight side by side with the British during those dark days.

With Leif's valuable experience, he quickly became an instructor at their base in Canada, Little Norway. Ole Reistad was in command of the base, and the construction of a more permanent establishment was completed in record-time. It was officially opened on 10 November 1940, very close to where the Maple Leaf baseball stadium once stood. The Norwegians used Fairchild Cornells, Douglas 8A-5s and Curtiss Hawk 75A-8s, the bomber pilots concentrating on the Douglas. Leif stayed on as an instructor for six

A photo of Leif
from his days
in Canada.
(*Morten
Lundsten*)

months before he left Canada on 10 May 1941, as part of what was called
the 1st Fighter Wing, with men such as Finn Thorsager, Rolf Arne Berg, the
Piltingsrud brothers Gunnar and Arvid as well as Jens Müller (of Great Escape
fame).

Tarald Weisteen arrived at Little Norway about six months after the camp
was opened. One day, he was given a ride up to the estate of Vesle Skaugum
where the 1st Fighter Wing was based, waiting for their journey across the
Atlantic. Weisteen tells of a warm welcome from the men, among them Leif,
as he mentions him in his book, *Nightfighter*. Weisteen felt, though, that some
of them were a bit lukewarm towards him, as they felt he should have arrived
in Canada sooner. Leif Lundsten was not of that opinion and greeted him with
open arms.

Leif left Halifax onboard a merchant vessel called *Aurania* and arrived in
Iceland on 23 May. The journey was eventful.

Rolf Arne Berg wrote in his diary:

> I had been standing on the deck for a few minutes when a torpedo hit a
> 12,000 tonner just 200 meters to the left of us. The torpedo was fired from
> a U-boat 200 meter to our right and, later, we heard it had just missed

our boat. A second after the first explosion, another torpedo hit the same boat from the other side, and, at the same time, a second boats was hit. This [second] boat was in our path and took the hit for us. In no time, the tanker was a burning inferno. Just after that, a tremendous thump rocked our boat violently. It was one of the U-boats bumping into us. We released a few explosives. The convoy was split up after that.[3]

Shockingly, twelve ships were sunk before the Norwegians finally reached Iceland.

Thirteen men from *Aurania*, amongst them Leif, arrived at Operational Training Unit 52 at Debden in Essex, just north of London, in the middle of June 1941. At Debden, Leif would fly a Hurricane for the first time.

No. 331 Squadron was officially formed at Catterick in Yorkshire a week before Leif was posted there. The Squadron was not formed without problems. The Norwegians felt that the British based at the station were working against them, making everything more difficult than it should have been to get the Squadron on its feet.

No. 331 Squadron had Hawker Hurricanes at their disposal, and these were well used. The Norwegians were disappointed over the quality of their Hurricanes. Dirty, tired and with daily leaks of glycol, pumps and hydraulics failed regularly.

On 20 and 21 August, the Squadron moved up to Castletown in Scotland. To most of the battle-hungry Norwegians, the Squadron was moving in the wrong direction. They wanted to go south, not north.

On 27 August, Leif had to perform a task that few, if any, had done before him; land a Hurricane with 90 per cent of the rudder and the elevator gone. Leif was flying Hurricane FN-K/Z5266. The squadron had taken to the air to practise formation flying, and they were split into two flights of six aircraft, in line abreast. To keep the formation tight in a turn, the inner pilot had to reduce his speed while the outer pilot had to increase his. In this situation, there are limits to how slow the inner pilot can fly and how fast the outer one can go, so the aircraft change positions in the formation during the manoeuvre. On this occasion, Jens Müller was on the inside and Leif was on the outside.

Müller later said, 'I increased my speed to glide outwards. At the same time, Lundsten was coming inwards. Soon we came to the point where we were to cross each other. Lundstens Hurricane was just a tad in front of mine, and then we hit.'[4]

Müller's propeller chopped off most of Leif's elevator and rudder. With a severely damaged propeller, Müller had to jump out. He got away with no serious injuries.

With Leif, the situation was a bit different. He decided to land his Hurricane at Castletown. The engine was running nicely, and Lundsten set course for

Above: The famous Hurricane landing, and the subsequent crash into a 124 Squadron Spitfire at Castletown in 1941. (*Morten Lundsten*)

Left: Another view of the tail of Leif's Hurricane after his emergency landing at Castletown. (*Helge Mehre*)

the airfield. With wheels and flaps out, he went in for landing almost like normal. Shocked mechanics could only watch as fabric from his tail flapped in the wind. He hit the ground perfectly but, with no rudder, he couldn't control his Hurricane on the ground. He then collided with a Spitfire from 124 Squadron.

Mechanic Ragnvald Myhre recalled, 'I was standing there, watching it all. It was a brilliant landing with no rudder. I still remember the crushing sound when he hit the Spitfire.'[5]

The Spitfire was badly damaged, and Leif's Hurricane likewise, but he got away without a single injury of any kind.

Leif is also the first pilot to grace 331 Squadron's Operational Record Book (even though many take offs and landings had been performed already). The Squadron moved next from Castletown to Skeabrae at the Orkney Islands, which cause further frustration to many of the pilots. At Skeabrae, their task was to protect the naval base Scapa Flow. With little vegetation and the weather constantly changing, life was tough at the island. When severe storms set in, the ground crews had to tie down anything of value. At times during winter, the entire airfield could be covered with a layer of ice. Apart from these setbacks, the Norwegians did several scrambles, but very rarely did they spot the high-flying Germans once they got up.

Arvid Piltingsrud, was from Søndre Land, a municipality within Oppland county in central-southern Norway and just an hour's drive from Leifs home town. On 15 September 1941, Leif and Arvid took off in their Hurricanes for a convoy patrol, which would turn out to be the first operational mission noted in the Squadron record book. Leif flew FN-C on this occasion, and the patrol took about an hour.

On 1 October, Leif was fortunate to be granted twelve days' leave. Stein Sem, from his class at Kjeller, got the same leave. At times, it could be very hard to even get over to the mainland from Skeabrae, so many pilots simply stayed around the airfield. Several days could be wasted simply travelling alone. It is not known where Leif went for his leave, but he may have gone to Edinburgh.

By November, the Norwegians finally got rid of their old Hurricanes. They would be using Spitfires from now on, and they all welcomed this already legendary aircraft with great pleasure. Leif did not fly any official missions during this time and, on 21 December, he was posted to Dyce in Scotland, together with Morten Ree, Rolf Arne Berg and Stein Sem. At Dyce, they would do night patrols for the coming months. Two days before they left Skeabrea, they celebrated their farewell with beers and cigarettes. The group did not manage to leave Skeabrae until 23 December, and then ran into trouble boarding the passenger ferry to Stromness. They were not given priority, even though Ree had a letter with him from Major Odd Bull which stated that they were travelling to an urgent posting. However, they did reach Dyce in time to celebrate Christmas Eve there.

On 15 February 1942, Leif had his first operational sortie in a Spitfire. Back from Dyce, he flew a night patrol together with Arnt Hvinden. They were both back at 0820. Leif flew FN-C/X4622 on this occasion. Another mission came the next day in FN-S/P7388. Throughout the spring of 1942, the Squadron replaced their older Mk II Spitfires with brand new MkVbs. On 23 February, Leif took part in a convoy patrol. After they arrived back at Skeabrae they received a message from the Admiral of the fleet to say that they had protected them and thanking them for a superb effort.

During large parts of March and April, Leif continued flying missions with 331 Squadron. Dawn patrols and dusk patrols were completed with no major incidents. The second anniversary of the German invasion of Norway, 9 April, was passed in silence.

Helge Mehre tells us, 'All personnel gathered together. I gave a very short speech. Then we sang a verse of "A Mighty Fortress Is Our God."'[6]

One phenomenon during Leifs days at Skeabrae was Weather Willy, a Focke Wulf Fw200 Condor coming from Stavanger in Norway, flying its regular recce sortie. It used to pass between the Orkneys and Shetland and head out into the Atlantic before it changed course and landed at Brest in France. For Leif and the Norwegians, Weather Willy became an obsession. It was decided to send one Spitfire up in the early morning, to 6,000 feet, to meet Weather Willy where they thought he would stand no chance. The controller tried his best to give the Norwegians the right vector so they could fire on this annoying German. They never did get close to the Condor, and they simply had to give up the task. According to Svein Heglund, they never got close because the area was simply too large for a Spit to cover and find the intruder.

Meanwhile, the RAF had planned a very different life for Leif Lundsten and 331 Squadron. They were about to finally leave Skeabrae. The boys went wild with excitement when they got the news that they were to move down south to North Weald, just outside London. The Squadron record book reported that never before had so many faces looked so pleased.

Leif Lundsten would once again record a first. He brought Squadron adjutant Erik Lynneberg down to North Weald in a Miles Magister on 1 May 1942, to make the necessary arrangements and preparations for the rest of the Squadron to follow three days later. The total flying time from Skeabrae was fourteen hours. No. 331 Squadron arrived with their Spitfires after a quick stop at Catterick, where 332 Squadron remained for the time being. No. 332 Squadron were insanely jealous and did not wish their 331 colleagues good luck. But it wouldn't be long until 332 Squadron arrived at North Weald as well. The 331 Squadron officers moved into Hill Hall, a large mansion. Leif stayed here with the rest of the officers until August of that year, when they moved again to the Officers' Mess at North Weald – the building is now called Norway House.

Leif was already flying offensive sorties as early as 9 May 1942. He usually flew Spitfire Mk Vb AR328, coded FN-O. For their first real taste of war, the Squadron would make a fighter sweep over enemy territory. Before taking off, they were all very tense and excited. Kristian Nyerrød wrote:

> The pilots gathered in the briefing room in good time before 1300 hours. Even those who would not participate showed up. The atmosphere was tense. Only the guys from 222 Squadron seemed relaxed and loud. They joked around and had fun. They were experienced. For them, this was routine. It was not routine for the Norwegians, but they all came back in one piece with Wing Commander David Scott-Maldon leading.[7]

On 17 May, Norway's national day, 331 Squadron escorted bombers to Bolougne and back. The flak was intense, and the Luftwaffe showed up in force. Twelve RAF fighters from other squadrons were shot down, with eight pilots lost. No. 331 Squadron seemed to get away from the mess with all pilots safe, but when they landed at North Weald, several pilots were missing. They were all worried. Amongst the missing pilots was Leif Lundsten. The anxiety over the missing pilots was serious, and people's faces did not light up until Leif and three other pilots finally showed up. Lundsten and his group of missing pilots reported that they had had to go down at other airfields in need of fuel. Leif and Kristian Nyerrød landed at Hawkinge, while Rolf Arne Berg crashed his Spitfire at Manston during landing.

In June, 332 Squadron came down from Catterick, with Wilhelm Mohr as their Squadron Leader, to take up permanent residence at the airfield alongside 331 Squadron. Tough and intense missions quickly started to wear on the young Norwegians. No. 331 Squadron had already lost a couple of pilots (including Jens Müller) before 332 Squadron even arrived. Author Cato Gunfeldt wrote, 'All pilots with the Norwegian squadrons were, to a larger or lesser degree, scared, just as they were in other squadrons. What separated one person from another was their ability to handle the fear.'[8]

In his book, *Nightfighter,* Tarald Weisteen wrote:

> Several calmed their nerves with alcohol. One of us, who could be extra keen on the bottle, was one day supposed to fly on a mission. He was far from sober. The ground crew managed to prop him up in the cockpit, and let him breathe 100 per cent pure oxygen from the Spitfire's oxygen tank. We thought this would help to make him sober quicker…When we landed after the mission, he had no idea where he had been.[9]

As the summer of 1942 wore on, Leif was given his own Spitfire to fly. It was common for most squadrons to give an experienced pilot a particular aircraft that they would maintain especially for him. For Leif, this Spitfire would be FN-O/AR238. Among his ground crew was mechanic Jon Slinning, who worked on the engine of AR238. For Leif, the summer continued with more missions and patrols over the channel and into enemy territory. On several occasions, he spotted Bf109s and Fw190s, but did not get within shooting range. Both 331 Squadron and 332 Squadron lost pilots that summer. No. 332 Squadron, for example, lost four pilots on the same mission, which had a lasting impact.

Leif Lundsten participated in the famous Dieppe raid together with the rest of the North Weald Wing. As usual, he flew AR238. No. 331 Squadron received Helge Mehre as Squadron Leader, and, on that dark day in August, they arrived over Dieppe early in the morning. It did not take long before the heavens are full of Messerschmitt 109s and Focke Wulf 190s. A dogfight took place, and several of the Norwegians claimed destroyed and damaged Luftwaffe fighters.

Leif did not participate on the second mission that day, and Fredrik Fearnley flew AR238 in his place. Both 331 Squadron and 332 Squadron got into dogfights again with German fighters and bombers. Leif was back on the roster for the third mission. Rolf Arne Berg was shot down by German fighters on this mission and had to bail out. Luckily, he was back with the Squadron sometime in the late afternoon. Leif did not claim any fighters shot down that day, and did not participate in the fourth and last mission that was undertaken around 1800 hours.

After the last Merlin was shut off, the Norwegians gathered at their forward base, Manston, and celebrated. They knew they had done well. Svein Heglund wrote:

> That night, the atmosphere was cheerful and happy in the mess at Manston. Everyone was very pleased for having made it to the end of this day alive. However, what had happened to those of us who had been shot down was still unknown. We were all surprised and very happy when Rolf Arne Berg unexpectedly showed up wearing Navy overalls after a little swim in the channel.

332 Squadron's Squadron Leader, Wilhelm Mohr, was hit in the leg during the first mission of the day, and had his foot in a cast while the rest of the boys flew over Dieppe. He did not want to miss the party, though. Reidar From remembered:

> Mohr hobbled around, pale but calm. After a while, he came over to me and asked for a drink from my beer. "Sure! Go ahead!" When I gave him my pint,

Leif Lundsten with a few Norwegian top brass. 331 Squadron had been on an escort mission for B-17s on this day, hence the Mae Wests. (*Riksarkivet*)

he threw up, beautifully, straight into it. Not a single drop hit the floor. Then he fainted. Everyone got up on their feet, a bit shocked. The doctor was furious. He thought Mohr was sleeping comfortably in his bed.[10]

On 27 August 1942, promoted to Lieutenant, Leif flew escort for eight American B-17 Flying Fortresses to Rotterdam. That same day, the Norwegians got a visit from their Chief of Defence, Generalmajor Wilhelm von Tangen. Leif Lundsten was one of the pilots he spoke to, and Leif can be seen in several photographs with von Tangen. They also had time for a little air show between the missions. On 5 September, King Haakon, Crown Prince Olav and Crown Princess Martha also paid the boys a visit.

During that Autumn, the Norwegians would wave goodbye to their Spitfire VBs and receive brand new Mk IXs. It was a change for the better as the ageing Mk V could not keep up with the Focke Wulf Fw190. As the Mk IXs came onto the scene, Leif had to give up AR238. He would fly many Mk IXs from North Weald, but the one he would fly more than any other was FN-R/BS467, a Spitfire that would stay with him until he left North Weald for a rest period a year later.

In December, Leif would suddenly find himself as the new leader of B-Flight. One December day, 331 Squadron would escort B-24 Liberators to

Leif Lundsten handles top Norwegian officials visiting at North Weald on 27 August 1942. (*Riksarkivet*)

Abbeville-Drucat. Leif, as usual, flew FN-R, with Stein Sem as leader of B-Flight. Somewhere over France, Sem reported engine problems and returned to base with Ottar Malm on his wing, who himself had reported problems with his oxygen supply. Malm also had issues with his radio and did not fully understand what was being said to him. Just as they crossed the French coastline, they were attacked by Fw190s. Sem was hit and had to bail out. Sadly, he was never found. He was reported as missing, believed killed. No. 331 Squadron now needed a new B-Flight leader, and Leif took over from the missing Sem. Lundsten was then promoted to Captain.

Christmas Eve was celebrated in regular Norwegian tradition at North Weald on 24 December. The start of the celebrations was normal procedure with dinner and the appropriate speeches but, as alcohol consumption increased throughout the evening, everything got more than a bit wild. The Squadron operations record book reported that all of their favourite Aquavit drink was now gone, which meant they simply had to get home to Norway by next Christmas!

As newly promoted B-Flight Leader, Leif most likely found it much easier to get within shooting range, and his results soon came. On 15 February 1943, 331 Squadron escorted B-24 Liberators to the continent. On their way back to England, Leif chased a Focke Wulf Fw190, and saw it crash into the sea.

Leif, as Blue One, was about 20 miles south-east of North Foreland when he spotted five Fw190s that dived back towards France at 12,000-15,000 feet. Leif made a sharp turn to the left and started to fire. He gave one short burst at long range. He then spotted his number two and three passing above and to the left of him. He was then on the point of breaking off his attack, as he was unable to get closer, when one of the 190s pulled up a hundred yards in front of him, trying to attack his number three. Leif gave the 190 a few seconds' burst and it went over on its back, diving steeply. He followed it down and then saw the enemy go straight into the sea. As Leif pulled up, he saw another splash about 1,000 yards in front, which he guessed was the 190 claimed by his wingman.

With a higher rank and a wealth of experience came more responsibility. Leif was put in charge of the entire 331 Squadron on several missions during the winter and Spring of 1943. On 26 February, he led 331 Squadron to St Omer in France. Their presence was reported on the German radios in the area, and Lundsten quickly spotted twenty Fw190s about 6,000 feet below them. He then called up 332 Squadron, flying below them somewhere, but they did not see the Germans. Leif then turned to Wing Commander Jameson and told him he would take the entire squadron down for an attack.

A few seconds later, Leif and 331 Squadron were in the thick of it. After some twists and turns, he went head on against an Fw190 which was flying straight and level. He opened fire at about 700 yards and closed in to about 100 yards firing the whole time. A big chunk of the 190 flew off the cockpit area and hit a wing on his number two's aircraft, damaging it slightly. By then, Leif had built up quite a high speed and he pulled up. The last he saw of his enemy was that he was diving down very steeply and on his back. To Leif, it appeared that the Fw190 was out of control, and he claimed a probable destroyed after this engagement.

On 12 March, Leif led Blue Section over England early in the morning. They were detailed to attack what Leif called The Hornchurch 190s, most likely a gaggle of 190s that had attacked the airfield. Leif chased the Germans all the way to the French coastline, and got within 600-700 yards from a formation of ten 190s. To Leif, they seemed to throttle back, thinking they were safe, as he was gaining on them considerably. He closed in very quickly and fired at one of them from 100 yards. After just a few seconds' burst, the enemy aircraft exploded and went into the sea. He then attacked another one of the 190s who had been flying line abreast with Leif's first victim. He gave this one a short burst of fire and observed strikes on the 190's fuselage, followed by clouds of black smoke. The Germans then finally reacted, and Leifs target quickly pulled up. He had to break away as the rest of the 190s were about to manoeuvre into a position where they could attack his Spitfire. Leif considered his second 190 as destroyed but did not see it go down and only claimed a probable.

Leif Lundsten flew regularly in March and April, and they flew far more 'ramrod' fighter sweeps over enemy territory than they had before. The intensity of American attacks against targets on the continent had increased dramatically. The Norwegians escorted them as far as they could, but the Spitfire was never designed as a long-range escort fighter.

On 13 March, Leif Lundsten was awarded the Distinguished Flying Cross (DFC). A month later, he reached the high mark of 100 sorties with 331 Squadron. The day would turn out to be bittersweet.

Again flying as Blue One, this time in FN-R/BS125, 331 Squadron got into a fight with famous German crack fighter unit. Cato Guhnfeldt wrote:†

It was the boys from [Squadron] 331 that did the job that day, represented by their Blue Section who all dived down on three Germans. These were flying in line abreast at 12,000 feet over the sea just off Vlissingen in Holland. What the Norwegians did not know was that they had big fish in front of them. The commander of II. Gruppe/Jagdgeschwader 1, Gruppenkommandeur Major Herbert Kijewski, and II. Gruppe/Jagdegescwhader's Hans Mohr. The Norwegians attacked from behind without any fuss. Leif Lundsten claimed one of them destroyed, Fredrik Eitzen another and Helner Grundt Spang claimed a third.

From German sources, it was reported that only two were missing, and so the Norwegians claimed one too many. However, it would be bittersweet as a newcomer to the Squadron, Gustav K. H. Koren, was killed the same day. From Leif Lundstens own report:

I was flying as Blue One when, over Walcheren island, Red Three reported some Huns at 3 o'clock below us. I saw them, and the whole of Blue Section went down to attack them. We saw three Fw190s flying in line abreast, the post [rear] one a little below. This was at 12,000 feet. I attacked the middle one. I started firing at about 800 yards, closing in to about 400 yards, when the Fw190 had an explosion and started burning. He went straight down. I saw afterwards three big splashes in the sea just off Walcheren Island. Blue Two and Three also saw these splashes.

Early on the morning of 8 May, Leif was scrambled together with this wingman Knut Bache. An unidentified aircraft had been spotted on the radar. With Bache neatly tucked under his wing, they roared off the runway at North

---

† Note that the R is not another Spitfire, but 'BS125' rather than 'BS467' would suggest that it was a different aircraft, given the same code letters, perhaps if BS467 was no longer airworthy, or had been transferred to another squadron.

Norwegians at North Weald. Reidar Haave Olsen, Knut Bache, Kristian Nyerrød, Leif Lundsten, Kaj Birksted, Knut Bache and Steim Sem, November 1942. (*Riksarkivet*)

Weald in pursuit of the unknown intruder. They quickly tracked him down and could easily identify the Junkers 88. Just six miles from North Weald, they shot the German down. It crashed in a ball of flame near Great Tawney Hall in the village of Stapleford Tawney in Essex. No one from the Junkers 88 survived their encounter with the Norwegians.

On 17 May, Leif flew FN-S/MA225 over the continent with no major incident taking place, on what was otherwise a very special day for the Norwegians as it was their national day.

June 6, 1943, would be the last time Leif Lundsten flew with 331 Squadron that year. Together with Gregers W. Gram, he did a convoy patrol over Barrow Deep off the Essex coast. Nos 331 and 332 Squadrons had, from the early days at North Weald, held competitions to see who could swallow beer the quickest. When Gregers Gram came on the scene with 332 Squadron, his Squadron always won as he had a way of drinking pints without swallowing. Three weeks after his patrol over Barrow Deep, Leif was sent on a rest period to Vickers-Armstrong as a test pilot. Six months later in January of 1944, Leif completed a fighter leader-training course as preparation for his upcoming task as a Squadron Leader.

Leif came back to 331 Squadron during spring 1944, and flew his first operational sortie on 23 March, taking over 331 Squadron from Arne Austeen. Leif would now lead the Squadron in preparation for the planned invasion of the continent. As part of the RAF's 2nd Tactical Air Force, The Norwegians of North Weald would now form 132 Wing with 66 Squadron at Hornchurch, 127 Squadron also at North Weald and (Dutch) 332 Squadron at Acklington in Northumberland. Leif was also promoted as a Major.

For most of April, 66, 331 and 332 Squadrons transferred to Bognor Regis in Sussex. With the Luftwaffe mostly absent from British shores, Leif led the squadron on several ground attack sorties over the continent. Unfortunately, they lost Knut Bache in May, the man that shot down the Junkers 88 with Leif the previous year.

On 6 June, D-Day, the day everyone had been waiting for, the entire Wing of forty-seven Spitfires took off from Bognor Regis to participate in Operation Neptune, the attack phase of Operation Overlord. Similar sorties were conducted over the next two days. To the Norwegians, it was a major disappointment that no German fighters or bombers were to be found. They all expected the days around D-Day to be filled with action like Dieppe in 1942. No Germans indeed and the losses would be on the Norwegians side.

On 9 June, Leif's life would come to a horrible end. He led the Norwegian squadrons into the air in support of the ground troops on the beaches of Normandy. Over France, 331 Squadron received a report of around six enemy aircraft in the area, at low altitude to the south. Leif led the Squadron down to the deck in search of the Germans. The Royal Navy mistook the Norwegians for the Luftwaffe and started to fire on them. Leif was then informed over the radio by the controller what was happening. They then got word to turn around and fly out of France the way the came in. Lundsten then turned the Squadron around and up into the clouds for cover. They had only just changed course when the Navy fired at them once again, and this time they didn't miss. Leif's Spitfire was hit and he told the rest of the Squadron over the radio that he had to bail out. He was last seen by Sergeant Steen flying into a cloud, weaving like mad with black smoke pouring out of his engine. Up until the very last moment of his life, he was a magnificent Squadron Leader. He gave his Squadron the order to return to base and gave them the course. The other pilots reported after landing that the Navy's anti-aircraft fire had been intense and precise. Major Leif Lundsten was never found.

Birger Tidemand-Johannessen, a fellow 331 Squadron pilot, later wrote a book about his time with the Squadron, including his participation in that fateful mission. He writes:

The two Norwegian Squadrons were among the first to be ordered to patrol over the beaches of Normandy. On the third day after D-Day, we patrolled the landing sites. We flew in over land, turned around and flew back towards the coast and the gathered fleet of ships just beyond the coastline. Through the thin, slightly hazy cloud cover, we saw hundreds, maybe thousands, of ships of all kinds – warships, torpedo boats and landing craft of all shapes and sizes. It was a truly impressive sight from the air.

It speaks for itself that such a large military operation can't be set into motion without complications. This also happened to us. A trigger-happy flak gunner from one of the vessels mistook our Spitfires for being German. He opened fire, and was soon joined by others. A firestorm of projectiles screamed past our Spitfires. We were being shot at by our own! I pressed the throttle all the way forward, pulled the stick all the way into my stomach, and cut upwards, straight up and over the massive fleet, while I was scared to death waiting for the first explosions. How many thousands of cannons and machine guns fired was hard for me to tell, but the air was thick with tracers. Then, the fleet realised their mistake. The firing stopped within seconds.

It is an honourable thing to be shot at by your enemies. One is always prepared to accept that a Messerschmitt 109 or a Focke Wulf 190 will do its absolute best to shoot you down. It's part of the game. But when one over-excited gunner on the same side as yourself makes a mistake it's not very pleasant. And, it wasn't just one single gunner, it was the entire fleet who had an absolute field-day.

Many of us literally shit in our pants that day, myself included. I had never been more scared in my entire life.

Squadron leader Leif Lundsten was shot down. He managed to give us the correct course for home before his Spitfire crashed and took his life. It was an experience that shook all of us, of how pointless it was that our popular and skilful Squadron Leader had been killed by our own; and not the least the fact that he thought of his boys and gave us the right course for home while his Spitfire was on fire. Only one in four shells was a tracer, the others we naturally never saw at all.[11.]

In Leif's official papers, there was a name, hand-written during the war where his next of kin were recorded. His father was originally named as the one to be contacted if something happened. But, some time during those years of war, he had met a British girl named Miss Lee. This is the name that was handwritten, and it is she who was to be contacted. Her phone number was FRO409. A Miss S. Lee did indeed live in Frobisher, London, confirmed by public records from 1945.

Back at 331 Squadron, it was Martin Gran who was given the sad task of collecting Leif's things and writing to his fiancée. Gran took over 331

Squadron after Leif, and he survived the war as one of Norway's most highly decorated fighter pilots.

After the war, the rumours of Leif's tragic death reached all the way to Toten, Norway. Some people told of how a Navy search had located the fuel tank of Leif's Spitfire, but nothing else. Others reported that Leif had said, 'Faen! They are shooting at me!' before he disappeared. Leif was not forgotten by the locals of Toten or by the younger generation that followed him. He has a well-deserved reputation as a legend and a hero among many aviation enthusiasts. Leif Lundsten was only 26-years-old when he was lost.

Spitfires flown by Leif Lundsten:
FN-S/P7388
FN-O/P7357
FN-Y/P7929
FN-S/P8199
FN-A/P7377
FN- J/P7384
FN- P/AD509
FN-O/AR328
FN- V/BL821
FN-N/AR289
FN- U/P8707
FN-X/AR296
FN-T/EN786
FN-R/BS467
FN-D/BS137
FN-Z/BS388
FN-T/BS471
FN-Z/BS470
FN-P/BR982
FN-M/BS466
FN-T/BS471
FN-Y/EP796
FN-R/BS125
FN-T/LZ917
FN-B/BM408
FN-S/MA225
FN-T/LZ920
FN-N/BM295
FN-B/MJ567
FN-Y/MK12

Epilogue

Many of the pilots featured in *Into the Swarm* were killed in action during the Second World War. This happened over 70 years ago now. In today's world it is all a long time ago, by anybody's book – except perhaps the men who were there, for whom it still feels like it was only yesterday. For them, their experiences have become vivid memories. Some handled post war life well, and kept going with little trouble, but there are others who suffered post traumatic stress disorder 30 years later. Some dealt with their experiences by writing books or released some of the tension by talking about it. Others simply did not cope with what they had been through at all and drowned their fears and memories in alcohol.

The British pilots were welcomed back from the war with full glory. They were and are heroes of their country, never to be forgotten. The Battle of Britain Memorial Flight soon emerged and is still flying today as a living tribute to those airmen and the historic Battle they fought in. The movie *Battle of Britain* also served as a revival for Warbirds from the Second World War in Britain.

Not so long ago I found myself speaking to a random, quite tired-looking, drunk local chap in a British pub in Cambridge. This man knew the names of Douglas Bader, Leonard Cheshire and Bob Stanford Tuck. Their names have stuck in most peoples' minds. I was surprised but very pleased.

For several other nationalities the post-war story was very different. For the veteran Poles from the RAF, they found themselves to be thought of as traitors, many of them being imprisoned by the Soviet Union when they came back to Poland. It was not until the end of the Cold War, that these brave men received the recognition they truly deserved, which is too late for most of them, who had already passed on.

For the Norwegians, they went home to Norway, proud of what they had been through and sad at the loss of young lives. The rest of the population did not understand, and many felt the Norwegians abroad simply had enjoyed a relaxed and nice time in Britain – they had not endure five years of tough occupation. Because of this attitude, many Spitfire veterans felt disappointed and bitter towards their own population and government.

It is my own personal theory that this is why it has been harder to some extent, to get Norwegian and Danish veterans to speak about their experiences. It wasn't until the 1990's that books started to pop up, largely due to the work of one single journalist. By then, it was almost too late. Much had already been forgotten, many keeping to their promise not to speak or write books about the subject at all. In my opinion, it's a crime that someone like Kaj Birksted was never appreciated more and talked into writing about his experiences at the end of the War.

One specific example of how veterans from different countries have been treated is something that happened to me at North Weald in 2012. With *Viking Spitfire* (author's book from 2012) in my arm, there were several Norwegian veterans in attendance for the 70th anniversary of arriving at North Weald in 1942. I went up to one of them (already having been in touch with him over the phone three years before), and started to introduce myself and my book. He stopped me mid-sentence, saying he had enough books about Spitfires and the war and did not need more of them. 'Oh no sir, you misunderstand, I simply wanted your signature!'

Afterwards I tried to work out, where had we gone so terribly wrong? When a veteran thought I was selling him a book rather than asking for a signature and a handshake from one of my heroes. It was a sobering and thoughtful encounter.

In Britain the books about Second World War aviation have not ceased. A whole culture has developed around the heroes of the air. Big air shows are still put on, many with veterans in attendance and paintings by expert artists have sold for big money. Ray Hanna flying MH434 low and fast over Duxford airfield has given so much joy to so many. I have attended many air shows, and I am jealous of how Britain has kept their veterans close to their hearts, while other nations simply have forgotten them. I know many in Britain also complain about school education not remembering its aviation history but to that I say, keep it in perspective. Think of the Poles, the Czechs and even the Norwegians. Then appreciate how a random drunk can speak of Douglas Bader, because I guarantee you no drunk Norwegian will speak of our top scoring ace Svein Heglund around these parts.

I often wonder what those that did not survive would have thought of us. What would Mungo Park or the Woods-Scawen brothers think if they knew they are still being talked of in 2013? What would Arne Austeen think if he had known that his life and tragic death is still a popular debate so many years later? On the internet, people are making models of his Mustang III and flying it in online simulation games. Would Arne Austeen be honoured? Proud? Or perhaps thinking we should drop it all together and find something else to do with our time? I don't know, but I like to think they would find it comforting that their names are not forgotten. Wilhelm Mohr, the grand old man of the

Royal Norwegian Air Force, never wanted a book about himself, but he was never shy of helping me writing about others. With his blessing, it's easier to write about those who lost their lives knowing that someone who knew them approves.

Norwegian saboteur Max Manus once said during an interview in the mid 1980s, 'All the heroes are dead, *we* are just the ones left behind.' From his perspective, it's perhaps easy to understand why should say such a thing.

With the release of this book, I can relax just a little bit knowing that the stories of all those heroes long gone will not be forgotten.

Endnotes

Chapter 1

1. Forrester, Larry, *Fly For Your Life*, Frederick Müller Ltd. London, 1956, pages 121-122
2. Forrester, Larry, *Fly For Your Life*, Frederick Müller Ltd. London, 1956, page 123
3. Barker, Ralph, *That Eternal Summer*, Collins, 1990, page 111
4. Barker, Ralph, *That Eternal Summer*, Collins, 1990, page 115
5. Barker, Ralph, *That Eternal Summer*, Collins, 1990, page 118
6. Bolitho, Hector, *Finest of The Few*, Amberley, 2010, page 90
7. Barker, Ralph, *That Eternal Summer*, Collins, 1990, page 126-127
8. Beedle, J, *43 Squadron*, Beaumont Aviation Literature, 1966, page 174
9. Townsend, Peter, *Duel of Eagles*, Cassell Publishers Limited, 1970, pages 372-373
10. Barker, Ralph, *That Eternal Summer*, Collins, 1990, page 134-135

Chapter 2

1. Cull, Brian, *249 At War*, Grub Street, 1997, page 12
2. Neil, Tom, *Gun Button To Fire*, Amberley, 2010, page 240-241
3. Neil, Tom, *Gun Button To Fire*, Amberley, 2010, page 96
4. Barclay, George, edited by Wynn, Humphrey, *Fighter Pilot, A Self-Portrait by George Barclay*, Crecy Books, 1994, pages 68-69
5. Neil, Tom, *Gun Button To Fire*, Amberley, 2010, page 117
6. Barclay, George, edited by Wynn, Humphrey, *Fighter Pilot, A Self-Portrait by George Barclay*, Crecy Books, 1994, pages 98-99
7. Neil, Tom, *Onward To Malta*, Airlife Publishing Ltd, 1992, page 46-47
8. Cull, Brian, *249 At War*, Grub Street, 1997, page 69
9. Neil, Tom, *Onward To Malta*, Airlife Publishing Ltd, 1992, page 135
10. Neil, Tom, *Onward To Malta*, Airlife Publishing Ltd, 1992, page 169

Chapter 3

1. Cossey, Bob, *A Tiger's Tale*, J&KH Publishing, 2002, page 51
2. Cossey, Bob, *Tigers*, Arms & Armour Press, 1992, page 85
3. Cossey, Bob, *Tigers*, Arms & Armour Press, 1992, page 87

Chapter 4.

1. Davidson, Martin, Taylor, James, *Spitfire Ace*, Channel 4 Books, 2003, page 97
2. Davidson, Martin, Taylor, James, *Spitfire Ace*, Channel 4 Books, 2003, page 99

3. Wellum, Geoffrey, *First Light*, Viking, 2002, page 97
4. Bartley, Tony, *Smoke Trails In The Sky*, Crecy, 1997, page 12
5. Davidson, Martin, Taylor, James, *Spitfire Ace*, Channel 4 Books, 2003, pages 53-54
6. Forrester, Larry, *Fly For Your Life*, Frederick Müller Ltd. London, 1956, page 103
7. In 1980, Cazenove's Spitfire P9374 emerged on the beach at Calais, where he force-landed it after a cannon shell went through his radiator on 24/5/1940. His aircraft was recovered in January 1981. On 13 October 2000, Thomas Kaplan and Simon Marsh purchased P9374 from a French aircraft enthusiast and, with the dedicated team at Aircraft Restoration Company in Duxford, England, began the long process of restoring the aircraft to its original condition and making it air worthy. With its return to the skies over its homeland on 30, August 2011, P9374 is the earliest Mark of Spitfire flying anywhere in the world.
8. Bartley, Tony, *Smoke Trails In The Sky*, Crecy, 1997, page 16
9. Bartley, Tony, *Smoke Trails In The Sky*, Crecy, 1997, page 17
10. Bartley, Tony, *Smoke Trails In The Sky*, Crecy, 1997, page 19
11. Wellum, Geoffrey, *First Light*, Viking, 2002, page 130
12. Davidson, Martin, Taylor, James, *Spitfire Ace*, Channel 4 Books, 2003, page 221-222
13. Robinson, Michael, *Best of The Few*, 2001, pages 73-74
14. Bartley, Tony, *Smoke Trails In The Sky*, Crecy, 1997, page 41
15. Bartley, Tony, *Smoke Trails In The Sky*, Crecy, 1997, pages 27-28
16. Robinson, Michael, *Best of The Few*, 2001, page 92
17. Robinson, Michael, *Best of The Few*, 2001, pages 92-93
18. Kent, J A, *One of The Few*, William Kimber & Co. Ltd. 1971, page 127
19. Bartley, Tony, *Smoke Trails In The Sky*, Crecy, 1997, page 56
20. Bartley, Tony, *Smoke Trails In The Sky*, Crecy, 1997, page 56
21. In Allan's combat report he stated: 'I have come to the conclusion that rate of fire of cannons, is too slow for chances of a hit, when doing deflection shooting, as I scored no hits'.
22. Duke, Neville, *Test Pilot*, Grub Street, 1992, pages 42-43
23. Duke, Neville, *Test Pilot*, Grub Street, 1992, pages 43-44
24. Duke, Neville, Franks, Norman, *The War Diaries of Neville Duke*, Grub Street, 1995, page 13

Chapter 5

1. Neil, Tom, *Onward To Malta*, Airlife Publishing Ltd, 1992, page 162-163
2. The Temple was the name of a building that Betty's Uncle had a flat in. With Pat living in RAF accommodation and Betty working at St Thomas's Hospital, they had single rooms, so when Pat was on leave in London they were able to stay at Betty's uncle's flat.
3. Oxspring, Bobby, *Spitfire Command*, Grafton Books, 1987, page 178
4. Oxspring, Bobby, *Spitfire Command*, Grafton Books, 1987, page 197-198

Chapter 7

1. Gunhfeldt, Cato, *Nattjager,* Wings, 2004, page 83-84
2. Gunhfeldt, Cato, *Nattjager,* Wings, 2004, page 84
3. (Spitfire Into Battle, 2002, p 180, 181).
4. *Opp med Spitfire,* p 94-95

Chapter 8

1. Guhnfeldt, Cato, *Spitfire Saga II*, 2009, page 66

Chapter 9

1. Arnesen, Finn, *Våre Flygere I Kamp*, 1962, page 90-91
2. Nyerrød, Kristian, *En Av De Mange*, 1995, page 33
3. Berg, Rolf Arne, *Spitfire Saga*, 2009, page 25
4. Guhnfeldt, Cato, *Spitfire Saga I*, 2009, page 47
5. Guhnfeldt, Cato, *Spitfire Saga I*, 2009, page 47
6. Guhnfeldt, Cato, *Spitfire Saga I*, 2009, page 162
7. Nyerrød, Kristian, *En Av De Mange*, 1995, page 80-81
8. Guhnfeldt, Cato, *Spitfire Saga I*, 2009, page
9. Gunhfeldt, Cato, *Nattjager,* Wings, 2004, page
10. Guhnfeldt, Cato, *Spitfire Saga II*, 2009, 232
11. Spitfire, norsk jagerflyger i kamp, 2001 Birger Tidemand-Johannessen

Acknowledgements

In no particular order I would like to express my sincere thanks to the following people for their help, contributions and general support: Martin Lardner-Burke, Tristan Woods-Scawen, Mark Lewis, Mijail Navarro, Jay Slater, Alan Sutton, Jasper Hadman, Jacqueline Scholefield, Ady Shaw, Bob Yeoman, David Pritchard, Kym Yeoman, Ben Montgomery, Bob Cossey, David Denchfield, Tom Neil, Geoffrey Wellum, Sarah Hanna, Carl Garnham, Joshua Hancock, Michael Robinson, Eddie Nielinger, Peter Ayerst, Arthur Westerhoff, Nils Hagemann, Chris Barker, Jaroslaw Gwardys, Andy Wright, David Duker, Gary Miller, Brad Hurley, Simon Welburn, Ashley Marie Morrison, Iain Morrison, John Maclachlan, Glenn Knight, Peter Cornwall, Lisanne Tullett, Mark Andrew, Vitor Santos, Marco Spinosa, Stu Bradley, Eddy Standaert, Rob Champion, Chris Brookes, Jan Broersma and Tor Idar Larsen.

Christopher Yeoman, 2013

I would like to thank the following people: John Clifford for his time spent correcting all my mistakes (once again!). You can truly and utterly only know how much work John did once you have seen my original texts! Thank you John! I would also like to especially thank Morten Lundsten, Sverre Anthonisen and Erland Hvalby for sharing their pictures with me.

For inspiration, support, or help during this project I would like to thank the following people: Noorit Larsen, Arne Austeen, Leif Lundsten, Kaj Birksted, Finn Eriksrud, Finn Thorsager, Wilhelm Mohr, Rolf M. Kolling, Anton Wang, Per Waaler, Gurli Thorsager, Cato Gunfeldt, Birger Tidemand-Johannessen, Kristian Nyerrød, Tarald Weisteen, Tore Erling Larsen, Peter Arnold, the aviation community at North Weald, and especially thanks to Chris Yeoman for inviting me to join this project.

Tor Idar Larsen, 2013

Major Leif Lundsten, standing proudly in front of his Norwegian-marked Supermarine Spitfire IX, sometime before D-Day. (*Author's collection*)

Tore E. Larsen's giant-scale RC model Supermarine Spitfire marked up as Leif Lundsten's BS467. The Spitfire flies at a small RC airstrip only 20 minutes away by car from where Leif Lundsten grew up. The photo was taken on 7 May 2013, 69 years and 2 days to the date Lundsten perished. It flies as a tribute to a brave young man. (*Tor Idar Larsen*)

Johan Nicolay Eide, June 1941. Eide was killed in January 1943 over Cambridge when his Spitfire was struck by lightning. The following quote is taken from a letter he wrote to his his parents: 'I do not care whether I will get through this or not, only that I know that I have laid a stone in the temple of freedom. I will strive towards that for as long as I can, because I have seen what oppression means.'